LANGUAGE AND DESIRE

WITHDRAWN

Language and Desire is an original and intriguing exploration into the language we use to talk about and express romantic and sexual desire.

The contributors use a rich variety of approaches to analyse the features and patterns of this discourse, including empirical linguistics and discourse analysis. They engage directly with issues in critical linguistics, women's studies and gender studies. In particular they investigate:

- the language used to encode romantic and sexual desire;
- the attitudes and assumptions about romantic and sexual desire that are embodied in English;
- the relations between language and the construction of identities based upon manifestations of desire.

Contributors include: Sara Mills, Joanna Channell, Mary Talbot and Michael Hoey.

Language and Desire will attract a varied readership including students of linguistics, women's studies, gender studies, and lesbian and gay studies.

Keith Harvey is a lecturer in Applied Linguistics at the University of East Anglia. **Celia Shalom** is a lecturer in English Language and Applied Linguistics in the English Language Studies Unit at the University of Liverpool.

RELATED TITLES

Also available from Routledge:

FEMINIST CRITIQUE OF LANGUAGE
Deborah Cameron

GENDER ARTICULATED
Kira Hall and Mary Bucholtz

LANGUAGE AND DESIRE

Encoding sex, romance and intimacy

Edited by Keith Harvey and Celia Shalom

London and New York

First published 1997
by Routledge
11 New Fetter Lane, London EC4P 4EE

Simultaneously published in the USA and Canada
by Routledge
29 West 35th Street, New York, NY10001

Typeset in Baskerville by
BC Typesetting, Bristol

Printed and bound in Great Britain by
Mackays of Chatham PLC, Chatham, Kent

British Library Cataloguing in Publication Data
A catalogue record for this book is available from the British Library

Library of Congress Cataloguing in Publication Data
Language and desire: encoding sex, romance, and intimacy/edited by
Keith Harvey and Celia Shalom.
  1. Language and sex.   I. Harvey, Keith, 1959–   .   II. Shalom,
Celia, 1953–   .
P120.S48L33   1997
306.44–dc21   96-37726
                                                  CIP

ISBN 0–415–13691–1 (hbk)
ISBN 0–415–13692–X (pbk)

CONTENTS

Part III Voices

ABOUT THE AUTHORS

Joanna Channell has been researching, teaching and writing about English language and applied linguistics since 1978. Recent applied work has included research on questionnaire design for Government surveys, and analysis of the language of National Vocational Qualifications. Her published work includes EFL materials, articles on language teaching and descriptive linguistics, *Vague Language* (1994) and editorial contributions to the 1995 *Collins COBUILD English Dictionary*.

Alice Deignan is a lecturer in TESOL at the University of Leeds. She is the author of *Collins COBUILD Guides to English: 7: Metaphor* (1995). Her research interests include metaphor and pragmatics.

Keith Harvey is a lecturer in Applied Linguistics at the University of East Anglia. He has worked in ELT as a teacher and teacher trainer in France and Hong Kong and as a lexicographer for Collins COBUILD. He has published articles in translation studies, lexicography and language learning and also written and presented three series of programmes on language-related issues for BBC English, World Service radio.

Michael Hoey is Baines Professor of English Language and Director of the Applied English Language Studies Unit at the University of Liverpool. His major publications are *Signalling in Discourse* (1979), *On the Surface of Discourse* (1983/91), *Patterns of Lexis in Text* (1991), which was awarded the Duke of Edinburgh English Speaking Union Prize for the best book on Applied Linguistics in 1991, and the edited collection, *Data Description Discourse* (1993).

Murray Knowles lectures in Applied English Linguistics at the Centre for English Language Studies, School of English, University of Birmingham. His research interests include language and ideology, and language and literature. His previous publications include co-authorship of *Language and Control in Children's Literature* (1996).

ABOUT THE AUTHORS

Charles Lambert teaches English at the Language Centre of the Third University of Rome. After leaving Cambridge in 1975 he worked in TEFL in Italy, Portugal and England. He completed an M.A. in Applied Linguistics at Birmingham University in 1991.

Wendy Langford is currently based in the Sociology Department at Lancaster University, where she carried out her Ph.D research – a study of women's experiences of romantic love relationships. She is the author of a number of articles on love and sexuality and a forthcoming book *The Subject of Love*.

Elizabeth Manning has been a lexicographer at COBUILD since 1984 and has taken a special interest in grammar. The publications she has worked on include the *Collins COBUILD English Dictionary*, the *Collins COBUILD English Grammar* and the *Collins COBUILD Grammar Patterns 1: Verbs*.

Sara Mills is Research Professor in the School of Cultural Studies, Sheffield Hallam University. She has published mainly in two distinct areas: feminist linguistics/literary theory and feminist postcolonial theory. Her publications include: (co-author) *Feminist Readings/ Feminists Reading* (1989); *Discourses of Difference: Women's Travel Writing and Colonialism* (1991); (ed.) *Gendering the Reader* (1994); (ed.) *Language and Gender* (1995); *Feminist Stylistics* (1996). She is currently working on a book on discourse theory and a book on gender and colonial space.

Celia Shalom is a lecturer in English Language in the Applied English Language Studies Unit at the University of Liverpool. Her research interests include discourse analysis, lexis, and language and gender. Flowing from ESP courses taught at the Central University of Barcelona, she is researching the spoken genres involved in academic conferences. She has a number of publications on genre and language teaching.

Mary M. Talbot is a postdoctoral fellow in the Media Arts Research Centre at the Southampton Institute, England. Previously she was a lecturer at Odense University in Denmark. Recent publications include *Fictions at Work* (1995) and contributions to a variety of collections on language in social life, particularly print media. She is currently working on *An Introduction to Language and Gender* and an edited collection on *Women in 20th Century Consumer Culture*.

Christine A. White is lecturer in Drama at Loughborough University and a professional lighting designer, with work most recently at Nottingham Playhouse, Leicester Haymarket and the Queen Elizabeth Hall, London. She is convenor of the Scenography Group for the International Federation for Theatre Research and her recent publications include *Scenography and the Fourth Dimension* available on the Internet (Http://www.dmu.ac.uk/In/4dd).

ACKNOWLEDGEMENTS

We would like to thank everyone who has given us advice and support during work on this book. The following people deserve a special mention: Richard Boggs, for his editorial input in the early stages of the project; Murray Knowles, whose 'Language and Ideology' postgraduate seminars at the University of Birmingham were the breeding ground for many of the ideas found here; Michael Hoey, for his encouragement. In particular, we are grateful to Julia Hall, formerly commissioning editor at Routledge, whose faith in the project was immediate and unswerving.

On a personal note, we would like to thank the following people for their love, support and encouragement throughout the project: Tony Cawley, Rob Colley, Jean Huèges, Fiona Maguire, Pete Morriss and Deborah Yuill.

The following individuals and institutions granted permission to reproduce copyright material:

'A person's most significant decision', copyright © John Diamond / *The Times*, 14/05/92.

Extracts from *The Chocolate War* by Robert Cormier, copyright © 1974 Robert Cormier. Reprinted by permission of Pantheon Books, a division of Random House, Inc.

Extract from *Forever* by Judy Blume, copyright © 1975 Judy Blume. Reprinted with the permission of Simon & Schuster Books for Young Readers, an imprint of Simon & Schuster Children's Publishing Division.

Extract from *Passionate Awakenings* by Diana Hamilton, used with permission from Harlequin Books S.A. First published in Great Britain 1990 by Harlequin Mills & Boon.

Extract from *Angels in America*, Part I: *Millennium Approaches* by Tony Kushner, copyright © 1992 and 1993 by the author. Published by Theatre Communications Group, Inc. Used by permission of the publisher.

ACKNOWLEDGEMENTS

Extract from 'Please Master' from *Collected Poems 1947–1980* by Allen Ginsberg, copyright © 1968 by Allen Ginsberg. Reprinted by permission of HarperCollins Publishers, Inc.

Extracts from *The Faber Book of Love Poems* edited by Geoffrey Grigson, and *Collected Poems* by W.H. Auden, used by permission of Faber and Faber Limited.

Extracts from *The History of Sexuality*, vol. 1: *An introduction* by Michel Foucault, translated by Robert Hurley (Penguin Books 1979, first published as *La Volunté de savoir*, 1976), copyright © Editions Gallimard, 1976. Translation copyright © Random House Inc, 1978. Extract from *The Penguin Book of Homosexual Verse* edited by Stephen Coote (Penguin Books, 1983), Introduction copyright © Stephen Coote, 1983, 1986. Reproduced by permission of Penguin Books Limited.

Extracts from *Selected Poems* and *Nerves* by John Wieners, used by permission of Jonathan Cape.

While the publishers and authors have made every effort to contact copyright holders of material used in this volume, they would be grateful to hear from any they were unable to contact.

INTRODUCTION

Keith Harvey and Celia Shalom

1 WHY LANGUAGE AND *DESIRE*?

'Love demands expression', notes the desiring narrator of Jeanette Winterson's *Written on the Body* (1992: 9). Less pithily but perhaps more precisely, we would concur that human beings need to give form in language to their desires for one another. For the experiencer of desire, there would appear to be at least two reasons for this. While uncompromising in its demand for attention, desire is also elusive and destined to fade. To attempt to encode it – to write it, to speak it – is a way of capturing it, of attempting to delay the onset of its decline, and of providing us with a trace of the vividness of our experience once it is past. But to give linguistic form to our desires for another human being is also, importantly, to try to understand an experience that overwhelms us and thereby threatens constantly to outmanoeuvre and outclass our verbal resources, the principal means at our disposal for ordering and making sense of our lives.

Lacanian psychoanalysis suggests that the compulsion to put our desires into speech stems from the insurmountable obstacle to our ever being able to fulfil them; we are thrown back onto language as a substitute for the blissful *jouissance* which we once knew in our union with the mother, but which we can now only aspire to vainly through an endless succession of simulacra (desire's 'metonymic' quality (Lacan 1977: 166–7)). At the same time, language is itself the *trace* of our separation from the original blissful state; thus, it is simultaneously the advantage we have gained and the price we have paid for entering the symbolic order. Lacan's speculations help to explain desire as a defining feature of the articulate mammals that we are and, importantly, as a challenge which feeds off its own articulation. In the words of literary and cultural critic Catherine Belsey:

> Writing about desire. It has, of course, been done before ... But something seems to remain unsaid. And it is primarily this that motivates still more writing. Desire eludes final definition, with the result that its

1

character, its nature, its meaning, becomes itself an object of desire for the writer.

(Belsey 1994: 3)

Naming it, renaming it, finding a verbal image for it, revealing it, recounting it . . . these are the verbal acts constantly repeated and refashioned by the desiring speaking subject.

Consequent upon the need to encode desire is the requirement to situate it in time, to represent its temporal dimension: desire's telling is often also its narrative. The prevalence of fictional narratives of love and desire is well documented in our culture. Stacey and Pearce (1995: 15–24) suggest that non-fictional, 'real-life' love *stories* also possess a 'textuality' by virtue of the conventional manner in which we conceive of them: that is, as sequences of events constructed around obstacles to be overcome and discoveries (relating to the self, to the other) to be made. It follows that love stories – the 'real' as well as the fictional – are apt to undergo similar processes of cultural construction. As Duncombe and Marsden have put it:

> even at what may feel like the most spontaneous and authentic moments in their lives – 'being in love' – people are performing or staging romance. Yet to realise this is not to invalidate their feelings of heightened everyday experience, for 'love' cannot be expressed completely outside the cultural forms of society.
>
> (Duncombe and Marsden 1995: 249)

Thomson's (1989) work on the narrative skills demonstrated by teenage girls recounting their early experiences of sex within formative relationships would seem further to confirm a tendency to encode desire in stories.

But language is not only the medium for desire's narrative representation, it is also pivotal in the expression of desire between two people. Seduction, for example, crucially involves a linguistic component, with 'chatting up' one of its central moves. Key aspects of intimacy are worked out and established through verbal signs (Barthes 1979 (1977) has illuminating comments to make on the pragmatics of the phrase 'I love you'). And lovers characteristically talk reflexively, recursively about their feelings for each other (the encounter, the realisation, the obstacles, the 'first time'). The verbal medium is thus central in the process of maintaining and deepening relations founded upon love and desire. Throughout this volume, suggestions are made as to the nature and function of the 'duolects' that develop between two people who are intimate.

If these concerns are located at the *micro*-level of human interaction, it is also important to note that in our culture desire has also become a player at the *macro*-level of social and political forces. The representations of desire within patriarchal and heterosexist paradigms inform debate in women's studies and in gay and lesbian studies. Indeed, the challenges offered to these paradigms have increasingly involved the designation of and mobilisation around identities predicated exclusively upon distinct types of desire. Thus, desire as that intimate, deeply compelling and profoundly *private* experience also has its public face, which emerges in controversies and arguments around issues of group identity, agency and justice. Typically, linguistic representations are key sites of contention in such struggles.

It is important at this point to clarify what we understand by the 'encoding of desire' by bringing out a thematic and pragmatic distinction between *language about desire* and *desire in language*. This distinction is similar to Abu-Lughod and Lutz's (1990: 10) contrast between 'discourse on emotion' and 'emotional discourse'. While the first is discourse that has emotion as its avowed topic and propositional content, the second has some affective 'effect' or outcome. In our terms, 'language about desire' produces texts where some account of desiring subjects, desired objects or the processes of desire itself is present, often (though not exclusively) through third-person narration. In contrast, 'desire in language' produces text that is designed to bring about a real-world change in the relationship between the participants (say, where one person publishes a personal advertisement to contact an as yet unknown other) or, indeed, to consolidate that relationship. Here, desire may or may not be present textually as propositional *content*, but desire for the other will be the underlying *motivation* behind the discourse for at least one of the participants.

An assumption has impelled the research reported on in this book: namely, that the encoding of desire results in distinct and describable linguistic features and patterns. These features and patterns may be attributed to the nature of the language code itself – how it impels us to say things – but also to the important ways in which we can inflect its exigencies. Alternatively, they may stem from external pressures: social constraints, contextual influences, the presence of taboo, the existence of ideological struggle, etc. Contributors have looked at language phenomena along both the paradigmatic and the syntagmatic axes, ranging from the formation of particular lexical systems to the elaboration of specific discoursal structures.

2 APPROACHES AND METHODS

How then can we study desire in language and language about desire?

This book is both exploratory and eclectic. The contributors come from a variety of disciplines and draw on different traditions to illuminate and explain the linguistic evidence they are studying. Not only will the reader find work from discourse analysts, text linguists, grammarians and corpus linguists, but also research in social discourse theory, gender politics, gay and lesbian studies as well as psychoanalysis. The book has no claim to be a comprehensive account of the linguistic encodings of desire in modern

3

English. Rather, each chapter opens up a topic area that is as yet largely un-explored within descriptive linguistics.

2.1 Describing language

A number of the chapters that follow subscribe to the theoretical imperative to describe the language from the evidence of real text. For researchers work-ing within this paradigm the examination of instances of *parole* is seen as the essential methodological prerequisite to any systemic abstraction at the level of *langue*. This descriptive approach links the work of Firth (Palmer (ed.) 1968: 96–113) with that of Halliday (1978; 1985/1994) and of Sinclair (1991). According to this tradition, descriptions based upon authentic text are more reliable and complete than those built up from the introspections of native speakers. Central also to this descriptive project is an attention to the extra-linguistic factors of the 'context of situation', a term which Firth (Palmer (ed.) 1968: 137–67) developed from the ethnographic work of Malinowski. This term has proved crucial to work in conversational analysis and to Halliday's accounts of language as social semiotic.

In an important sense the assumption of this book – that the linguistic encodings of desire constitute distinct and describable phenomena – also takes its cue from an aspect of Michael Halliday's descriptive-theoretical work. This has increasingly sought to explore the lexico-grammar of English as the principal means by which speakers construe aspects of experi-ence. Language – and, in particular for Halliday, grammar – transforms experience into meaning through the choices that speakers make from the system (see, for example, Halliday 1978: 60–92). Recently, Halliday has attempted to describe the 'grammar of pain' through an analysis of authentic doctor–patient dialogue and corpus evidence.[1] In this work, the possible encodings of physical suffering and discomfort are described as a system of structural choices through which 'pain' is construed in three distinct ways: as an entity, as a quality (of a participant) and as a process. Language is thus a network of formal and functional operations in which certain patterns are more or less implicated in the realisation of particular areas of meaning potential. Our attempts to isolate and describe those patterns involved in the realisation of utterances about or motivated by desire clearly draws on the Hallidayan framework of analysis.

For Halliday, lexis and grammar are situated on a descriptive continuum. Accounting for their relationship has benefited considerably from the devel-opments of corpus linguistics. The computerised corpus-based analysis of large collections of text represents one of the most important developments in British descriptive linguistics in recent years (see Aarts and Meijs (eds) 1984; Sinclair (ed.) 1987; Hoey (ed.) 1993). Importantly, corpus software enables the analyst to operate with frequencies, opening up to empirical description the varying tendencies of, say, particular genres of written text (journalism, fiction, etc.) to employ particular lexis. The potential value of such evidence for those working in sociolinguistics and critical linguistics is clear, although it is striking that so far corpus description has remained largely the province of research into lexical semantics and grammar. The contributors to this volume who work with corpora each attempt to develop their analyses beyond statements about the language-as-system to bring to bear speaker-related issues or social and ideological representations within texts. The possible variations in language used by and about women and men surfaces repeatedly as a focus for analysis in this respect.

2.2 Language, gender and critical theory

Initially, linguists working in language and gender developed a research paradigm within classical sociolinguistics, correlating the variations noted in the performance of particular language features with the speaker variable of gender (see Coates and Cameron (eds) 1988 and Graddoll and Swann 1989 for accounts of this tradition within language and gender research). It is significant, though, that researchers in this area have increasingly looked to disciplines outside linguistics in order to account for the evidence of systematic variation they have found. Sociolinguistic methods might indicate a differential distribution of variants; they will, however, be less apt for explaining them. Thus, feminist theory and practice themselves have come significantly to inflect debates around 'difference' and 'dominance' in language behaviour (Cameron 1985). Indeed, feminism's radical eclecticism and interdisciplinarity – drawing on psychoanalysis as readily as on Marxism – stands as an important example for linguists when dealing with the complexity of social practice.

More recently, work in language and gender (see, for example, Hall and Bucholtz 1996) has challenged the view that the language we produce is simply a function of our social selves. This has led to a questioning of the assumption that the gender we 'are' *produces* the language we use. Drawing on post-structuralist critical theory, Deborah Cameron remarks:

> Whereas sociolinguistics would say that the way I use language reflects or marks my identity as a particular kind of social subject . . . the critical account suggests that language is one of the things that *constitutes* my identity as a particular kind of subject. Sociolinguistics says that how you act depends on who you are; critical theory says that who you are (and are taken to be) depends on how you act.
>
> (Cameron 1995: 15–16)

Many contributors to this volume work with this conception of the constitutive relation between language and social identity. Some illustrate how work in gay and lesbian studies has also found this formulation of a 'construction-ist' link between discourse and self productive in its elaboration of a disciplin-ary paradigm.

Evincing a similar disciplinary eclecticism to feminism, critical work in linguistics has drawn on the Hallidayan descriptive tradition and combined it with the insights of French thinkers on the left such as Foucault and Althusser. Critical linguistics has introduced an agonistic dimension into the description of text. For a critical linguist 'language' is not a consensual, uni-tary instrument of communication; rather, at any one time, competing uses of language are present within the so-called 'speech community'. (Critical linguists have found Bakhtin's (in Morris (ed.) 1994: 73–80) anti-unitary concept of 'heteroglossia' theoretically useful here.) The relative status of such competing discourses – with their associated generic forms and rhetori-cal conventions – is both an expression of prevailing social hierarchies and tensions as well as an important way in which these hierarchies come to be established and perpetuated.

Furthermore, like much feminist work in language, critical linguistics is not merely a disinterested recorder of differences in language practice; its advocates are often committed to exposing the mechanisms of hegemony in order to facilitate the access to a language of empowerment by marginalised groups:

> Moving beyond passive awareness to action means learning to choose when to conform to the conventions as they are, or to challenge them, and so help to break new ground. Action involves knowing how to choose, when to choose and whether to choose.
>
> (Janks and Ivanič 1992: 317)

The element of political engagement marks out this current in modern lin-guistics from the purely descriptive schools.

Critical linguistics also recognises the need for an eclectic use of method-ologies in order to uncover the differential workings of power in language. Informant attitudes, explored through questionnaire and interview, are a valuable clue to the state of linguistic and political play within a society:

> It is a strength of ethnographic approaches to linguistic research that the study of language attitudes of members of a community is seen as an essential complement to and part of the study of their sociolinguistic practices. Practices and attitudes fuel each other.
>
> (Fairclough 1992a: 51–2)

Ethnographic methods feature in this collection where the attitudes that underpin the evidence of text require interpretation and explanation if they are to be made explicit.

6

2.3 Foucault, linguistics and discourse

Much of the work in gender and critical linguistics which demonstrates a constructionist turn draws on the theoretical work of Michel Foucault. Foucault's books – and in particular his last volumes on the history of sexuality in the West – have been influential throughout the humanities. For example, recent work in gay and lesbian – 'queer' – studies has used Foucault to describe the supple and intricate ways in which 'identities' predicated upon categories such as 'homosexual' are constructed and reproduced by 'discourses'. Social constructionists argue that such identities are sustained and transformed within specific cultural and historical configurations and do not have a transhistorical or transcultural validity (see Stein (ed.) 1992 for a full account). Foucault's work on discourses as expressions of – as well as devices at the service of – power/knowledge has been crucial in the elaboration of constructionist arguments.

For descriptive linguists, misunderstandings might occur when approaching this work in the social sciences as the two traditions share key terms but use them to signify rather different meanings. Two critical overlaps concern the terms 'discourse' and 'agency'. The reader of this volume will find that contributors will use them differently depending on the tradition within which they are working. For the linguist, 'discourse' is a supra-sentential descriptive category used for the discussion of authentic, situated utterances (written or spoken). For the social scientist, discourses (note the inflection as a count noun) are – in the celebrated definition offered by Foucault himself – 'practices that systematically form the objects of which they speak' (Foucault 1972: 49). In other words, they are networks of convention, knowledge and practice that determine one's perception of – and behaviour in – the (social and natural) 'real'. Language is thus *one* – albeit arguably the most important – of the practices that constitute a discourse.

Turning now to 'agent', in functional grammar this term designates a component of the grammar of the clause. Specifically in Halliday (1985: in particular 144–9), 'agent' is used in an ergative interpretation of the clause to refer to the 'external cause' of a (verbal) process. Within the social sciences, on the other hand, the term 'agency' refers to the subject's ability to resist, challenge and indeed contribute to the transformation of a 'discourse'. Thus, in a critique of Foucault, Fairclough argues: 'Foucault's insistence upon the subject as an effect of discursive formations has a heavily structuralist flavour which excludes active social agency in any meaningful sense' (Fairclough 1992b: 45). And Butler's philosophical objections to an exclusively determinist view of discourse ('that to be *constituted* by discourse is to be *determined* by discourse' (Butler 1990: 143)) employ similar terms: 'Construction is not opposed to agency; it is the necessary scene of agency, the very terms in which agency is articulated and becomes culturally intelligible' (*ibid.*: 147).

It is hoped that this brief account of the theoretical and methodological traditions that feed into the chapters in this book will provide a useful back-drop for the reader and enable her or him to gain some sense of the validity and complementarity of the approaches that are present. We would now like to discuss some of the major themes and issues that emerge from the collection as a whole.

3 THEMES AND ISSUES

3.1 Taboo and transgression

It is significant that the very nature of the language dealt with in this volume has given rise to difficulties for a number of the contributors. Many of us have variously experienced feelings of embarrassment, guilt, arousal and, even, repulsion while working on the 'data'. These may have manifested themselves in a reticence to be explicit in citation; some of the texts are apt to excite and arouse both researcher and reader, providing an added challenge to the task of analysis and objectivity. Similarly, we may have felt an awkwardness about intruding into that private sphere over which a veil of linguistic silence is often drawn. So, the intimate and personal nature of the material and the issues it raises bring us up against questions about the nature of our own engagement as well as about the potential reaction of members of our own academic discourse community.

How can the strength and persistence of these feelings of unease be accounted for? It is commonplace to hear that the expression of sexual and romantic desire in our language is marked by the presence of a taboo. And it is generally accepted by linguists that taboo entails particular linguistic phenomena which are consequent upon the absence of a so-called 'unmarked' term in processes of naming and referring (Adler 1978: 35). The obsessive coinage of alternative items for a single 'unnameable' concept – or 'over-lexicalisation' (Halliday 1978: 165; Carter 1987: 93) – is taken as evidence of a problem area. Thus for sexual intercourse, the language offers a plethora of terms ranging from the technical (*fornicate, have carnal knowledge of*) to the vulgar (*fuck, screw, bonk, give someone a shafting*). Euphemism (*go to bed together, sleep with, know in the biblical sense*) and discourse-specific strategies of circumlocution and avoidance are also characteristic. The occurrence of such terms always gives rise to unease between addresser and addressee.

But what exactly is meant by 'taboo'? And how can it explain the fact that iteration of a marked term – even within the context of academic research – does not diminish its power to disturb? It is worth noting that the 'strong' conception of taboo derives from anthropology (Lévi-Strauss 1969 (1949)) and psychoanalysis (Freud 1950 (1913)). Thus, according to Rycroft (1972) 'taboo' is a term 'for the setting apart of an object or a person or for the absolute prohibition of some class of acts on the grounds that it would be a violation of the culture's whole system of thought' (Rycroft 1972: 164).

A taboo in this sense is not simply something unseemly or inappropriate in certain social contexts; rather, it is a founding principle and guarantor of 'society'. For Bataille (1987 (1957)), there is a crucial distinction between a transgression of the interdict and a violation of it. Transgression is socially sanctioned to take place in the context of special events and ceremonies, often of a religious nature. During these, the society paradoxically reasserts its founding principles and its cohesion by a collective involvement in the transgression of the taboo. In short, transgression is cathartic. Thus, for instance, human sacrifice transgresses the taboo of murder. However, it is important to note that transgression does not lessen the force of the taboo. On the contrary, it reinforces it. The utterance of linguistic signs linked to the taboo object or act can similarly be invested with transgressive power during the designated rituals. In contrast, violation of the taboo – or an unauthorised utterance of the associated word – constitutes an inadmissible act that brings down upon its perpetrators a severe sanction, often death or ostracism.

Although this account of taboo can be useful to explain the persistent negative power that attaches to the utterance of certain words, it has been challenged by some commentators for its universalising tendencies; it seems to preclude the possibility that taboos can change and, indeed, disappear through time and across cultures. Walter (1993) mentions a number of recent developments to the taboo thesis with regard to the representations of death; many are also pertinent to a discussion of the continuing relevance of taboo in contemporary discourses on sex. One argument, for example, asserts that the taboo thesis might well have been applicable before the 1960s but that 'in tune with those expressive elements of the counter culture that have since become institutionalised as part of postmodern culture' (Walter 1993: 36) this is no longer the case. The taboo is thus conceived *ipso facto* as modifiable.

Another argument suggests that taboo might operate differentially within a given culture, with certain groups affected more or less by it according to their social class, age, professional status and so on. In this connection, Walter's discussion brings out the important and often paradoxical role of the media on subjects said to be taboo. Thus, the media can be said to constitute the modern arena for the ritualised transgressions of the very taboos that they also uphold and reinforce. Importantly, we would like to suggest that the language used by lovers in private, intimate contexts provides evidence of another differential operation of linguistic taboo within the speech community. Indeed, it may well be a defining feature of intimate discourse that within it taboos (concerning bodily waste, for example) are transgressed and 'played with'. Menstruation, for example, persists still today in Western societies as a locus of taboo. (Not only will advertisements for tampons avoid any mention of the bodily process the product is manufactured to deal with, but blue writing will be employed to deflect awareness of the redness of menstrual blood.) Women, through the generations, have been taught to exercise discretion and secrecy around their monthly 'period'. Yet, this is just the type of taboo that lovers may transgress within the linguistic space they create, as Joanna Channell's paper in this volume demonstrates.

In short, we would like to offer a conception of taboo that, while preserving the useful link with transgression, does not universalise its influence and impact. Linguistic taboos do indeed persist, but their variable influence needs to be understood through the filters of genre, context and media.

3.2 Intimacy and linguistic innovation

So contexts of intimacy allow participants to transgress taboo. But such contexts do not only have consequences on the propositional level; it is striking also that in the speech of those involved in loving, sexual relationships formal features within the language code are also played with, extended and subverted. Lovers push back the boundaries of the code, thereby compensating for what may be seen as a kind of 'linguistic deficit' of intimate language within the public sphere. These experiments in language form – in which structures can be reinvented through, say, recursiveness or through processes analogous to pidginisation – share features with what Lecercle (1990) has called the operations of the 'remainder' (the 'linguistically repressed' (*ibid.*: 51)) in certain 'marginal' and even 'pathological' uses of the code. Their functions are multiple, as we will suggest, but recall that delight in linguistic game-playing – freed from the constraints of rational propositional meaning – that Freud (1960 (1905)) famously identified as the source of pleasure in jokes.

Linguists committed to empirical methods face a problem, of course, when wishing to study the features of intimate language. If they do manage to assemble some evidence it is likely either to be slight and unrepresentative, obtained by unethical means, or to represent the public – and thereby 'transformed' – transcription of what is really said behind closed doors. (We do not, as yet, know of a corpus of pillow talk!) However, as language users we are all aware that playing with the code forms part of the game- and role-playing we participate in with those we are close to. Typically, lovers when employing a private feature will be signalling powerfully to each other the strength and the length of the relationship by implicitly recalling all those other times that it has been used. Indeed, the moment of coinage of a term specific to the duolect may become an important date in the history of the relationship.

This creation of a domain specific to a couple is not the only function of the linguistic creativity manifested in intimate contexts. In the desire to link the body with the word and to find words for our most powerful emotions, we are to a large extent obliged to chart new territory. On one level, this may be a consequence of a social system that circumscribes expressions of wonderment in the body and of intensity and subtlety of physical and emotional response to a small repertoire of stock tokens. One might also speculate – echoing Lakoff's (1973) work on gender differences in the designation of colour – that in our culture women more than men are encouraged to develop a vocabulary of emotional response that goes some way to recognising the complexity and shifting nature of such feelings. But on another level, it needs to be reasserted that it is also in the nature of the experience of love and sexual desire to be *in excess of* any linguistic code that we could conceive of. Indeed, the pleasure-providing function of this experience might well directly depend on its outstripping of the resources of the code.

There are chapters in this collection that explore the creative use of language in encoding sex, romance and intimacy. Wendy Langford's chapter, for example, not only gives us a glimpse of the renaming practices (of the self, of the other, of the context of intimacy itself) that take place between many couples. Beyond the furry animal names, there are examples of lexical creativity in fully fledged 'sentences' that would not be out of place in Lecercle's corpus (*Dow Bowow ow lowv mow bowbow lowv bowbow*). Other examples that explore the limits of the code through creative usage are suggested by the authors and their friends: the exploitation (and violation) of morphological rules (*Darlingest*); the coinage of lexis (*fuckywucky*); the establishing of untypical collocations (*my absolute sweetheart*); the exploitation of word order (*Now up-get time*); grammatical simplification not unlike that tried out by children and non-native learners (*You go out now. Come back soon?*). At the level of discourse, we also speculate that a particularly high frequency of conventional and unusual vocative use within speech turns is also characteristic (*Cherub, Nutmeg, Pigeon, Chicken*, etc.). And between lovers conversational rituals develop whose idiosyncracies draw on rules and intertextualities that are unique to them.

The starting point for research in this area is clearly the productive tension that exists between the resources available to language users to give form to their desires, and users' wishes to express meanings that are unique to their experience of intimacy with another person. Such research will occupy a central place in a more general inquiry into the linguistic and cultural forms employed in the encoding of pleasure.

3.3 Private worlds, public words

The boundary between public and private is currently undergoing a process of redefinition and *public* renegotiation in our society. It has become commonplace, for example, to postulate a general movement of private language and experience into the public domain, particularly via the mass media (Fairclough 1992b: 110–13). On the other hand, feminists (for example, French 1986: 582) have attacked the private/public distinction itself as an arbitrary one that has served carefully to circumscribe and naturalise the (non-public) role of women in the patriarchal order.

We wish to argue that our culture is not so much witnessing a simple movement of private language into the public domain as registering the effects of a more complex process along two related but distinguishable axes. First, there has been a general change – both quantitatively and qualitatively – in the language used to encode intimacy and private experience. This is the consequence of various social and intellectual trends, from the spread of psychoanalytic and therapeutic discourses since the beginning of the century to sexual liberationist movements in the post-war world. All of these movements can be reduced to a simple postulate, namely that there is something 'within' an individual that needs to be verbalised (see Giddens 1992 on the concept of the self). Indeed, it is often asserted that personal and societal disease can result from the blocking of this verbal channel (see Sontag (1991: 44–58) on repression as a 'cause' of cancer). Thus, in our analysis, an individual today obeys an imperative consequent upon an important historical shift. As a result, subjects register an increased need to talk about their emotional needs and to 'discover', through a specific type of language, the nature of their desires.

Alongside therapeutic and liberationist discourses, however, there are other specific societal events which have resulted in significant shifts in the quantity and quality of language available to individuals to describe publicly their sexual behaviours and needs. Two notable examples in recent decades are the availability of chemical contraceptives, and the spread of HIV and AIDS. To be effective and useful, public education campaigns in these areas have had to break new ground in their representations of human sexualities. The indirect spin-off has been the increased availability of an explicit, non-judgemental language with which individuals can articulate in public their sexual desires and practices.

The second element of the process we wish to sketch out relies on an important distinction between the practices, linguistic and otherwise, of the media and those current in other domains of public life. While it is true that there are few aspects of public life that are not subject to media commentary today, it is important not to conflate the discourse of the media with the whole of 'public life'. The press, television and radio dispose of highly specific public means for accessing, informing and influencing the individual, thereby bypassing and subverting the distinction between private and public. In Celia Shalom's paper, for instance, the cross-media 'genre chains' of the personal ad are seen as both a generic as well as a technological development highlighting complementary yet distinguishable areas of the public/private overlap.

The media's ability to range freely across the boundary between public and private explains in part why they have played a central role in the problematisation of the distinction itself (Kress 1986). However, while they have been able in performance to appropriate and *public*ise those developments within the private discourses of intimacy and desire described above, they largely remain the guardians of the sanctity of the distinction through the often conservative social positions they adopt.

3.4 Desires and identities

Another factor that contributes to the contemporary transformation of the relation between public space and the private world is the increasing tendency to conceive of aspects of sexual behaviour as a foundation stone of individual identity: 'homosexuality' as a type of activity congeals into 'the homosexual' as a selfhood. Once such selves are recognised – and, importantly, *self*-recognise – the possibility is open for the formation of group identities and for the concomitant public articulation of a specificity of experiences, needs and rights (Whisman 1996: 121–5).

The idea that the individual 'has' a sexuality and that this is a – perhaps *the* – defining feature of her or his being is, according to Foucault, a recent historical development. It is related to the idea that in order to find out what is essential about ourselves we need to bring to light the latent truth inscribed within sex: 'We tell it [sex] its truth by deciphering what it tells us about that truth; it tells us our own by delivering up that part of it that escaped us' (Foucault 1979 (1976): 69–70). It is significant that modern 'scientific' accounts of sex – starting with the probings of late nineteenth-century sexology – originated in discussions of sexual behaviours that fell *outside* the regime of adult reproductive heterosexuality. These involved the construction of a descriptive apparatus to account for homosexuality, infant sexuality, fetishism, onanism and so on. As Weeks has pointed out, citing Laplanche and Pontalis (1980: 307):

> Freud opened his *Three Essays on the Theory of Sexuality* in 1905 with a discussion of homosexuality and other 'sexual aberrations' precisely because he believed that their existence transformed conventional views as to what constituted sex. He used them, as Laplanche and Pontalis put it, 'as a weapon with which to throw the traditional definitions of sexuality into question'.
>
> (Weeks 1986: 70)

Thus, reproductive heterosexuality, as a construct, was always in a relationship of systemic dependency upon a network of desires to which it *owed* its definitional status (see also Sedgwick 1994: 9–11).

Today, as same-sex desire appears more or less comfortably to have congealed around the identities 'gay man' and 'lesbian' – interacting with, yet

13

not fundamentally destabilising gender –, so a whole plethora of categories have emerged to complicate this binarism, suggesting a continuing explosion in identities grounded upon the shifting terrain of desire: 'bisexual', 'men who have sex with men' (but who do not identify as 'gay') and 'queer' (which may exclude mainstream, 'assimilated' gay people and include certain marginalised 'straight' sexualities) are examples of terms whose invention is a consequence of these diversifying pressures. It is also remarkable that within lesbian and gay communities, a whole 'masquerade' of consciously adopted 'identities' proliferates and is signified through the systems of fashion, accessories and language: 'butch' and 'femme' (for lesbians), 'queen', 'clone', 'bear' (for gay men) are examples of the labels that stand in hyponymic relation to the categories 'lesbian' and 'gay'. These various identities also signify – although do not necessarily in reality entail (a measure of their 'playfulness') – an orientation towards certain preferential sexual practices (fetishism, s/m, 'active'/'passive' role distribution, etc.).

Thus, it is not surprising that those chapters in this book that deal with same-sex desire – chapters by Keith Harvey, Charles Lambert, Sara Mills and Christine White – explore the problems of identity formation most fully. It is worth noting, however, that an epistemic regime of desire/identity is not without dangers. Such a regime might be inextricably bound up with a ruse of power intent on regulating still further the way we use our bodies. Hence, a more diffuse and shifting configuration of 'bodies and pleasures' is occasionally glimpsed in the later Foucault (1979 (1976): 159), freed from the limitations that desire as the 'core' of identity threatens to impose.

Important theoretical work on 'identities' is also going on in gender studies. Butler, in particular, has produced a dynamic modification of a constructionist theory of gender identity and difference with the concept of gender as 'performative' (Butler 1990: 134–41). According to this concept, the discursive effect of stability within and across genders is a consequence of their constantly *repeated* performance. The idea of repetition is crucial here: it not only allows one to explain how gender roles are consolidated, but also opens up a space in which variation, modification and subversion become possible. 'Performance' is thus the means by which agency can be reintroduced into social discourse theory. Those chapters in this text which concentrate on linguistic description (such as Alice Deignan's and Elizabeth Manning's) have, by implication, something important to contribute to the idea of a performative fabrication of genders and sexualities. If language is the chief means through which discourses are articulated and naturalised as 'truths', then the evidence of large corpora of authentic texts – samples of the 'verbal habitats' in which our speaking selves exist and change – can show us exactly how such articulations and naturalisations are *repeatedly* accomplished through an attention to contexts and frequencies.

Other implications for the notion of identity and its relation to sex and sexuality are raised in this collection. Again, they involve the problematisation of the categories of public and private, but unlike those centripetal forces towards identity formation invoked above, they suggest a certain fragmentation and undermining of the concept of unitary identity. Wendy Langford's examination of alter personalities has already been discussed: traversing, through their newspaper publication, the boundaries between the home and the world, these 'other selves' suggest that the speaking subject adopts and adjusts to multiple personae in the course of her or his daily verbal trajectory. However, unlike the features of register variation that are a commonplace source of commentary within discourse analysis and sociolinguistics, the language these speakers employ remains largely opaque to other members of the speech community. Perhaps more radical still is the multiplicity of parallel selves suggested by the texts of first-person erotic fantasy examined by Michael Hoey. Here, heterosexual men and women recount the 'inner discourse' of sexual fantasy that exists alongside their public, outer selves. In these texts it is clear that individuals play out sexual fantasies of power, domination and submission that remain secret from those around them, and that might well contrast with their actual sexual behaviour. The pleasure taken in the language used to encode them is, one suspects, in inverse proportion to – and largely dependent on – the public identity that contrasts so markedly with them.

4 THE STRUCTURE OF THE BOOK

These then are some of the major threads that run through this collection. The book has been divided into three parts – 'Words', 'Narratives', 'Voices' – but issues and approaches will often cross over those boundaries.

Part I, 'Words', contains three chapters by lexicographers. Each chapter concentrates on various aspects of lexical meaning and usage. Alice Deignan considers metaphors of desire; Elizabeth Manning looks at a category of reciprocal verbs; Keith Harvey investigates male speakers' word choice when referring to partners.

Part II, 'Narratives', moves out from the level of word to the story. The three chapters in this section examine written narratives. Michael Hoey discovers a new discourse pattern in the text of erotic fantasy; Mary Talbot explores the encoding of women's desire in Mills & Boon romantic fiction; Murray Knowles focuses on the account of one adolescent's desire in a novel for teenage readers.

In Part III, 'Voices', the chapters explore the articulations of desire in language within their various generic, situational and societal contexts. Joanna Channell analyses an example of intimate spoken discourse on the telephone; Wendy Langford offers an interpretation of intimate alter personalities between the couple by examining the terminologies they employ; Celia Shalom looks at the levels of interaction at work in the written personal advertisement; Charles Lambert discusses the search for a distinctive voice for gay male desire in lyric poetry; Sara Mills and Christine White investigate feminists' negotiation of labels within relationships.

Finally, it is more than just a conventional signal of closing for us to remark that much more work remains to be done in this area. We hope that this collection will go some way towards stimulating such future research.

Keith Harvey and Celia Shalom

Edinburgh and Liverpool, September 1996

NOTES

1 We are grateful to Michael Halliday for sending us a copy of his paper 'Grammar and daily life: construing pain'. It was given as a talk at the Fourth International Symposium on Critical Discourse Analysis at the University of Athens, December 1995.

REFERENCES

Aarts, J. and Meijs, W. (eds) (1984) *Corpus Linguistics*, Amsterdam: Rodopi.

Abu-Lughod, Lila and Lutz, Catherine A. (1990) 'Introduction: emotion, discourse, and the politics of everyday life', in Catherine A. Lutz and Lila Abu-Lughod *Language and the Politics of Emotion*, Cambridge: Cambridge University Press; Paris: Editions de la Maison des Sciences de l'Homme.

Adler, M.K. (1978) *Naming and Addressing: A Sociolinguistic Study*, Hamburg: Helmut Buske.

Barthes, Roland (1979 (1977)) *A Lover's Discourse: Fragments*, London: Cape.

Bataille, Georges (1987 (1957)) *Eroticism*, London: Marion Boyars.

Belsey, Catherine (1994) *Desire: Love Stories in Western Culture*, Oxford: Blackwell.

Butler, Judith (1990) *Gender Trouble: Feminism and the Subversion of Identity*, London: Routledge.

Cameron, Deborah (1985) *Feminism and Linguistic Theory*, Basingstoke: Macmillan.

—— (1995) *Verbal Hygiene*, London: Routledge.

Carter, Ronald (1987) *Vocabulary: Applied Linguistic Perspectives*, London: Unwin Hyman.

Coates, Jennifer and Cameron, Deborah (eds) (1988) *Women in their Speech Communities*, London: Longman.

Duncombe, Jean and Marsden, Dennis (1995) '"Can men love?": "reading", "staging" and "resisting" the romance', in Lynne Pearce and Jackie Stacey (eds) *Romance Revisited*, London: Lawrence & Wishart.

Fairclough, Norman (1992a) 'The appropriacy of "appropriateness"', in Norman Fairclough (ed.) *Critical Language Awareness*, London: Longman.

—— (1992b) *Discourse and Social Change*, Cambridge: Polity Press.

Foucault, Michel (1972) *The Archeology of Knowledge and the Discourse on Language*, New York: Pantheon.

—— (1979 (1976)) *The History of Sexuality*, vol. 1: *An Introduction*, Harmondsworth: Penguin.

French, Marilyn (1986) *Beyond Power: On Women, Men and Morals*, London: Abacus.

Freud, Sigmund (1950 (1913)) *Totem and Taboo*, Standard Edition, vol. 13, London: Hogarth Press.

—— (1960 (1905)) *Jokes and their Relation to the Unconscious*, Standard Edition, vol. 8, London: Hogarth Press.

—— (1962 (1905)) *Three Essays on the Theory of Sexuality*, Standard Edition, vol. 7, London: Hogarth Press.

Giddens, Anthony (1992) *The Transformation of Intimacy: Sexuality, Love and Eroticism in Modern Societies*, Cambridge: Polity Press.

Graddol, D. and Swann, J. (1989) *Gender Voices*, Oxford: Basil Blackwell.

Hall, Kira and Bucholtz, Mary (eds) (1996) *Gender Articulated: Language and the Socially Constructed Self*, London: Routledge.

Halliday, M.A.K. (1978) *Language as Social Semiotic*, London: Edward Arnold.

—— (1985/1994 2nd edn) *An Introduction to Functional Grammar*, London: Edward Arnold.

Hoey, Michael (ed.) (1993) *Data, Description, Discourse: Papers on the English Language in Honour of John McH. Sinclair*, London: HarperCollins.

Janks, Hilary and Ivanič, Roz (1992) 'Critical language awareness and emancipatory discourse', in Norman Fairclough (ed.) *Critical Language Awareness*, London: Longman.

Kress, Gunther (1986) 'Language in the media: the construction of the domain of public and private', *Media, Culture and Society* 8: 395–419.

Lacan, Jacques (1977) *Ecrits: A Selection* (trans. Alan Sheridan), London: Routledge.

Lakoff, R. (1973) *Language and Woman's Place*, New York: Harper & Row.

Laplanche, J. and Pontalis, J.B. (1980) *The Language of Psychoanalysis*, London: The Hogarth Press and the Institute of Psychoanalysis.

Lecercle, Jean-Jacques (1990) *The Violence of Language*, London: Routledge.

Lévi-Strauss, Claude (1969 (1949)) *Elementary Structures of Kinship*, Boston: Beacon Press.

Morris, Pam (ed.) (1994) *The Bakhtin Reader: Selected Writings of Bakhtin, Medvedev, Voloshinov*, London: Edward Arnold.

Palmer, F.R. (ed.) (1968) *Selected Papers of J R Firth 1952–1959*, London: Longman.

Rycroft, Charles (1972) *A Critical Dictionary of Psychoanalysis*, Harmondsworth: Penguin.

Sedgwick, Eve Kosofsky (1994) *Epistemology of the Closet*, Harmondsworth: Penguin.

Sinclair, J.M. (ed.) (1987) *Looking Up: An Account of the COBUILD Project in Lexical Computing*, London and Glasgow: Collins ELT.

—— (1991) *Corpus Concordance Collocation*, Oxford: Oxford University Press.

Sontag, Susan (1991) *Illness as Metaphor, Aids and its Metaphors*, Harmondsworth: Penguin.

Stacey, Jackie and Pearce, Lynne (1995) 'The heart of the matter: feminists revisit romance', in Lynne Pearce and Jackie Stacey (eds) *Romance Revisited*, London: Lawrence & Wishart.

Stein, Edward (ed.) (1992) *Forms of Desire: Sexual Orientation and the Social Constructionist Controversy*, London: Routledge.

Thomson, Sharon (1989) 'Search for tomorrow: or feminism and the reconstruction of teen romance', in Carol S. Vance (ed.) *Pleasure and Danger: Exploring Female Sexuality*, London: Pandora.

Walter, Tony (1993) 'Modern death: taboo or not taboo?', in Donna Dickinson and Malcolm Johnson (eds) *Death, Dying and Bereavement*, London: Open University/ Sage Publications.

Weeks, Jeffrey (1986) *Sexuality*, London: Routledge.

Whisman, Vera (1996) *Queer by Choice: Lesbians, Gay Men and the Politics of Identity*, New York and London: Routledge.

Winterson, Jeanette (1992) *Written on the Body*, London: Cape.

Part I

WORDS

1

METAPHORS OF DESIRE

Alice Deignan

1 INTRODUCTION

The aim of this chapter is to show how metaphor plays a part in creating and reinforcing stereotypical images of sexual desire in its different manifestations. I shall argue in this introduction that speakers can use metaphor to express value judgements implicitly and without rational justification. These may be value judgements which many people would find unacceptable if stated in non-metaphorical language, or judgements which at the very least would require discussion. In the rest of the chapter I shall discuss examples of metaphors which are used to talk about sexual desire, exploring the attitudes towards desire and its manifestations which appear to be tacitly encoded in them.

Metaphors work by writing or talking about one entity or concept in terms of another: 'Treating X as if it were, in some ways, Y' (Low 1988: 126). Following Low, the entity or concept treated in this way is referred to in this chapter as the *topic* of the metaphor; the entity or concept used to talk metaphorically about the topic is referred to as the *vehicle*. For example, in the common metaphor DESIRE IS FIRE, DESIRE is the topic of the metaphor; FIRE is the vehicle. Following convention in writing on metaphor (see, for example, Lakoff and Johnson 1980), capital letters are used to talk about the underlying general, or conceptual, metaphor.

The topic of a metaphor is often abstract or otherwise difficult to understand, while the vehicle is often concrete, or at least more familiar to speakers in some way. Henderson (1986) shows how the economy is often treated as a machine; here the topic, THE ECONOMY, is abstract, and the vehicle, A MACHINE, is concrete. Comparing the economy to a machine enables speakers to visualise its workings and make inferences about it from their understandings of machinery. THE ECONOMY IS A MACHINE is realised in linguistic expressions such as *oil the wheels* and *to pump money into the system*, which facilitate discussion and thought.

It is argued by some researchers that metaphor is central to human thought and language (for example, Sweetser 1990; Lakoff 1993, 1987;

21

Lakoff and Johnson 1980). Evidence for this position consists of data of three types. First, in the field of cognitive science, researchers test speakers' understanding of and responses to metaphors in texts, often comparing this to literal language (see, for example, Gibbs and O'Brien 1990; Gibbs 1993). The second type of evidence is typified by much of the work done by Lakoff and his co-researchers, which is based on introspective studies of linguistic expressions. Third, other studies of linguistic expressions are based on corpora of various kinds (see, for example, van Teeffelen 1994; Rohrer 1995; Patthey-Chavez et al. 1996). This present study is of the third kind. The main difference between this and the other corpus-based studies referred to is that I have used a large existing corpus of non-specialised language (such as newspapers and radio broadcasts) for my research, whereas van Teeffelen, Rohrer and Patthey-Chavez et al. have all built their own corpora of a specific type of text, such as political speeches or erotic fiction.

Studies of linguistic expressions used to talk about abstract fields have shown that some areas of life are talked about almost entirely using one or more metaphors. Reddy (1993), for example, has shown that many of our ways of talking about communication involve a conduit metaphor, which is realised linguistically by expressions such as *I couldn't get through to them* and *Try to get your message across*. While metaphors enable us to think and talk about topics in comprehensible terms, there is never a complete match between topic and vehicle; to use Reddy's example, communication has something in common with physical transfer but it is not the same thing.

This partial matching means that metaphors will highlight some aspects of their topic and hide others. The metaphor THE ECONOMY IS A MACHINE mentioned above, for example, highlights the systematic, rule-governed nature of the topic while down-playing its social aspect. Reddy argues that the conduit metaphor for communication presents messages as if they were packages passed from speaker to hearer. The nature of a non-metaphorical parcel is determined by its packer and not by its unpacker, and the conduit metaphor implies that this is also true of communication. Reddy argues that this is not in fact the case, and that in communication the receiver has as much responsibility for the success of the message as the sender. In this way, he argues, the conduit metaphor presents a distorted view of communication, highlighting the role of the sender and downplaying the role of the receiver.

However, if we accept Lakoff and Johnson's (1980) argument that metaphors are central to thought, there can be no 'real', metaphor-free way of talking about an abstract notion such as communication. Reddy does not suggest that we can talk about communication without metaphor, rather he puts forward some alternative metaphors. Mey (1994: 64) also takes the view that metaphors can distort understanding, and argues that almost any unanalysed metaphor is dangerous if uncritically accepted; it is important to examine metaphors and their assumptions and entailments.

Many metaphors have social significance. Lakoff and Johnson write: 'Metaphors may create realities for us, especially social realities' (1980: 156). They show how the use of a WAR metaphor for the search for cheap energy resources affected the perception of an energy crisis in North America by the inferences suggested, though not made explicit, in the metaphor. These inferences include:

- There is a tangible enemy.
- The issue has top national priority.
- Lack of energy threatens the survival of the country.

The public perception of the energy crisis influenced thought and behaviour; a different metaphor might not have created the same inferences and might have led to different courses of action. Metaphors, then, are not only a reflection of mental processes; the relationship is a dynamic one and metaphors can both expand and limit thought and action.

Fairclough (1989: 120) has shown how the common metaphor of DISEASE for social problems or 'ills' highlights the majority interests; these are metaphorically represented as the 'health' of the society. Problems often discussed through this metaphor are crime and drug addiction. A DISEASE metaphor can be used to suggest a 'cure' that is not in terms of rehabilitation of criminals or addicts, but in terms of 'elimination' or 'surgery' on the 'body' of society. Similarly, a WAR metaphor for social problems may characterise certain individuals and situations as 'the enemy' and be used to justify aggressive 'military' action. Sontag (1991), in her discussion of the metaphors used to talk about cancer and AIDS, argues that by using metaphors of war for illness, an existing tendency to stigmatise and marginalise sufferers is legitimised.

It follows that ownership of widely used metaphors conveys power, and it is recognised that control of the prevalent metaphors used to talk about a topic can contribute to the control of how the topic is generally considered. Bolinger (1980) writes of different interest groups seeking to promote their rival metaphors in order to persuade the public to accept the entailments of these metaphors.

One of the assumptions on which this research is based is that an investigation into the metaphors that are used frequently to talk and write about a topic can yield insights into the way in which that topic is understood within a culture. By looking at metaphors which are established within the language (as opposed to new, poetic metaphors which call attention to themselves) and considering their inferences, it may be possible to make explicit views that are communicated implicitly through metaphor and which are often unchallenged.

2 THE STUDY: METHODOLOGY AND OUTLINE

This study was conducted using the Bank of English, a 211-million-word corpus consisting of naturally occurring, current English, such as casual conversation, radio journalism, newspapers, books and letters. The Bank of English is owned by Collins COBUILD, a division of HarperCollins Publishers, and is held at the University of Birmingham. A number of words and expressions from the corpus were studied using concordancing software. Metaphorical expressions which are used in the discussion of sexual desire were noted, and the semantic patterns which emerged were studied. The initial search began with items such as *desire*, *sex* and inflected and derived forms of these words. Writing on metaphor and the expression of emotion was also used as a source of words to study; studies by Lakoff (1987), Emanatian (1995) and Patthey-Chavez *et al.* (1996) suggested the investigation of lexis from the semantic fields of fire, animals, food and plants. Previous corpus research into metaphor undertaken in order to produce an English-language learner's guide (Deignan 1995) also suggested semantic fields to be investigated. Except where indicated, all the examples cited are taken from The Bank of English; an indication of the source (for example, 'fiction', 'broadsheet journalism', etc.) is given in parenthesis after each citation.

Because the aim of this study is to investigate conventional metaphors, metaphorical uses which occurred fewer than five times were disregarded. The study of innovative or otherwise rare metaphorical expressions is interesting in itself, but not relevant for this chapter which concentrates on established, widely used metaphor. Of especial interest were cases in which several different but semantically related lexical items were used metaphorically. An example of this is the cluster of items associated with fire, such as *flames*, *smoulder* and *fiery*. The existence of different but semantically related linguistic metaphors suggests that there is an underlying conceptual metaphor, in this case, DESIRE IS FIRE. Lakoff and Johnson (1980) describe such metaphors as 'live', in that they generate new linguistic expressions and play a role in organising our thinking.

For obvious reasons, it is difficult to gather examples of intimate language, and the corpus used for this study is largely 'public' language. In this chapter I do not attempt to discuss the metaphors used in intimate language, and therefore the focus is on the discussion and description of desire rather than on the expression of desire.

In section 3 some of the metaphors used to discuss sexual desire in general terms are looked at. In section 4 I look at the metaphor DESIRE IS FIRE, which is of particular interest because it is also used to talk about anger and hate. Section 5 examines metaphors which are used to distinguish different manifestations of desire, and often to make value judgements about these. Finally, in section 6, I summarise these points and draw some tentative conclusions.

24

3 METAPHORS FOR SEXUAL DESIRE

3.1 Desire is an external force

Desire is often talked about as if it were a separate being from the person who experiences it. This is common to other strong feelings, such as anger, which are sometimes talked about as invaders of the rational self. Whether desire is welcomed or not, it is often talked of as outside the control of its experiencer. Lexis such as *live* and *die* realise this view, as in the following citation:

> Does desire ever die?
> (fiction)

Desire can be an invader of the body of the person who feels it:

> Her body was full of endless desire.
> (fiction)

> A strange, troubling desire stirred in her.
> (magazines)

While in the above citations, it seems possible that sexual desire is welcomed, desire is often talked of as unwelcome, malicious, dangerous and a force to be struggled against if possible, as in the following citation:

> He fell for the charms of a woman member of staff at his college. It was a dangerous passion that could have played havoc with his final years of education and blighted his early career.
> (*Today* newspaper)

Desire then can be an invader which moves into the body of the experiencer, or a force external to its experiencer, one which he or she is almost powerless to resist. Another image of desire which shares some of these features is that of an irresistibly strong natural force such as moving water. Patthey-Chavez *et al.* find several examples of WATER metaphors for sexual desire in their corpus of erotic fiction for women; their examples include:

> With a force that left her breathless, a wave of pleasure washed over her.
> (Patthey-Chavez *et al.* 1996: 89)

There is evidence in the Bank of English of WATER metaphors for desire, as in the following citation:

> It is so easy to tip over and fall into a torrent of passion that sweeps you away.
> (non-fiction book)

25

Here the experiencer of desire is metaphorically taken away from their everyday self by a powerful external force. Fire and electricity are other natural forces which are important metaphors for desire (discussed in section 4). Fire and water are, of course, elemental, though opposing forces, used as metaphors for desire probably because they epitomise human helplessness in the face of nature. Unlike FIRE metaphors, which highlight energy and destructiveness, WATER metaphors seem to suggest a passive experiencer of desire, overwhelmed by the force of a dominant partner, and Patthey-Chavez *et al.* (1996) show these are common in writing about women's desire.

3.2 Desire is falling (into a container)

In the last citation in the previous section, the metaphor of desire as moving water is combined with the metaphor of falling. Lakoff and Johnson (1980) discuss orientational metaphors at length, and produce linguistic evidence for the metaphor UP IS RATIONAL. *Tip over* in the above citation seems to be a linguistic realisation of this; the experiencer of desire loses the ability to behave rationally, and metaphorically falls over.

The FALL metaphor for sexual love often appears with a CONTAINER metaphor, which is commonly used to talk about various states. Used of sexual love, it takes the form LOVE IS A CONTAINER, and is realised by the expression *be in love*. The metaphors are combined in expressions such as *fall in love*, but either can be used alone. The two most common adverbs modifying *fall* and *be in love* are *deeply* and *madly*. *Deeply* is used to emphasise the intensity of feelings by comparing them to the depth of the metaphorical fall, while *madly* seems to be an allusion to the DESIRE IS INSANITY metaphor (discussed below). Examples of adverbial modification from the corpus are:

> This was a man who was deeply in love with his wife.
> (non-fiction book)

> In Spain, where they had lived for three years, he met a beautiful blonde Norwegian and they fell madly in love.
> (broadsheet journalism)

Another expression which frequently modifies the FALL metaphor is *head over heels*:

> Janet had fallen head over heels in love with another woman.
> (fiction)

This emphasises the powerlessness and upheaval of experiencing sexual love suddenly; if UP IS RATIONAL, then *head over heels* expresses complete loss of rationality.

The CONTAINER and FALL metaphors are important because their linguistic forms are very frequent in English; *fall in love* is one of the most usual ways to talk about the beginning of sexual love. *Fall for* is also used to refer to sexual love; the emphasis is usually on the feelings of one partner rather than both people involved:

> How, they ask, can a woman who looks like that fall for a man with a haircut like that and those teeth.
>
> (*Today* newspaper)

Fall for is also frequently used to talk about individuals being deceived or misled by an illusion. Citations suggest that a person *falls for* something which is either untrue, or will prove damaging to them, or both. The connection between love and deception is underlined by the number of these citations which refer to deception by sexual partners:

> She painted pictures of us living in our house with our children and having friends over for dinner, having a fire and talking about political issues. I fell for the dream. I fell for it hook, line and sinker.
>
> (magazines)

> No, they're not divorced yet, but they don't sleep together any more and he has promised me he'll leave her. And so another woman falls for the oldest lie in the book.
>
> (magazines)

The group of FALL metaphors suggest an image of sexual love as loss of rationality and surrender of control over events. In the next section I discuss an image of discovery of sexual desire that has very different implications.

3.3 Experiencing desire is awakening; desire is an awakened sleeper

Many individuals can recall one significant experience or person that brought about a sudden realisation of their sexuality or capacity for desire. This moment is often talked about using metaphors from the field of sleep and awakening, suggesting, incidentally, an interpretation of the Sleeping Beauty and Snow White fairy tales. (The fact that versions of this story are told throughout Western culture may provide evidence that the metaphor is significant conceptually.)

Citations alluding to sexual awakening include:

> Seventeen was the age when I woke to the realisation that I was gay. Was this also the case for you? I was awakening to my homosexuality.
>
> (fiction)

When he takes a job as a waiter in a Calgary restaurant run by husband and wife Matt and Violet, he falls in love with Matt, awakening
in the young man feelings where he never even knew he had areas.

(broadsheet journalism)

This metaphor seems to take two patterns. In the first of the above citations,
the experiencer of desire is talked about as if he were asleep until the moment
of his realisation of his sexuality. In the second, desire itself sleeps until
awoken. Desire as discussed in the texts in the Bank of English is for the main
part heterosexual, whereas the sleep and awakening metaphor is used to
describe homosexual desire in more than half of the thirty citations expressing this metaphor in the corpus. The metaphor suggests a positive evaluation of sexual desire; it can be inferred from this metaphor that to be without
desire, or not to know one's sexual orientation, is to be semi-conscious.

A SLEEP metaphor is also used to talk about the disappearance of sexual
desire some time after it has first been experienced. In contrast to the
'awakening' metaphors just discussed, citations on this topic mainly refer to
heterosexual desire. What is more, desire itself, and not the experiencer, is
the sleeper in all these citations.

Your sex life may be dormant, but that doesn't mean it's dead. Trudy
Culross talks to three women who reawakened their desire.

(magazines)

'It was a great relief,' he admits, 'to discover that normal sex drive can
just lie dormant for a while.'

(non-fiction book)

These metaphors are similar to those discussed in 3.1 in that they represent
sexual desire as an independent being whose presence or absence is not
entirely controlled by the experiencer.

3.4 Experiencing desire is physical weakness

Sexual desire is also talked about using the lexis of pain, illness and madness.
The entailments of the metaphors from these three areas are distinct, so they
are treated separately here.

3.4.1 Desire is pain

Nouns which are used to talk about sharp pain are also used to refer to
sexual desire; in the following citations *twinge* and *stab* are used:

I had felt a twinge of desire.
(fiction)

28

A stab of pleasure, or its anticipation, pierced her. She felt weak with desire.

(fiction)

Metaphors of piercing are mainly used to describe women's desire. Literal pain is for most people a negative experience; in these citations, desire is, like some kinds of pain, a sudden, distracting and invasive sensation, but unlike pain, physically pleasant.

3.4.2 Desire is an illness

Disease is a metaphor for a range of topics, mostly those regarded as social ills. *Cancer*, for instance, is used to talk about topics such as the following in the corpus: civil litigation, gambling, juvenile delinquency, inflation, racism, unemployment, violence. While some of the lexis of illness is used to talk about sexual desire, DESIRE IS ILLNESS is significantly different from the metaphor SOCIAL PROBLEMS ARE A DISEASE. In the case of desire, suffering from metaphorical illness is not evaluated negatively, but ambivalently, as the following citations suggest:

. . . a fever of desire.
(fiction)

I am sick with love.
(fiction)

The use of *fever* and *sick* to express DESIRE IS ILLNESS seems to draw on the loss, common to both states, of complete, rational control of body and mind. A link between desire and illness is also present through physical sensations such as heat and dizziness, which are sometimes associated with desire, and are also symptoms of illness. (There is corpus evidence to show that *feverish* is used to talk about other states involving lack of control or judgement, such as thoughtless gambling.)

Healthy and *unhealthy* are also used to talk about desire; but they refer and evaluate in a different way and are discussed in a separate section below.

3.4.3 Desire is madness

The loss of rational control which is an element of pain and illness metaphors and which underlies falling metaphors, is brought to the fore in the MADNESS metaphor. This metaphor is highly ambivalent in its evaluation. Historically, sexual desires and acts which infringed prevailing moral standards were linked, negatively, with insanity as recently as early in the twentieth century. The high degree to which the expression *sex maniac* is

29

established in the language may also be a reflection of this link. In the following citation, its collocation with *branded* shows that it is intended as a highly negatively evaluating term:

> I got slapped very hard. I was four years old and already I had been branded a sex maniac.
>
> (broadsheet journalism)

Sex maniac is sometimes used to refer to people whose sexual desires lead them to seek unwilling partners and/or to acts of violence:

> She was a girl in the wrong place at the wrong time and she fell victim to a convicted sex maniac.
>
> (*Today* newspaper)

The above citations, taken alone, would suggest that the MADNESS metaphor negatively evaluates; however, DESIRE IS MADNESS has several interpretations.

In informal conversation, for example, *sex maniac* is used frequently in a jocular sense. Other expressions of DESIRE IS MADNESS reflect the common experience that the abandonment of everyday, rational control, becoming 'mad', is at the heart of sexual pleasure:

> . . . a disruptive love which is perfect, a blissful insanity without guilt, explanations or neat Freudian logic.
>
> (*Independent* newspaper)

> The dance grew quicker and simpler and more forcefully intimate until nothing separated her from him. There was only love and this insane freefalling bliss.
>
> (fiction)

Metaphors from the areas of pain, illness and madness, then, stress to varying degrees lack of rational control and physical sensations of desire. Although the vehicles of these metaphors generally refer to undesirable states, the metaphorical uses are not negatively evaluating for the most part, but on the contrary often encode the experiencer's pleasure at losing touch with his or her rational self.

3.5 Desire is appetite

It seems unsurprising that appetite for food is used to talk about sexual desire, given that hunger and desire are two of our most basic physical wants, and that satisfying each is a source of pleasure. The metaphors used in English focus largely on desire for sex or for a partner rather than on the act of sex. *Hunger* is a common linguistic expression of this metaphor in fiction:

> Her body hungered for him.
> (fiction)

30

I just never expected him to be so virile, so hungry for sex.

(fiction)

Sex-starved is also used to refer to unsatisfied desire; unlike *hunger* and *hungry*, it has humorous connotations:

The popular image of sex-starved singles or marauding lager louts is certainly called into question.

(broadsheet journalism)

. . . every sex-starved boy scout's fantasy back in the 70s.

(magazines)

Appetite can be also used to talk about sexual desires:

John Kennedy's sexual appetite is reputed to have been gargantuan.

(non-fiction)

The logical entailment of the metaphor of DESIRE IS HUNGER is that the desired partner is a pleasant food. Sexual partners are often described as *tasty*, or referred to as types of food. Anecdotal evidence suggests that in intimate or otherwise very informal settings, an enormous variety of terms is used, most of which refer to parts of the desired person's body (*melons, figs*, etc.) rather than the whole person. The only institutionalised terms in the corpus are *tart* and *crumpet*, which are probably untypical of more intimate use, and are used to talk, usually in a derogatory way, about a woman:

. . . a couple of girls, some drinks, all of which was very welcome at the time. Pleasant girls, too, not obvious tarts.

(fiction)

Crumpet is less negative, but an inevitable entailment of a metaphor which equates people with food to be consumed is to downplay their personalities and desires:

Men know they fancy that bit of crumpet. They recognise boredom and seek variety.

(journalism)

The metaphor of sexual desire as appetite and the desired person as food would suggest that sexual activity would be spoken of in terms of eating. In fact, this is rare in English; the following citation is unusual:

He'd called her a whore, thrown her on the bed and devoured her body as he would a piece of meat at the market.

(fiction)

In a cross-linguistic study of English and Chagga, a Bantu language of Tanzania, Michele Emanatian (1995) finds that while eating itself is not

31

usually a metaphor for sex in English, it is used as a metaphor for sexual intercourse in Chagga; his examples include (Chagga transcription omitted):

Does she taste good?
(literally: Is she a good sexual partner?)

Give me a taste (of) there, woman.
(literally: Let me try you out sexually.)

If I eat her, I won't have to eat again.
(literally: If I have sex with her, I'll be satisfied forever.)

(Emanatian 1995: 168)

It is not difficult for an English speaker to interpret these metaphorical uses, as they are logical extensions of the appetite and food metaphors used in English. However, they would be innovative in English; the DESIRE IS APPETITE metaphor is conventionally focused on anticipation of pleasure, or pleasurable anticipation.

3.6 The experiencer of desire is an animal

A very widespread metaphor in Western culture [is] PASSIONS ARE BEASTS INSIDE A PERSON. According to this metaphor, there is a part of each person that is a wild animal. Civilised people are supposed to keep that part of them private, that is, they are supposed to keep the animal inside them.

(Lakoff 1987: 392)

The notion of people having an animal side to their nature is sometimes employed to talk about sexual desire. However, corpus evidence does not show that desire is talked about as if it were an animal separate from its experiencer, as Lakoff's description might lead one to expect. The metaphor is mainly realised in the use of *animal* to premodify words such as *passion*, as in the following citation:

Newman sprawled back on the bed. It had been sheer animal passion for him.

(fiction)

Like the MADNESS metaphor, this seems to highlight the lack of rational control associated with desire, and here it seems to evaluate positively. Where *animal* or *beast* is used as the head word in a nominal group, the evaluation is usually negative, especially where *beast* collocates with *sex*, a frequent tabloid press usage:

Sex Beast Jailed
> (headline, tabloid press)

Where the collocation is with *sexy* however, the evaluation is positive:

> He's an urbane, elegant, sexy beast who perhaps studies champagne vintages.
>
> (*Today* newspaper)

In the following citation, the topic of *beast* is not a single individual but a way of behaving. The writer of this text shows the common tendency to extend a metaphor with other words from the field of the vehicle, in this case *roam* and *slay*:

> In San Diego last night, Anita Hill told about 1,000 women politicians that women should slay the sexual harassment beast that she says still roams the American workplace.
>
> (radio journalism)

Beast and *animal* are also used metaphorically to talk about violence. Aspects of meaning highlighted by both metaphors are loss of rational control and uninhibited expression of feelings, characteristics which are associated with animals. Examination of citations above shows that these qualities, when associated with desire, are not always negatively evaluated; different writers use them to encode different values, which can be traced through an examination of collocates and wider context.

In this section, I have discussed and illustrated some of the metaphors which occur frequently in discussion of desire in the Bank of English. It has emerged that desire is often placed metaphorically away from the self, either as an external, often elemental force, or as an animal temporarily taking over the experiencer. Desire is often talked of in terms of other physical experiences and disruptions, such as hunger and illness, pain and madness. Each conceptual metaphor can be used to express positive or negative evaluation.

4 DESIRE AND ANGER

DESIRE IS FIRE is looked at separately in this section because of the strong linguistic connections it has with metaphors for anger; the degree to which the metaphorical expressions of both groups of feelings are shared is, as Lakoff (1987) argues, suggestive.

4.1 Desire is fire, desire is electricity

Fire and heat as metaphors for desire have been analysed and commented on by several writers (for example, Lakoff 1987; Patthey-Chavez *et al.* 1996).

There is a good deal of evidence for the existence of this metaphor in the Bank of English; a number of words from the domain of heat and fire are used to talk about desire. Desire is referred to as *fire* or as *flames*, and quantified using words such as *flicker*:

> In her the fires of passion didn't just burn, they raged.
> (fiction)

> ... to keep the flame of passion alive indefinitely.
> (fiction)

> ... a flicker of desire.
> (fiction)

Knowledge of fires is mapped onto desire at many points; desire can start with *a spark*, *be ignited*, and then be kept going by *stoking* or *fuelling*. Events can *dampen* or *extinguish* desire as water can dampen or extinguish a fire:

> ... to stoke the flames of your desire.
> (magazines)

> How do you keep the embers of passion stirred in your own relationship after fifteen years?
> (fiction)

> ... extinguishing their passion.
> (magazines)

The metaphor seems to have been established in English for some time, shown by the existence of the words *ardent* and *ardour*. Indeed, these are now so well established as to have lost both their literal sense of 'fiery' and any sense of metaphoricity when used to talk about desire.

In English, fire as a metaphor for sexual desire highlights the notion of desire as a dangerous or even destructive force, which can spread rapidly in a way that is difficult to control. Positive entailments of this metaphor are connotations of vitality and the warmth associated with fire. Like food, warmth is one of our basic physical needs, which may provide a further reason for the frequency and range of expressions of this metaphor. Lakoff (1987) believes that all basic metaphors have their origin at some point in physical experience, and that this metaphor is grounded in our physical experience of desire, which includes feelings of raised body temperature.

A physiological connection may also underlie the related metaphor DESIRE IS ELECTRICITY; citations relate the sensation of an electric shock to the feeling of being near a person who evokes sexual desire. The lexis of electricity used to talk about desire includes words such as *charge*, *crackle* and *current*:

> Richard sensed the crackle of desire between them.
> (fiction)

You meet an ex-lover and there's still a charge between you. Even though you're both married to other people by now, you're tempted to go to bed together.

(journalism)

4.2 Anger is fire

Several researchers have looked at fire as a metaphor for anger and hatred (Lakoff 1987; Yu 1995). There is corpus evidence that this metaphorical expression is frequently realised. Citations of *flames of* for example show almost half of these uses to be non-literal, and more than half of those uses to be associated with anger or conflict; the other metaphorical uses are associated with sexual desire. In a corpus which contained less journalistic material (with its frequent reports of fires and war) metaphorical uses might be even more frequent. The following citation is typical of metaphorical use:

. . . with the tabloid press cynically fanning the flames of mindless anger.

(radio journalism)

As with desire, fire is mapped onto anger and hatred at many points; anger is *sparked* or *ignited*, bursts into *flames* which are *fanned* or *fuelled*, and can be *dampened*. In the following citation, hatred is *stoked* as desire can be:

At a time when the vast majority of South Africans are mourning the loss of a leader, it will not do to stoke the fires of racial hatred.

(broadsheet journalism)

However, the lexis used to realise ANGER IS FIRE is not identical at every point with that used to realise DESIRE IS FIRE. In the following citation, the items *fiery* and *heated* are used to talk about anger; only *fiery* is found in citations about sexual desire:

One insider reported that the two players had a fiery exchange of words in the club foyer, 'it was very, very heated,' he said.

(*Today* newspaper)

Exploring the use of fire as a metaphor for both anger and desire shows that our prototypical anger and desire scenarios have much in common; the feeling develops rapidly once sparked, it can lead to loss of control, it can sometimes be deliberately fed (*stoked, fuelled*) and it can be destructive, although this can have positive implications sometimes, in clearing away emotional debris. Lakoff (1987) explores the metaphorical connections between fire and lust in detail; his belief in the importance metaphors have in framing our thought and actions leads him to speculate that the shared metaphor may lead to mental connections between sexual desire and hate and anger, which, he suggests, may not be present in all cultures.

35

5 MANIFESTATIONS OF DESIRE

In the previous sections, sexual desire has been discussed in general terms. In this section I look at two groups of metaphorical expressions which are often used to evaluate different manifestations of desire, especially to compare and contrast homosexual and heterosexual desire.

5.1 Clean desire and dirty desire

Lakoff (1987; 1993) argues that certain conceptual metaphors are 'basic-level'. A basic-level metaphor is one which is grounded in direct physical experience and so may be deeper and more central to our thinking than culturally learned metaphors. He cites SIN IS DIRTY, VIRTUE IS CLEAN as a basic-level metaphor, arguing that it is widespread if not universal across cultures, and that it is grounded in everyday physical experience; dirty objects are usually unpleasant and possibly dangerous. The metaphor is used to talk about many states or forms of behaviour regarded as either virtuous or wrong. The following citation shows the use of *clean* to mean 'without corruption':

> The country seemed on the brink of a new era of clean, democratic, civilian-led politics.
>
> (*Economist*)

Dirty is frequently used to talk about corruption in politics; the word occurring to its right most frequently is *tricks*. *Dirty* is used more frequently than *clean* as a metaphor; although *clean* occurs more than twice as frequently as *dirty* in the corpus, its literal uses are very frequent. Approximately 35 per cent of citations for *dirty* are metaphorical, 10 per cent alluding to sexual desire or behaviour. Only around 7 per cent of citations of *clean* are metaphorical, with less than 1 per cent of citations alluding to sexual desire or behaviour. A number of near synonyms for *dirty* are used with a similar metaphorical meaning; these include *filthy*, *grubby* and *smutty*.

Clean is used to describe behaviour, talk and texts which do not deal with sexual desire. The evaluation is usually positive, as in the following citation:

> Written and produced by John Hughes . . . , the film is good clean family fun.
>
> (magazines)

In contrast, *dirty*, *smutty* and *filthy* are used to express negative judgements about sexual desires and behaviour. The same relationship holds between the three items when they are used literally and metaphorically; *smutty* is mildly dirty and has overtones of childishness, while *filthy* is extremely dirty and has very unpleasant connotations.

Dirty stories and *dirty talk* contain more explicit sexual details, or include taboo words for sexual behaviour. In the following citations, this is viewed negatively by the writer:

> . . . coarse and crude but no more erotic than a kid yelling dirty words.
>
> (broadsheet journalism)

> Somehow the presence of her up there and talking dirty can be desperately humiliating for most men.
>
> (broadsheet journalism)

The evaluation is more negative where *filthy* or *filth* is chosen:

> It was the most violent film that I have ever seen, and I was equally appalled by some of the constant filthy language.
>
> (*Today* newspaper)

> . . . his sustained outpouring of filth and innuendo.
>
> (*Today* newspaper)

These items can also be used to describe any form of sexual behaviour which is not approved of. *Filthy*, in particular, is used to express strong condemnation of various forms of sexual behaviour:

> . . . the filthiest acts imaginable, baiting boys and looking for trouble.
>
> (fiction)

> He was a filthy pervert. God knows how many women he molested.
>
> (fiction)

It has been suggested that *clean*, *dirty*, and their derivations and near synonyms are used by writers to encode their negative value judgements about sexual desire and behaviour. However, this orientation can be exploited. In the following citations, *dirty* is used to describe activities which the writer evaluates positively:

> . . . a summer of dirty weekend visits to country hotels.
>
> (broadsheet journalism)

> They claim to be a reflection of the way women really think and talk about sex, but we all know that in reality women's conversations are far dirtier and far funnier than anything we ever see in print.
>
> (broadsheet journalism)

It may be that this metaphor allows speakers to put forward a covertly positive evaluation of sexual desire and erotic talk; to talk about these topics in more explicitly approving terms might be unacceptable or simply embarrassing. The use of the metaphor also suggests that fundamental ambivalence in our attitudes to sex which was noted above in connection with the metaphors of madness.

5.2 Healthy desire and unhealthy desire

The other central metaphor used to evaluate manifestations of desire is that of health, expressed mainly in the items *healthy* and *unhealthy*. These were not looked at in the section on illness above as the metaphors dealt with in that section are used to describe the physical effects of experiencing sexual desire; *healthy* and *unhealthy* in contrast are used to talk judgementally about sexual desire and behaviour. In this metaphor, GOOD DESIRE IS HEALTHY, BAD DESIRE IS UNHEALTHY. Judgements about good and bad desire are subjective in most cases whereas judgements about literal health or ill-health can often be made more scientifically. Using *healthy* as metaphor for good, and *unhealthy* as a metaphor for bad, then, plays down the subjectivity of the evaluation and suggests that, as with literal health, objective judgements can be made about desire.

As is the case for the CLEAN/DIRTY metaphor, the negative term is employed proportionately more frequently as a metaphor. This point, and the following observations about frequency, of course reflect the texts contained in the Bank of English. It is possible that a corpus of a different kind would show different patterns of use.

There are fifteen times as many citations for *healthy* as for *unhealthy* in the corpus, probably reflecting the number of magazine and newspaper texts on diet and exercise. The main use of *healthy* is literal; lexical words occurring most frequently immediately after *healthy* are, in descending order, *eating*, *diet*, *people* and *person*. *Unhealthy* is also used in its literal sense, but the most frequent lexical word occurring immediately after it is *interest*, suggesting metaphorical use. This is followed by, in descending order, *diet*, *obsession*, *foods*, *relationship*. These collocational patterns give a useful general overview of usage as both *healthy* and *unhealthy* are mainly used as attributive adjectives.

In its non-literal use, *unhealthy* is used to evaluate interpersonal relationships and expressions of these, such as sexual practices and desires. Where *healthy* is used metaphorically about sexuality, it appears to describe heterosexual desires and relationships within the 'normal' limits of conventional acceptability; i.e. excluding pornography, incest or relationships with partners who are much older or younger:

> Sex education is necessary for them to be informed and build up healthy attitudes about sex.
>
> (magazines)

> She had her sights firmly set on a career and, despite a healthy interest in boys, concentrated on training as a State Enrolled Nurse.
>
> (fiction)

Within the Bank of English, homosexual desire is sometimes described as *unhealthy*:

Society needs women because it wants the leavening that only they can provide. There is something very unhealthy about the homosexual world; no wonder they arouse such antagonism.

(non-fiction)

In the following citation, *unhealthy* is used to describe sexual desire in teenage women, which the writer finds dangerous:

[This behaviour] is tailor-made to induce teen infatuation, unhealthy sexual fantasies and pandemonium at gigs.

(magazines)

Interest in pornography or masochism is also often described as *unhealthy*:

He had an unhealthy interest in pornographic pictures.

(*Today* newspaper)

He had developed unhealthy sexual fantasies while at a boarding school where corporal punishment was carried out in the presence of other boys, the court was told.

(broadsheet journalism)

The same item is used to talk about desire based on coercion, such as paedophilia:

That area would be attractive to a man with an unhealthy interest in young children.

(*Today* newspaper)

In the following two citations writers use *unhealthy* to encode judgements as to an appropriate level of interest in sex. The first writer considers that 'excessive' interest in sex is bad, while the second writer condemns fear of sex:

There's an unhealthy preoccupation with sex.

(*Today* newspaper)

It would seem that advertising campaigns evoked an unhealthy fear of sex rather than providing practical advice.

(broadsheet journalism)

In summary, it seems that *healthy* desire means no more or less than desire which the writer approves of, while *unhealthy* desire is usually desire which the writer disapproves of or fears. It is significant that the range of desires described as *unhealthy* by various speakers and writers ranges from homosexual and teenage desire to such damaging desires as paedophilia. If words create and reflect mental categories as Lakoff (1987) argues, then it is alarming that this one word is used as a way of grouping these distinct phenomena. The result is an insidious blanket condemnation of them all.

6 SUMMARY AND CONCLUSIONS

In this chapter some of the major metaphorical networks used to talk about sexual desire have been discussed. The evidence presented has been taken from a corpus of current English, and the findings inevitably reflect the bias of the texts in that corpus. The texts are, however, reasonably representative of the public language encountered by most of us in our everyday lives, being taken from genres such as newspaper and radio journalism, fiction and non-fiction. Few of us are not daily exposed to language like that of the corpus in large quantities. While we may as individuals contest some of the values espoused by the writers of these texts, they must to an extent form a backdrop to our own value systems, even if it is one which we consciously challenge rather than accept.

It was argued in the introduction that an examination of the metaphors frequently used to talk about a topic can give us an insight into the ways in which that topic is constructed by the language. A complex picture emerges through this study of the metaphors used to talk about sexual desire. An examination of several groups of metaphors suggests that we fear desire, possibly for its potential to disrupt the established patterns of our lives; desire is talked of metaphorically as a wild animal, and as the dangerous and elemental forces of water, fire and electricity. Another entailment of these metaphors, and a general tendency in the discussion of powerful emotions, is a denial that desire is a part of ourselves; we project it linguistically onto objects or forces outside ourselves. Thus desire appears uninvited and takes us over; we are not responsible. This both reflects our physical perception of desire and allows us to disclaim responsibility for 'sinful' desire.

None of the metaphors used to discuss desire in general terms is wholly positively or wholly negatively oriented, however; each metaphor is complex and can be used to highlight several different facets of desire. Thus, while the metaphor of being taken over by a powerful invader sometimes presents a frightening and unwelcome experience, it is sometimes a description of great and unexpected pleasure. While insanity, illness and pain in their literal senses, and in some metaphorical uses, represent dreadful suffering, strangely, they can also be used to highlight the joys of desire. Metaphors of HUNGER are similarly ambivalent. Likewise, FIRE metaphors can highlight the destructive potential of desire; they can also positively evaluate its physical experience.

If a strong view of the centrality of metaphor for thought is taken, it follows that topics which share a metaphorical vehicle may be linked conceptually. FIRE metaphors are of interest and concern because they are shared with the discussion of anger. Also of concern here is the use of metaphorical expressions such as *dirty* and *unhealthy* to describe different manifestations of desire.

It has also been argued that metaphor is used, consciously or unconsciously, to encode subjective judgements in a way that hides their sub-

40

jectivity. The groups of expressions realising VIRTUE IS CLEAN, SIN IS DIRTY and GOOD DESIRE IS HEALTHY, BAD DESIRE IS UNHEALTHY often have this function. Speakers use a metaphorical expression to encode their approval, or – far more frequently – their disapproval, of a manifestation of desire. Hearers and readers are invited to apply their knowledge of literal cleanliness and health (desirable) and dirt and ill-health (undesirable) to the topic. The evaluation, thereby, takes on the appearance of objectivity. Gradual changes in our attitudes towards the expression of sexual desire mean that the entailments of these metaphors are not as readily accepted as they may have been in the past. It remains to be seen, however, whether these two conceptual metaphors will lose their evaluative force.

ACKNOWLEDGEMENTS

I would like to thank Carmen Rosa Caldas-Coulthard and Rosamund Moon for their comments on the first draft of this chapter; all remaining shortcomings and omissions are my own.

REFERENCES

Bolinger, D. (1980) *Language: The Loaded Weapon. The Use and Abuse of Language Today*, London: Longman.

Deignan, A. (1995) *Collins COBUILD Guides to English: 7: Metaphor*, London: Harper-Collins.

Emanatian, M. (1995) 'Metaphor and the expression of emotion: the value of cross-cultural perspectives', in *Metaphor and Symbolic Activity* 10(3): 163–82.

Fairclough, N. (1989) *Language and Power*, London: Longman.

Gibbs, R. (1993) 'Process and products in making sense of tropes', in A. Ortony (ed.) *Metaphor and Thought* (2nd edn), Cambridge: Cambridge University Press.

Gibbs, R. and O' Brien, J.E. (1990) 'Idioms and mental imagery: the metaphorical motivation for idiomatic meaning', *Cognition* 36: 35–68.

Henderson, W. (1986) 'Metaphor in economics', in R.M. Coulthard (ed.) *Talking about Text*, University of Birmingham ELR Monographs no. 13.

Lakoff, G. (1987) *Women, Fire and Dangerous Things: What Categories Reveal about the Mind*, Chicago and London: University of Chicago Press.

—— (1993) 'The contemporary theory of metaphor', in A. Ortony (ed.) *Metaphor and Thought* (2nd edn), Cambridge: Cambridge University Press.

Lakoff, G. and Johnson, M. (1980) *Metaphors We Live By*, Chicago: University of Chicago Press.

Low, G. (1988) 'On teaching metaphor', *Applied Linguistics* 9(2): 125–47.

Mey, J. (1994) *Pragmatics: An Introduction*, Oxford: Basil Blackwell.

Patthey-Chavez, G., Clare, L. and Youmans, M. (1996) 'Watery passion: the struggle between hegemony and sexual liberation in erotic fiction for women', *Discourse and Society* 7(1): 77–106.

Reddy, M.J. (1993) 'The conduit metaphor: a case of frame conflict in our language about language', in A. Ortony (ed.) *Metaphor and Thought* (2nd edn) Cambridge: Cambridge University Press.

Rohrer, T. (1995) 'The metaphorical logic of (political) rape: the new wor(l)d order', *Metaphor and Symbolic Activity* 10(2): 115–37.

Sontag, S. (1991) *Illness as Metaphor/AIDS and its Metaphors*, Harmondsworth: Penguin.

Sweetser, E. (1990) *From Etymology to Pragmatics: Metaphorical and Cultural Aspects of Semantic Structure*, Cambridge: Cambridge University Press.

van Teeffelen, T. (1994) 'Racism and metaphor: the Palestinian-Israeli conflict in popular literature', *Discourse and Society* 5(3): 381–405.

Yu, N. (1995) 'Metaphorical expressions of anger and happiness in English and Chinese', *Metaphor and Symbolic Activity* 10(2): 59–92.

2

KISSING AND CUDDLING
The reciprocity of romantic and sexual activity
Elizabeth Manning

1 INTRODUCTION

Language both reflects and shapes our view of the world. This applies to grammar as well as lexis – to the way that people choose to put words together as well as to the actual words they choose to use. This chapter will show the link between lexis and grammar as it relates to verbs and phrases indicating romantic, affectionate, or sexual activities and relationships, and the link between these verbs and phrases and people's view of the events they represent. I will focus on verbs and phrases that can be classified grammatically as 'reciprocal' because of the structures or patterns in which they are used, since these seem to constitute the largest subgroup of lexical items relating to the semantic area of romantic and sexual activity.

The data described here is based on the 211-million-word Bank of English Corpus held at the University of Birmingham by Collins COBUILD. This is a general corpus of current English which contains texts from a variety of sources, both British and American – books, magazines, newspapers, leaflets and so on – and a large quantity of spoken data – broadcasts, phone-ins, lectures, and ordinary conversation. The corpus is thus a broad representation of the culture from which the texts are taken and can be analysed to provide information about that culture. All the examples cited here are taken from this corpus.

Analysis of corpus data makes possible a more reliable, objective, and informative description of a language than one based on the observation, memory, and intuition of individuals. As well as clearly showing the patterns a word has – both grammatical and collocational – corpus data can show the relative frequency of these patterns. This relative frequency is linked to the meaning of the word and the effect that this has on how people choose to use it. The more data an analysis is based on, the more reliable it is, and the more certain one can be that a sample of data which is analysed is representative of the usage of the word one is interested in (see Sinclair 1987, 1991).

This chapter will first give an introduction to the concept of the 'reciprocal verb' in section 2 and then deal more specifically with verbs of romantic and sexual activity that fall into this category in section 3, focusing on their grammatical patterns and the semantic differences between these patterns. This section will also introduce verbal phrases, such as *fall in love*, which relate to this semantic area and have reciprocal patterns (3.4). In sections 4 to 6, selected verbs and phrases are analysed with regard to the gender and sexuality of the participants, and to the relative frequency of the patterns with which the verb or phrase occurs. The paper also includes considerations of verbs that are almost reciprocal in their patterning (section 7) and of those verbs that are non-reciprocal (section 8) yet belong to this particular semantic area.

I will be using both the basic grammatical terms Subject and Object, and the terms used by Halliday when talking about the functions of clause elements: Actor (the person or thing that performs an action) and Goal (the person or thing affected by an action); and, on the analytical level of the clause as message, Theme (the person or thing that is mentioned first in a clause – 'the point of departure of the message' (Halliday 1994: 37)), which may or may not be the same as the grammatical Subject or the Actor (*ibid.*: 30–6, 109–12). I will be referring to the people involved in a particular action or activity as the 'participants'.

2 RECIPROCAL VERBS

It has been recognised that the concept of reciprocity comes into the analysis of a number of verbs and other expressions. For example, Quirk uses the term 'mutual participation' when describing one of the different possible meanings of noun groups co-ordinated with *and*, giving the examples 'John and Mary played tennis' and 'Margot and Dennis are in love' (Quirk *et al.* 1985: 943, 954–5). There are further references in publications by Dixon (Dixon 1991: 59–61) and Levin (Levin 1993: 36, 44, 58–65), and in the *Collins COBUILD English Grammar* (1990: 157–9). A recent comprehensive account of reciprocity in relation to verbs may be found in Francis *et al.* (1996: 455–73).

This chapter is based on the categorisation of reciprocal verbs that is used in the *Collins COBUILD English Dictionary* (1987, 1995). The label 'reciprocal' is used to identify verbs that have particular combinations of patterns, as described below, and this label is also given to some verbal phrases. The categorisation is basically grammatical, but also has a semantic component. Verbs which have the specified combinations of patterns can be seen to relate to actions and processes which are, semantically, of the same basic type. These are actions and processes in which two or more people, groups, or things do the same thing to each other, have a relationship, or are linked because they are participating jointly in an action or event. This is a broad classification, and the category of 'reciprocal verbs' can be subdivided according to a more delicate semantic analysis. As well as the semantic areas of romantic and sexual activity, reciprocal verbs are used to construe the semantic areas of conversing and discussing things; fighting; competing; collaborating; meeting; and forming, ending, and having relationships in general. These semantic areas can be seen to have a basic similarity with regard to the number of participants that are necessarily involved in the action or process, and the roles of these participants, i.e. there must be more than one participant, and it is possible for both participants to be actively involved to the same extent.

In the COBUILD analysis, a reciprocal verb has two basic patterns. First, it can be used with a plural Subject – that is, a Subject consisting of a plural noun group or two or more co-ordinated noun groups. When it is used with this plural Subject, the meaning is that the people, groups, or things involved are interacting in some way with each other. For example, two people can *fight*, can *have a chat*, or can *meet*. This pattern is used to represent both participants as having an equal role in the action or process.

Second, it can also be used with a Subject which refers to one of the participants, and a clause element which indicates the other participant. This clause element may be one of three things:

- A prepositional Object (that is, an Object consisting of a prepositional phrase). For example, in *He was fighting with his brother*, the other participant is indicated by the prepositional Object *with his brother*.
- An Adjunct. For example, in *I had a chat with him*, the other participant is indicated by the Adjunct *with him*.
- An Object. For example, in *I met him at university*, the other participant is indicated by the Object *him*.

This pattern is used to focus on the involvement of the first participant mentioned, or to imply that they have a more active role or greater responsibility for what happens. Usually the action or process is reciprocal even when this pattern is used, so 'He was fighting with his brother' implies that his brother was also fighting with him. However, sometimes this pattern is used because the action or process is not, in the particular instance concerned, reciprocal, as when, for example, 'The woman kisses a baby' or 'A car collides with a tree': in this instance the baby does not kiss the woman and the tree does not collide with the car. The primary participant is clear, and the speaker does not have the option of taking the other participant as the Subject ('The tree collided with the car'), or of using the verb with a plural Subject ('The car and the tree collided').

Note that the noun group in the second basic pattern may be a reciprocal pronoun – *each other* or *one another*, as in 'They were fighting with each other' or 'They met each other at work'. In this case, the second pattern is equivalent to the first pattern – there is a plural Subject referring to both participants. The reciprocal pronoun serves to emphasise, rather than indicate, the reciprocity of the action, since with these reciprocal verbs the use of the plural Subject by itself indicates reciprocity. However, the form of the pattern – whether the verb is used with a prepositional Object, an Adjunct, or an Object – itself conveys something about the relationship of the participants, as it does when the Subject refers to one participant (see section 3.2 below).

It should be noted that the reciprocity, or potential reciprocity, of the action is essential to the classification. For example, the verb *wait* can have a plural Subject, as in 'They waited', and can be used with a prepositional phrase referring to someone else who is also performing the action, as in 'She was waiting with a friend', but it is not considered to be a reciprocal verb because the reciprocal meaning is absent – there does not have to be more than one person involved in the action of waiting. For each reciprocal verb, one pattern may be more frequent than the other, depending on the meaning of the verb and what people want to focus on when they use it. This issue is explored further in section 6.

3 RECIPROCAL VERBS OF ROMANTIC AND SEXUAL ACTIVITY

Many verbs relating to romantic and sexual activity have patterns of the two kinds described above. In the case of the second kind of pattern, there are two versions:

- Noun group + verb + *with* + noun group (where the verb is used with a prepositional Object – the preposition used is *to* rather than *with* in the case of a couple of verbs)
- Noun group + verb + noun group (where the verb is used with an Object)

Some of these verbs have one version of the second kind of pattern, and some have the other, and the significance of this difference will be discussed later. Table 2.1 shows a list of all verbs and phrasal verbs relating to romantic and sexual activity which can be classified as reciprocal. These verbs, along with other verbs, were identified as reciprocal in the course of the compilation of the *Collins COBUILD English Dictionary* (1995 edition), which covers all words in general use. Note that they belong to various register levels and indicate various levels of intimacy. The verbs *breed*, *copulate*, and *mate* are usually used when referring to animal rather than human behaviour.

3.1 Patterns

I will now explain and illustrate the patterns of these reciprocal verbs of romantic and sexual activity.

Table 2.1 Reciprocal verbs of romantic and sexual activity

bonk	intermarry
breed	kiss
canoodle	marry
cohabit	mate
copulate	neck
court	screw
cuddle	shag
date	smooch
elope	snog
embrace	
fornicate	cuddle up
fuck	go out
get married	make out
hug	

Pattern 1 Plural noun group + verb

In this pattern, the verb is used with a plural Subject. All the verbs previously listed have this pattern. Here are some examples:

We hugged and cried.

She gave a fractional smile. *They kissed.* She drove away.

We'd only *been going out* for about six months at the time.

When *we married* we vowed to be together, to live together, and to die together, she said.

It may be that *some couples cohabit* initially because they are uncertain about the strength of their relationship.

John flew to be at her side after her fight with Browne, and *they* have been seen *smooching* in New York.

The 'plural noun group' may in fact be two co-ordinated noun groups as in this example:

Eighteen months after meeting, *Jessica and Todd got married.*

As can be seen from the examples above, if a speaker chooses to use this pattern, they represent both participants as being equally involved in the action or activity. The action or activity is construed as unambiguously reciprocal.

Pattern 2(i) Noun group + verb + *with* + noun group

In this pattern, the verb is used with a Subject referring to one participant and followed by a prepositional phrase indicating the other (the

47

prepositional Object). In most cases, the preposition is *with* (the exceptions are mentioned below).

Table 2.2 shows the verbs and phrasal verbs indicating sexual activity or relationships that have this pattern, which is illustrated by the following examples:

Widows' benefits are not payable if the widow remarries or if *she is cohabiting with a man* as his wife.

The 23-year-old tennis heart-throb smooched with Blue Lagoon star Brooke during breaks in a TV show he was filming.

He used to go out with Kylie Minogue.

In the case of the verb *cuddle up*, the preposition is more often *to* (34 occurrences in the Bank of English corpus) than *with* (10 occurrences). If *to* is used, it is the physical closeness involved in the activity that is focused on, rather than the fact that the two people involved are doing something together:

'When I met Kev, I thought, mmm, nice,' laughs Paula, as *she cuddles up to her man*.

Elvis Presley's daughter Lisa Marie, 24, cuddles up with music writer husband Danny Keough, 27.

With the passive verb (or phrase) *get married*, the preposition is always *to*, not *with*. Again, this shows that the action is not seen as people doing something together, but as one person becoming metaphorically joined with or connected to another. This pattern with the preposition *to* is shown in the following example:

I'm getting married to my American girlfriend, Ginny, in September.

Table 2.2 Verbs and phrasal verbs of romantic and sexual activity with pattern 2(i)

breed	mate
canoodle	neck
cohabit	smooch
copulate	snog
elope	
fornicate	cuddle up
intermarry	go out
get married	make out

Pattern 2(ii) Noun group + verb + noun group

In this pattern, the verb is used with a Subject referring to one participant and followed by a noun group referring to the other (the Object).

Table 2.3 shows verbs indicating affectionate or sexual contact, or sexual relationships, that have this pattern, which is illustrated by the following examples:

Table 2.3 Verbs and phrasal verbs of romantic and sexual activity with pattern 2(ii)

bonk	hug
court	kiss
cuddle	marry
date	screw
embrace	shag
fuck	snog

He wanted to *hug her*.

She kissed me and turned out the light.

She married a barrister, and died childless in 1864.

Note that *kiss* also has the patterns 'plural noun group + verb + noun group' and 'noun group + verb + noun group + noun group'. The noun group which follows the verb, or follows the first noun group, is something such as *goodbye* or *goodnight*, which indicates the purpose, meaning, and context of the kiss:

They kissed goodnight before splitting up to avoid photographers who spotted them.

He kissed me goodnight and then went off to check on something in the kitchen.

Kiss is the only verb which has this combination of patterns. Other verbs which have the pattern 'noun group + verb + noun group + noun group' – for example *bid* and *wave* – do not have the reciprocal pattern 'plural noun group + verb + noun group', i.e. 'They waved goodbye' does not mean that they waved goodbye to each other. For these verbs, the action is, for some reason, not seen as one which is primarily mutual or clearly reciprocal.

3.2 Difference between the two 'two-participant' patterns

There seems to be a difference in connotation between the prepositional Object pattern and the Object pattern. With the prepositional Object pattern, there is the implication that the activity is a joint one, although the focus is on the participant mentioned as Subject. In Hallidayan terms, this participant is taken as the Theme (the element that comes first in the clause), because they are the person the speaker is concerned with and wants to say something about. The Subject is, in this case, the same as the Actor, i.e. it refers to the person who performs the action concerned. This pattern unambiguously represents the activity as reciprocal: the participant that is mentioned as the Object must be reciprocating the action or taking an active role in the activity. If one person is *canoodling with* another, for example, the second person mentioned must also be canoodling with the first.

With the Object pattern, there is the implication that one person is doing something to someone else, although the second person, despite being presented as the Goal, may in reality take an equally active role. The action being mentioned is the action performed by the person the Subject refers to, and the fact that the other participant may be reciprocating the action is irrelevant. It should be noted that the more informal verbs referring to sexual intercourse have this pattern rather than the prepositional Object pattern, which may indicate something about the attitude of the kinds of people who use these verbs to the activity involved – it is seen as an activity in which there is one main participant rather than one with two equal (or nearly equal) participants.

In the case of the verbs referring to less intimate forms of contact – *cuddle, embrace, hug, kiss, snog* – when they are used with a Subject referring to one participant, the meaning is usually that the other participant does not do the same thing back – the action is not reciprocal. For example, if you say 'She kissed him', the implication is that he did not kiss her. The same sometimes, but not always, applies to the verb *court*. With the other verbs, the actions or processes are of such a kind that both participants have to be reciprocally involved. With *date* and *marry*, mentioning one of the participants as Subject is just done to put the focus on that person, because that is the person you are interested in. For example, you are much more likely to say 'My sister married a Frenchman' than 'A Frenchman married my sister' because you are much more likely to want to focus on your sister than on an unspecified Frenchman.

Most of the verbs we have been discussing have only one of these patterns. The only verb of sexual activity which frequently occurs with both patterns in the Bank of English corpus is *snog*, which shows an interesting ambivalence in people's minds about what kind of activity it is: one with one main participant or one with two equal participants. There are also a couple of examples of *screw with* and *fuck with* referring to sexual activity, and *shag with* also seems possible, although it does not occur in the corpus. (Most of the occurrences of *fuck with* have the meaning 'mess with', as in 'Don't fuck with us', rather than referring to sexual activity.)

50

3.3 The passive

There is potentially a passive for the prepositional Object pattern, with the pattern '*be* + past participle + *with*', but it very rarely occurs. The passive of the Object pattern – '*be* + past participle' or '*get* + past participle' – occurs slightly more often, as in 'He was kissed by everyone' or 'I didn't get shagged by anyone', but again it is not common. Using the passive voice enables the speaker to put the focus on a participant who is passively involved in the activity, by mentioning them first, as the Subject of the clause. The significance of this comparatively rare occurrence of passive structures with these verbs is that it does not often happen that a speaker who is referring to romantic or sexual activity wants to focus on the person who has a passive role by taking them as the Theme of the clause.

3.4 Reciprocal phrases

There are a number of phrases which refer to romantic or sexual activity and have similar patterns to reciprocal verbs. They are shown in Table 2.4. They can all either be used on their own with a plural Subject or be followed by a prepositional phrase beginning with *with* which refers to the other participant. Here are some examples:

There, between lunch and tea on a sunny afternoon, *they fell in love* beside the pool at the exclusive Monte Carlo Beach Club.

She saw the Bolshoi company perform 'Giselle', the tragic tale of *a sweet, naive girl who falls in love with an aristocrat*.

Any alien life-form watching us will soon believe that the human race is doomed to extinction, as it consists almost entirely of *Gold Blend drinking couples who* take seven years to kiss and never actually *have it off*.

I've only just heard that *Tom's been having it off with his secretary*.

In addition, *make love* can be followed by the preposition *to*. If one person makes love *to* another, there is the implication that the first person is taking a more active role. If one person makes love *with* another, the implication is that each person takes an equal role. This explains why, although someone

Table 2.4 Phrases for romantic and sexual activity that have reciprocal patterns

fall in love	have it off
go steady	have sex
go to bed	hold hands
have it away	make love

can *be made love to*, the expression *make love with* is not passivised: with *make love with*, the second person is equally involved, so if you want to focus on them, you make them the Subject.

Go to bed is often followed by *together*, but the other phrases are not. This is because it is often felt necessary to make it clear that the two people involved are going to the same bed (and having sex), since *They went to bed* could just mean 'They went to bed separately (to sleep)'.

3.5 Summary of description

We have shown how the grammatical patterns of verbs and phrases relating to romantic and sexual activity affect our perceptions of the reciprocity of the activity involved:

1 Total reciprocity is construed by the pattern 'plural noun group + verb' or the pattern 'noun group + verb + *with* + noun group', although the latter pattern puts one of the participants as Theme rather than both participants.
2 Ambiguous reciprocity is construed by the pattern 'noun group + verb + noun group' – this pattern does not clearly convey whether the second participant reciprocates, although sometimes it is clear from our real-world knowledge of the type of activity involved that the second participant must be reciprocating to some extent.
3 Non-reciprocity is construed by the passive – the non-active participant (the Goal) is taken as the Theme.

In patterns where one participant is mentioned before the other, that is, where one is indicated by the Subject and the other by the Object or prepositional Object, it is obvious that the choice of participant as Subject is crucial.

We will now consider evidence relating to the use of particular reciprocal verbs and phrases; cases where the other participant is not mentioned; the relative frequency of the different patterns; and verbs relating to the semantic field we are discussing which do not fall into the class of reciprocal verbs.

4 MALE AND FEMALE PARTICIPANTS

Corpus lines can be analysed to see how often the person encoded by the Subject and the Object or prepositional Object is male and how often it is female.

This is particularly interesting in the case of the phrase *make love*, where the other participant can be encoded in a prepositional phrase beginning

Table 2.5 Analysis of *make love to* (489 lines altogether – all verb forms included)

Out of 100 randomly selected lines:

male to female: 62
  e.g. 'She knew that he would make love to her.'

female to male: 20 (including 2 passive lines)
  e.g. 'She made love to him in a cramped room.'

male to male: 4
  e.g. 'He knew the man wanted to make love to him.'

female to female: 3
  e.g. 'I made love to a woman and it appealed to me.'

either to either: 4
  e.g. '. . . people making love to each other.'

other: 7

Note: The 'either to either' lines are ones where the activity is being referred to in general terms, rather than when a specific instance is being mentioned. The 'other' lines are mostly ones where the other participant is inanimate, as in, for example, 'I'm, you know, making love to my violin and all that'.

Table 2.6 Analysis of *make love with* (114 lines altogether – all verb forms included)

Out of 100 randomly selected lines:

male with female: 9
  e.g. '. . . a video of him making love with two girls.'

female with male: 45
  e.g. 'I should have made love with him,' Cathy thought.

male with male: 0

female with female: 5
  e.g. '. . . women making love with women.'

either with either: 12
  e.g. 'Who you love or make love with is a purely personal matter.'

other: 29

Note: The 'other' lines are mostly ones where *with* is part of an Adjunct, as in, for example, They probably always made love with the lights out.

with either *to* or *with*. Tables 2.5 and 2.6 show an analysis of the phrase when used with the 'prepositional Object' pattern. (For an analysis of all the patterns of this phrase, see Table 2.11 below. The tables relate to the complete Bank of English corpus.) The figures show that the more 'active' pattern, involving the preposition *to*, is used to encode male heterosexual activity more than the more 'co-operative' pattern involving the preposition *with*, whereas the opposite is true for female heterosexual activity. The evidence is sparser for references to male and female homosexual activity, but the same difference seems to occur.

We can compare these figures with the figures for two other reciprocal verbs/phrases which also refer to sexual activity. Tables 2.7 and 2.8 show figures for *have sex with* and *shag*, respectively. The figures show that, with the patterns indicated, both items are used to encode male and female heterosexual activity to a roughly equal extent, although the more neutral term *have sex with* is used to encode female heterosexual activity slightly more often than male heterosexual activity. The opposite is true for the more informal term *shag*, which has the 'noun group + verb group + noun group' pattern, with its connotations of 'doing something to someone'. This difference does not seem to occur with the references to homosexual activity – both items are used with these patterns to encode male homosexual activity more often than female homosexual activity.

Table 2.7 Analysis of *have sex with* (842 lines altogether – all verb forms included)

Out of 100 randomly selected lines:

male with female: 34
e.g. '. . . during which time I had sex with another woman a few times.'

female with male: 38
e.g. 'If I ever find my wife having sex with another man I will kill him.'

male with male: 9
e.g. 'He had sex with two young teenage boys.'

female with female: 2
e.g. '. . . photographs explicitly depicting women having sex with each other.'

either with either: 13
e.g. 'You will only catch the virus if you have sex with an infected partner.'

other: 4

Table 2.8 Analysis of *shag* (101 lines altogether – all verb forms included)

Out of 100 randomly selected lines:

male . . . female: 35
    e.g. 'I pity the poor woman that he does shag.'

female . . . male: 30
    e.g. 'All women wanted to shag him.'

male . . . male: 7
    e.g. 'I've never actually shagged a man.'

female . . . female: 1
    e.g. 'I've shagged her.'

either . . . either: 9
    e.g. 'Eventually, everybody shags everybody else.'

other: 18

---

5 NON-RECIPROCAL USES OF RECIPROCAL VERBS AND PHRASES

A few of the reciprocal verbs and phrases mentioned above can be used with a singular Subject in patterns where the other participant is not mentioned, as in 'I married young' and 'He's fallen in love'. When used like this, the focus is usually on the activity or action itself, rather than on the other person (or people) involved, as in the examples below. The other person or people are indefinite, if the activity or action in general is being referred to, or are just not mentioned, because their identity is not considered to be important:

He never *married.*

Sometimes *he had sex* as often as ten or twelve times a day.

Sometimes, however, the other person involved has already been mentioned and so their identity is clear, as in the example below:

She grew up in a middle-class New York City home, attended college, became an editor of children's books in a major New York publishing house, met Joel, a nice-looking lawyer, and *fell in love*.

Only in the case of the phrase *fall in love* does the non-reciprocal use of the phrase sometimes indicate that the other participant does not reciprocate:

He probably saw a girl across the quadrangle and *fell in love*, but she never looked at him, so he closed that door.

Table 2.9 Verbs and phrases for
romantic and sexual activity used
non-reciprocally

cohabit	have sex
date	get married
fall in love	make love
fornicate	marry
go steady	mate

In the case of the other verbs and phrases which are used non-reciprocally, the activity must be reciprocal – for example, if someone *gets married*, the other person involved must also *get married*.

The verbs and phrases in Table 2.9 are frequently used non-reciprocally.

6 RELATIVE FREQUENCY OF PATTERNS

Once it has been established what patterns we can expect verbs and phrases of this kind to have, the corpus data can be used to compare the relative frequency of patterns for reciprocal verbs and phrases. Tables 2.10 and 2.11 show two analyses of relative frequency, for the phrases *fall in love* and *make love*, respectively. It can be seen that the distribution of patterns is different for different reciprocal verbs and phrases, and depends on the action or activity in question. For example, it more frequently happens that people talk about one person falling in love with another than about two people falling in love, whereas this difference is less marked when it comes to talking about people making love. This is because falling in love is an action that is often one-sided, whereas making love necessarily involves both participants.

Table 2.10 Analysis of relative frequency of patterns for *fall in love* (2,426 lines altogether – all verb forms included)

Out of 100 randomly selected lines:

plural noun group + verb: 5
  e.g. 'It had taken six months for them to fall in love.'

noun group + verb + *with* + noun group: 52
  e.g. 'How could you fall in love with someone else?'

noun group + verb (non-reciprocal):   28
  e.g. 'I had fallen in love head over heels.'

other: 15

Note: The 'other' lines are ones which refer to people falling in love with places or things rather than with people.

Table 2.11 Analysis of relative frequency of patterns for *make love* (1,925 lines altogether – all verb forms included)

Out of 100 randomly selected lines:

plural noun group + verb: 29
    e.g. 'Every time we made love I was convinced it was the last time.'

noun group + verb + *with* + noun group.   7
    e.g. '. . . when I make love with my lover.'

noun group + verb + *to* + noun group: 30
    e.g. 'I wanted to make love to him.'

noun group + verb (non-reciprocal):   34
    e.g. 'He recently boasted he made love while cutting a record.'

Thus, the frequency patterns – the frequency of the grammar of the phrases – occur because of the semantics of the phrases.

7 VERBS THAT ARE ALMOST RECIPROCAL

There are a few verbs indicating that two or more people have a relationship which are not regarded as true reciprocal verbs because they must be followed by the adverb *together* when used with a plural Subject. These verbs are: *live, sleep, move in, run away, run off*. As can be seen from the examples below, the word *together* itself gives the clause a reciprocal meaning:

The relationship blossomed. *They* decided to *live together* the following year.

We'd been seeing each other for a year when he suggested *we should move in together*.

However, like some reciprocal verbs, these verbs can have a singular Subject referring to one of the participants and be followed by the preposition *with* and a noun group referring to the other participant:

She lives with her boyfriend in a terraced house in Chiswick.

When *Janice's lover, Aaron, moved in with her and her two pre-teen children,* her mother Marjorie was terribly upset.

Why do these verbs not have the 'plural noun group + verb' pattern? It may be because they would be ambiguous without the word *together* as they can be used with a plural Subject without a reciprocal meaning; or, because the verbs, which are basically to do with residence or movement (or in the case of *sleep*, where someone sleeps), seem to require an adjunct after them.

8 NON-RECIPROCAL VERBS

Having established the link between verbs with reciprocal patterns and verbs referring to romantic or sexual activity, it is interesting to consider verbs covering the same broad semantic area which are not reciprocal.

In some cases, for example *woo*, *seduce*, *chase*, and, at an extreme end of the scale, *rape*, the relationship, by definition, has to be one-way. These verbs have only a pattern in which they are followed by a noun group referring to the person with the passive role (the Goal):

A husband was cleared yesterday of attacking the vicar who *seduced his wife*.

She *has* always *chased famous men* – she is known for it.

In other cases, for example *caress* and *fondle*, it seems arbitrary that the verb cannot be used by itself with a plural Subject, since people can and do fondle or caress each other at the same time. With these words, as with transitive verbs referring to other areas of activity, the only way to indicate reciprocity is to have a plural Subject and to use *each other* or *one another* as the Object.

They kissed and felt and *fondled each other*, her hair splayed over the pillow.

In other cases, for example *see*, as in 'We've been seeing each other for some months', the verb perhaps has too many meanings, or its primary meaning is too prominent, to allow it to have the plural Subject pattern. Alternatively, the reason could be that it is never intransitive with any other meaning (except in expressions like 'I see'), although this need not necessarily affect the grammar of a different meaning.

One phrasal verb in this semantic area which usually has the pattern 'noun group + verb' is *sleep around*. Here the other participants are represented not by a noun group or a prepositional phrase containing a noun group, but by the adverbial particle *around*, which indicates the promiscuity of the behaviour by construing it as going to various places rather than as doing something with various people. There are three occurrences in the Bank of English corpus of this verb with the pattern that some of the reciprocal verbs have – 'noun group + verb + *with* + noun group' – but the noun group always refers to a general group of people, rather than to specific or named people. The exact identity of the other participants is never considered important when this type of sexual activity is being construed in this way.

9 CONCLUSION

It is clear that verb patterns, while not rigidly tied to meaning, are generated by meaning and act as broad pointers to it. This can be seen when considering the class of reciprocal verbs (and verbal phrases), and many verbs which are used to encode the semantic area of romantic or sexual activities and relationships have a particular combination of patterns which puts them in the category of reciprocal verbs. The pattern with a plural Subject indicates or emphasises the reciprocity of the action; the pattern where there is a singular Subject and the other participant is mentioned as Object or prepositional Object focuses on one of the participants or implies that they have a more active role. In some cases, different shades of meaning can also be conveyed by the choice of preposition: *with* or *to*. The speaker thus has a choice as to how to present such an activity or relationship, although in the case of particular verbs and phrases they will be influenced by the typical use of the verb or phrase – that is, by the choice that society in general has made as to how to present that activity or relationship.

ACKNOWLEDGEMENTS

The author would like to thank Susan Hunston and Gill Francis for their helpful suggestions and comments on this chapter.

REFERENCES

Collins COBUILD English Dictionary (rev. edn 1995), London: HarperCollins.
Collins COBUILD English Grammar (1990), London: Collins.
Collins COBUILD English Language Dictionary (1987), London: Collins.
Dixon, R.M.W. (1991) *A New Approach to English Grammar, on Semantic Principles*, New York: Oxford University Press.
Francis, Gill, Hunston, Susan and Manning, Elizabeth (1996) *Collins COBUILD Grammar Patterns 1: Verbs*, London: HarperCollins.
Halliday, M.A.K. (1994) *An Introduction to Functional Grammar*, London: Edward Arnold.
Levin, Beth (1993) *English Verb Classes and Alternations*, Chicago: University of Chicago Press.
Quirk, Randolph, Greenbaum, Sidney, Leech, Geoffrey and Svartvik, Jan (1985) *A Comprehensive Grammar of the English Language*, London: Longman.
Sinclair, J.M. (ed.) (1987) *Looking Up: An Account of the COBUILD Project in Lexical Computing*, London: Collins.
—— (1991) *Corpus Concordance Collocation*, Oxford: Oxford University Press.

3

'EVERYBODY LOVES A LOVER'

Gay men, straight men and a problem of lexical choice

Keith Harvey

EMILY   [. . .] You his . . . uh?
LOUIS   Yes I'm his uh.
(Kushner 1992, Act Two, Scene three)

1 PRELIMINARIES

I embarked upon the research reported in this chapter for reasons both personal and linguistic. Realising how unstable my own use of terms such as *my boyfriend, my lover* and *my partner* was, I sought to explore the issues behind this instability without relying exclusively on my own intuitions. I did not, however, wish to deny that these intuitions played an important role in the research process and in the analysis of the findings. As William Leap (1996) has pointed out in relation to his own extensive explorations into gay men's English, 'personal associations with the subject matter unavoidably reach deeply into data gathering and analysis and color the process of interpretation and representation' (*ibid.*: xiii). Indeed, where human, social and ideological issues are under consideration, the researcher's personal associations *should*, I believe, be taken account of and invoked in the research process.

The lack of stability, then, which I noted in my own usage of the terms mentioned above is not exactly that which other linguists and word-watchers have commented upon in the heterosexual usage of items such as *my girlfriend* and *my partner*. My discomfiture seems to me also self-evidently a consequence of (internalised) homophobia. Through the use of these words, a gay man runs the risk of violences ranging from subtle rejection to open discrimination and the impact of the homophobe's fist. As a linguist I wanted to be able to talk about this situation, to put gay use of the available terms on the lexical map (unsurprisingly, in no dictionary that I have consulted does a gay example occur under the headwords *boyfriend, girlfriend, lover, partner*, etc.) and to show that the 'anecdotal' problem of what to call the person you love and make love to when you are a gay man is in fact a consequence of highly charged social, moral and ideological issues.

60

However, in order to do this I could not rely entirely on a comparison of the 'evidence' of attested utterances by gay and straight men. This evidence might tell me *what* is said and, arguably, *how often* it is said and *by whom*; but such evidence is unlikely to illuminate the reasons *why* one word is used rather than another. I have also been interested, therefore, in exploring the extent to which the text-descriptive paradigm that is gaining ground in lexical studies – largely through the use of computerised corpora – is the product of an ideological position that marginalises and excludes aspects of linguistic meaning that are not straightforwardly quantifiable. (See Béjoint (1983: 73) for a previous challenge to an exclusively corpus-based approach to lexical meaning.)

To achieve these research aims, I employed a classic and (in its own way) simplistic ethnographic methodology of questionnaire and interview with two groups of male speakers of English, one identifying as gay, the other as straight. I hope that it will become clear, however, that this methodology was seen as a way of prising open some elusive issues and unarticulated questions. I do not consider methods such as these as windows onto the truth about language use but rather as techniques for opening up discussion about 'difference' (here, of sexualities) in and through language.

In exploring what is at risk for gay men when they use words to refer to the men they love, I try here to give the men themselves the space to comment upon their usage. As one of their number, I seek to tease out the issues that lie behind what they have told me. Through their words, I attempt, inevitably, to explain an aspect of my own experience. I am, incidentally, grateful to them for the opportunity to do this.

As I am to my lover, Floyd.

2 FOR WANT OF A BETTER WORD

2.1 A problem of lexical choice

Modern English, then, provides its users with a whole array of lexical items to refer to a person with whom one is 'having a relationship' of a non-marital – rather than extra-marital – kind. *Partner, lover, boyfriend, girlfriend* and *friend* are some of the more common, although strategies of circumlocution (e.g. *the person I'm having a relationship with*) and avoidance (e.g. *a friend of mine* or an unglossed use of a proper name) are also frequently attested. Evidence that this range of available terms generates insecurity in individual performance and is not merely a resource for stylistic variation is provided by the commentaries of language users themselves. Two different sorts of commentary can be distinguished: (1) metalinguistic (i.e. reflexive) comment by users of the language when engaged in discourse that has other avowed purposes; (2) longer speculations on the subject by non-specialist commentators, often journalists. (Interestingly, extensive and systematic treatment of the problem by linguists seems to be lacking: see the typically brief comments in, for example, Cameron 1985: 81; Fairclough 1989: 221–2.)

2.2 A case of public language awareness

Here are examples of the first type of metalinguistic comment (the data and emphasis are mine):

> I think it's unfair of a partner or boyfriend or lover *or whatever* to put that kind of pressure on you
>
> (gay man speaking)

> I'm a bit confused I mean I'm not a married man I live with my lover *for want of a better word*
>
> (straight man speaking)

In the first of these examples, the throwaway *or whatever* is used to bring to an end a list of potential labels that threatens to self-perpetuate. In the second, *for want of a better word* is a conventional fixed phrase that distances the speaker from what is perceived to be an unhappy choice of term.

Longer explorations of the problem by journalistic 'word-watchers' form our second type of public language awareness. Philip Howard, literary editor of *The Times*, was one of the first to discuss it over fifteen years ago when he wrote: 'We desperately need a word for those who are cohabiting without benefit of clergy . . . or register office' (Howard 1980: 88). Howard's is typical of 'popular' discussions in that it centres upon a certain number of available terms without exploring the significance of those variables of age, gender or sexuality that might influence choice. He is chiefly interested in relationships that involve co-habitation, and asserts that he can safely discount *lover* because it does not 'convey the meaning that anybody is living with anybody else' (*ibid.*: 95).

John Diamond's article in *The Times* (14 May 1992) is marked by an underlying tone of ideological panic. The following passage, for example, despite its avowedly humorous purpose, fails to mask the real unease felt by some male heterosexuals in a world where their hegemony is no longer taken for granted:

> The progression had once been so simple: my date became my girl-friend, became my steady girlfriend, became my fiancée, became my wife, became my former wife and everyone knew what I meant. But then the rot set in. (Rot set in? What am I becoming? . . . Any minute now I'll start wearing bow ties and complaining that 'gay' was a perfectly useful word which I dropped into my ordinary conversation at least three times a day until the shirtlifters got hold of it.)
>
> (John Diamond, 'A person's most significant decision',
The Times, 14 May 1992)

In order to find this funny, one has to share a number of values: those of a particular type of British male heterosexual. The assumption that one does indeed share them lies behind the revealing comment that once 'everyone knew what I meant'. In fact, such discourse masquerades as a send-up of exclusionary rant. Its aim is still the suppression of the threatening presence of differences.

More recently, Carl Miller in *The Independent* (23 March 1995) wrote an open letter to the actor Nigel Hawthorne after the press had publicised the fact that he was going to the Oscar ceremonies with his 'longstanding live-in boyfriend' – in the words of another newspaper. Miller begins his article thus: 'I am pleased to hear that you are taking your lover to the Oscar ceremonies.' The article starts with a term that leaves no doubt about the nature of the relationship. What is more, it affirms that – for gay men at least – *lover* can indeed be applicable to a long-term, co-habiting relationship.

Later in the article, Miller's own anecdote about his use of *lover* gives us a useful insight into its potential explosiveness for dominant heterosexual norms:

> A lady in Horsham once ticked me off for calling Jonathan my lover. 'You'll never fit in if you go on about the physical aspect,' she scolded. It's true that in the twilight world of the heterosexual, 'lover' implies hotel rooms and oral sex, but I've always thought 'partner' too like a pair of solicitors, and I can't really carry off 'boyfriend', now I've hit 30.

The unconscious irony of this last comment is that earlier in the same article he does indeed 'carry off' *boyfriend* when referring to a certain 'Jonathan' in his own life. This demonstrates that even for an individual language user with a heightened awareness of this problem the instability of terms remains unresolved.

It becomes apparent from these commentaries that the problem is perceived differently by distinct sociosexual groups within the so-called speech community. We need therefore to produce a description of word meaning in this area that does not fall into the trap of mistaking hegemonic meanings for 'consensual' meaning, and which recognises that meanings exist in a constant state not merely of diachronic flux but also of synchronic contestation.

3 METHODS

In order to produce an account of the unstable and problematic use of these lexical items, I carried out an investigation in two stages: questionnaire and interview. By limiting myself to male informants, I sought to draw attention to the effects, if any, of the gay/straight variable without the added complication of gender.

3.1 Questionnaire

To complete the questionnaire the respondents were to be aged 18 or over, currently in a relationship (defined loosely as 'romantically and sexually involved with another person') but not married (in the case of straight men) to the other person. Part I of the questionnaire required respondents to self-identify according to the following variables: age of respondent; sexuality of respondent (three options given: bisexual, gay, straight); gender of the other person in the relationship; length of the relationship; whether the relationship involves co-habitation.

In Part II of the questionnaire, an alphabetical list of twenty-five possible responses (plus an 'other: please specify' slot), respondents followed the instruction to put a circle around the term or terms used 'to refer to the other person in the relationship'. The list of terms follows:

a friend	my loved one
a friend of mine	my lover
my affair	my man friend
my better half	my old man
my bloke	my other half
my boyfriend	my partner
my fella	my relationship
my fiancé	my significant other
my fiancée	my wife
my friend	the person I live with
my girlfriend	the person I'm going out with
my husband	the person I'm seeing at the moment
my lady friend	

A final question asked respondents to specify which *one* term 'you think you use most frequently'. The items that emerged as the most frequent responses to these questions were to provide the focus for the interview stage. Although I invited respondents to supply me with a name and contact number for the interview stage, I stressed that this was optional and that the questionnaire could be sent back anonymously.

3.2 Interview

The interviews were to be the heart of the investigation. The information they yielded would contain personal views, contradictions, anecdotes and material that was generally not susceptible to statistical processing. It might, however, for these very reasons approach the personal, group and societal issues that underlie the variety of terms and their differential use.

Table 3.1

Interviewee	Age group	Length of relationship	Co-habitation	'Scatter' of items chosen in questionnaire
G1	18–29	over 2 years	Yes	*my boyfriend* *my partner*
G2	30–39	over 2 years	Yes	*my boyfriend* *my other half* *my partner*
G3	18–29	over 2 years	Yes	*my boyfriend* *my lover* *my partner*
G4	40–49	over 2 years	Yes	*a friend of mine* *my boyfriend* *my other half* *my partner* *my relationship*
G5	30–39	less than 6 months	No	*my boyfriend* *my lover* *my other half* *my man* *my boyf*
G6	30–39	less than 6 months	No	*my boyfriend* *the person I'm going out with* *'his name'*
S1	18–29	over 2 years	Yes	*my girlfriend* *my partner* *the person I live with* *the person I'm going out with*
S2	30–39	over 2 years	No	*my girlfriend* *my partner*
S3	18–29	over 2 years	Yes	*my girlfriend* *my partner* *her indoors*
S4	30–39	over 2 years	Yes	*my girlfriend* *my partner*
S5	50–59	between 1 and 2 years	No	*my friend* *my girlfriend*
S6	30–39	over 2 years	Yes	*my girlfriend* *my partner*

Note: G3: This respondent crossed out the terms offered on the questionnaire and added a fourth category 'queer'. It emerged during the interview that although he would 'never' identify as 'straight', and would 'rarely' label himself 'bisexual', he would use 'gay' as a self-descriptor 'at work' and 'probably with my parents'. In the context of the current study (and given that the person he is having a relationship with is male), I include him in the gay category. (The complex issues involved in defining the sample group and finding appropriate ways of sampling representative populations when researching into lesbians and gay men are usefully explored in Donovan (1992).)

Twelve interviews were conducted (six with gay men, six with straight men), each lasting between 10 and 20 minutes and following a similar pattern. First, interviewee reactions to the lexical items most often selected in the questionnaire were elicited out of context. Second, a gap-filling exercise sought to determine in the opinion of the interviewee which of the items seemed most likely to appear in a selection of linguistic environments. Lastly, interviewees were asked about their own questionnaire responses. Questions were not rigidly scripted as the objective was to explore issues which were not necessarily foreseeable.

Table 3.1 gives information about the interviewees according to their self-identification as either gay (G) or straight (S).

4 THE QUESTIONNAIRES

4.1 Questionnaire results

One hundred questionnaires were distributed; 53 were returned completed. The distribution took place on an ad hoc basis through networks of friends and contacts. Most respondents lived in London, the south-east of England and the West Midlands. Most were not known to me personally.

A profile of the typical respondent for this study emerged from the data collected: 50.9 per cent are in the 30–39 years age group (30 per cent are in the 18–29 years age group); 66 per cent are involved in relationships that have lasted for more than two years; 64.2 per cent co-habit with the other person; the number of respondents that identify as gay or straight is almost exactly equal (straight: 26; gay: 25, with 1 'bisexual' and 1 'queer').

Our typical respondent is therefore in his thirties and co-habiting with a long-term partner.

Thirty-two lexical items were indicated as possible lexical choices by the sample group in response to the request to put a circle around 'the one or ones you use'. Table 3.2 presents the choice of items in order of frequency. The 'scatter' of items selected by the sample of 53 men totals 155. The average number of items selected per respondent is therefore 2.9.

It is worth noting that although *my partner*, *my boyfriend* and *my girlfriend* between them account for approximately 46.5 per cent of selections, this leaves around 53.5 per cent of items chosen ten times or fewer. Indeed, 9 per cent of the total were only chosen once. This gives some idea of the degree of instability of lexical choice in this area.

4.2 Deviations and reappropriations

The calculation of the simple average number of different choices by variable is revealing of certain tendencies in the sample. (Here averages are only calculated where a subgroup of the sample has at least ten members.) While

Table 3.2

Item	Total	Bisexual	Gay	Straight	Queer
my partner	31	1	16	13	1
my boyfriend	21	0	20	0	1
my girlfriend	20	0	0	20	0
my friend	10	0	5	5	0
my lover	10	0	6	3	1
a friend of mine	7	0	6	1	0
my other half	7	0	4	3	0
the person I live with	6	0	3	3	0
the person I'm going out with	5	0	4	1	0
a friend	4	0	2	2	0
'his/her name' only	3	0	1	2	0
my loved-one	3	0	1	2	0
my relationship	3	0	2	1	0
her indoors	2	0	0	2	0
my husband	2	0	2	0	0
my wife	2	0	2	0	0
the missus	2	0	0	2	0
the person I'm seeing at the moment	2	0	2	0	0
my boyf	1	0	1	0	0
my companion	1	0	0	1	0
my concubine	1	0	0	1	0
my date	1	0	1	0	0
my fella	1	1	0	0	0
my fiancée	1	0	0	1	0
my little baby	1	0	1	0	0
my man	1	0	1	0	0
my mrs	1	0	0	1	0
my old man	1	0	1	0	0
the boy	1	0	1	0	0
the guy I'm going out with	1	0	1	0	0
the person I share a house with	1	0	1	0	0
my woman friend	1	0	0	1	0

neither the age of the respondents nor the fact of co-habitation seems to affect the average number of different choices made, sexuality does appear to have an impact, as Table 3.3 shows. The sexuality variable gives rise to the largest deviation from the average (2.9). A difference of 0.9 opens up between gay and straight men, with gay men 0.5 above the average 'scatter' of items and straight men 0.4 below it.

I wish to suggest a number of possible explanations for this result. First, it could be argued that gay men are out of necessity more sensitive to the demands of context than straight men and therefore draw on a wider range of items to suit the shifting context. This was made explicit by one gay interviewee when shown a list of the five items that emerged as the most frequent

Table 3.3

Variable	Category	Av. no. items
Age	18–29	2.9
	30–39	2.7
Co-habitation	Yes	3
	No	2.8
Sexuality	Gay	3.4
	Straight	2.5

choices in the questionnaire and asked which of them were part of his vocabulary (note that all interview extracts are transcribed without grammatical 'idealisation' or the addition of written conventions of punctuation and emphasis):

> it all depends on who I'm talking to about it really I mean at work I don't mention I don't say that I'm gay so they've no idea really but basically I use most of them I've used them all

(G4)

Thus, in homophobic or unknown (and therefore potentially homophobic) company, a term that obscures the nature of the relationship such as *a friend of mine* (indicated six times by gay men and only once by a straight man) might be deemed more appropriate. On the other hand, gender-specific items such as *the guy I'm going out with, my old man, my fella* (each indicated once) can be used without fear in gay-friendly environments.

However, there are signs that an explanation of lexical variation amongst gay men as a context-dependent, defensive strategy is not the whole story. In some of the low-frequency choices, items appear that point to a dimension of lexical use that is unavailable to straight men for the very reason that straight relationships alone in our society enjoy institutional sanction. While a straight use of *my mrs* (indicated once) and *the missus* (indicated twice) each represents a humorous reference to a woman to whom the speaker is not married, the terms are nonetheless both consonant with the gender of the referent and allude to a societal and institutional transformation of the relationship which remains possible. In contrast, the parodic 'appropriation' by gay men of terms from the institutional structures of the dominant group (such as *my husband* and *my wife*, each indicated twice) gains its subversive irony from the dissonance it creates in the restricted and prescriptive configuration of gender, sexuality and desire imposed by 'the epistemic regime of presumptive heterosexuality' (Butler 1990: viii). I would suggest also that the gay use of a term such as *my date*, while more oblique, realises a similar subversive irony in its allusion to the traditional narrative of adolescent heterosexual courtship.

Such a strategy of *reappropriation* – the lexical equivalent of the process sometimes referred to as 'queering' (see Leap 1996: 22–3) whereby objects and institutions are 'reread' from a gay perspective – constitutes an aspect of 'alternative' language use that Halliday (1978) does not consider in his classic study of 'antilanguages'. Yet, such reappropriation is relevant to Halliday's concerns. Halliday distinguishes a category of 'relexicalisation' (glossed as 'new words for old' (*ibid.*: 165)) in the language of certain criminal classes and 'antisocial' subcultures. Although not mentioned by him, the antilanguage known as 'Polari', developed and used by many gay speakers in the middle of this century, represents a fully relexicalised example of such an alternative code in which entirely new signifiers replace those of Standard English: *eek*, for example, is Polari for *face* (see Cox and Fay 1994 for a recent discussion of Polari). In contrast to relexicalisation, reappropriation invests recognisable English signifiers with alternative meanings and values. But like relexicalisation, reappropriation also operates in areas that are 'central to the activities of the sub-culture and that set it off most sharply from the established society' (Halliday 1978: 165). In our case, same-sex love constitutes such an 'activity'.

Furthermore, antilanguages are, according to Halliday, 'the bearer of an alternative social reality' (*ibid.*: 167). This 'alternative' is linguistically present and signalled by a highly metaphorical quality in the antilanguage. 'An antilanguage is a metaphor for an everyday language; and this metaphorical quality appears all the way up and down the system' (*ibid.*: 175). Dominant societal norms and institutions, if not ignored, are inevitably given *metaphorical* meaning by those who are alienated by them. I suggest that the gay uses of *my husband* and *my wife* constitute just such a metaphor. It is significant in this respect that if the straight choices of *my mrs* and *the missus* turn upon potentially 'contested' and context-restricted items (drawn from an informal register and carrying derogatory and sexist values), *my husband* and *my wife* are probably chosen by gay men for the very reason that they are *un*marked, context-*in*dependent and *central* to the institutions to which they allude. Their metaphorical power is thereby further enhanced.

5 THE INTERVIEWS

5.1 The interview material

In the interview data there is evidence of social- and context-related factors determining item choice that go beyond a strict attention to lexical semantics and into pragmatic considerations. I have grouped these factors under two broad headings: (1) 'strategies and contexts' focuses on those situational and interactional factors that impact upon item choice; (2) 'awarenesses' includes both 'language awareness' alongside a more social 'awareness of others'.

5.2 Strategies and contexts

If it is well known that items such as *my partner* and *my friend* afford a degree of discretion to a speaker consequent upon their potential ambiguities, this discretion is not identical for the same reasons if one is gay or straight. While the straight men distinguish between contexts in which they know their interlocutors and those in which they do not, the gay men overlay this with the distinction between gay and non-gay contexts.

> I do say sometimes my partner but that's usually in you know political places and where I don't know the other person either
>
> (S1)

> I might use my friend in the company of straight people I don't really know where I don't think of my sexuality as any of their business
>
> (G5)

Similarly, the same gay interviewee commented that *my lover* was a word he would use

> more with close gay friends than anywhere else

Strategies of discretion reveal other factors across the variable of sexuality. The following straight interviewee prefers to use *my friend* to guarantee the privacy which he judges appropriate to romantic and sexual life:

> the one I'd prefer to use is neutral as it were and could be interpreted in a range of ways which suits my privacy in a sense so that we don't know the full force and nature of the relationship and that's my friend
>
> (S5)

He recognises, however, that in actual use its ambiguity can lead to confusion and a negative perception of its user's coyness:

> I can remember one embarrassing moment when I introduced her when we arrived at a hotel we were off for it was the first sort of weekend away together and it was one of these private hotels you know sort of six bedrooms in a posh country house and the host and hostess came out to meet us and I got out of the car and I said hello I'm [name] and this is my friend [name] and there was something odd about that we didn't know what it was we tried to work it out whether I'd said too much or too little
>
> (S5)

Aged between 50 and 59 years old, this interviewee is probably encountering the problems set up by the expectations of a heterosexual life narrative, namely that by this age a man is married, widowed or divorced. That he might have only just begun a new romantic and sexual relationship is dissonant with such expectations.

Another straight interviewee finds *my partner* convenient in certain contexts particularly now that he and the woman with whom he lives have a child:

> now we've got a child partner is better I suppose I tend not to like if people are bothered about the fact we're not married partner will leave them with no clear idea I suppose I could just call her [name]
>
> (S6)

In an analogous way to that of the previously discussed interviewee, the expectations that heterosexual culture sets up for this man render problematic any term other than *my wife*. In both cases, the ambiguities of *my friend* and *my partner* offer a precarious and unsatisfactory solution in contexts where interlocutors are not privy to their love lives.

If these strategies of discretion are due to the renegotiation of schemata *within* heterosexuality, the 'tact' necessary for gay men when referring to their sexual partners is consequent upon a stepping outside of the romantic and sexual schema imposed upon them. Terms like *my friend* and *my partner* can be perceived as useful ways of avoiding the sanctions reserved for such a transgression. The following interviewee would normally use *my boyfriend* in gay company, but 'not in normal company':

> if we were in a group of mixed people we didn't know then maybe partner would be more appropriate
>
> (G6)

Similarly, another interviewee specified:

> at work it would be my friend it's being discrete
>
> (G4)

This instance of discretion of course is different in kind from that involved in the straight cases. Whereas the latter concerned the problem of interaction with strangers with whom the interviewees were likely to have little long-term contact, this gay man is talking about colleagues with whom he works on a daily basis but with whom discretion is nonetheless judged to be the wisest long-term strategy. Furthermore, while the straight instances of discretion were consequent upon variables (age, parenthood) that were essentially secondary 'attributes' of the desire involved, gay discretion results from the fear of hostility to the nature of same-sex desire itself.

In direct contrast to these strategies of discretion, the use of *my boyfriend* is cited by some gay men as a way of making their sexuality clear to their interlocutors:

71

boyfriend is the one I would use most boyfriend is clearly my gay partner . . . it makes it clear it's a gay partner I'm always kind of quite keen
to be absolutely straight as it were it states that I'm gay without having
an overtly sexual content

(G2)

Here, *my boyfriend* establishes a central component of the identity of the
speaker at the same time as it describes the nature of the relationship he
is involved in. This is because the confessional aspect that attaches to an
explicit act of coming out is problematic and many gay men will find other
indirect ways to perform the act:

I use that [my boyfriend] at work it can be useful as a way of coming
out I never actually say to people I am gay I hate that

(G3)

Such a strategy is an assertive (although indirect) act of self-categorisation
realised through the declaration of the speaker's living out his sexuality
within an established relationship. This double move achieved through the
use of a single term operates to wrongfoot any potentially negative reaction
to the speaker's sexual identity on the part of the addressee. If a confessional
'I am gay' seeks approval from the addressee, the use of *my boyfriend* at this
point forecloses the possibility of an addressee-controlled space of appro-
bation or objection.

5.3 Awarenesses

Gay men are acutely aware of the language used by the 'other' (and dominant) group in the modern polarisation of sexuality and also of the way in
which this language relates to an established, institutionalised 'life narrative'
for straight people.

as a teenager the heterosexual language is boyfriend and girlfriend boy
meets girl obviously and I think part of my insistence on my being gay
on being absolutely acceptable or valid is to use that same terminology
and to use boyfriend it's a feeling that it's no different a girl having a
boyfriend and me having a boyfriend I think it's taking the most
natural heterosexual word I suppose from teen days and actually identifying with that I think that's also a very direct way of making a point

(G2)

A different, and consciously more challenging, awareness of the impact of
the same items was articulated by the 'queer' interviewee. When discussing
my boyfriend he remarked:

it does have a shock potential I use it because girls use it a lot I'm being
subversive with it

(G3)

Thus, for these non-straight men such items are tokens in a value system to
which they wish variously to claim a participatory right (thus confirming
their sense of exclusion) and also to subvert.

I would suggest that, as the socially dominant group, straight men have
little conception of their language as an index of 'difference'. Not a site for
the elaboration of 'variants' based on a distinct or emerging identity, their
language is lived by them as commensurate with language per se. It is not
surprising that the only straight interviewee to make reference to the linguistic habits of the 'other' group did so not as a language user reflecting upon
the implications for his own language practice but as an observer of that
group of 'others'. While discussing *my partner*, this interviewee commented:

probably more than the others as well my partner is the one I've heard
most commonly used among you know gay relationships

(S1)

Interestingly, this interviewee's perception of the particular frequency with
which gay couples use *my partner* is not borne out by gay men's own intuitions.
According to the questionnaire, 12 out of 25 gay respondents chose *my boyfriend* as the term they used 'most frequently' while only 4 chose *my partner*.
The item attributed to gay men by this straight man (S1) suppresses the
gender of the object choice while that selected by gay men themselves
fronts it.

In the discourse of the gay interviewees, reference also occurs to the life
narrative that is bound up in our culture with other-sex object choice.

a previous partner who was fifteen years older I think I would probably
have used boyfriend I don't think there's quite the same ageing process
in gay men I don't think there's that striving to be an adult to reach
middle-age I think that perhaps because of the lack of one's own family
perhaps because you don't have the same mapped-out stages of
approaching adulthood

(G2)

It is important here to note the degree to which a critical angle on the values
and schemata of straight society plays an *active* part in defining what it is to
be gay. Without the ability to postulate what it 'is' to be straight, this speaker
would be deprived of the leverage necessary to opening up his own specific
definitional space. At no point during the interviews with the straight men,
however, do we find explorations of the specific life narratives of gay people
or of the way in which their 'otherness' might contribute to the formation of
a straight 'identity'.

KEITH HARVEY

6 MEANINGS AND VALUES OF INDIVIDUAL ITEMS

I turn now specifically to the following lexical items, each of which constituted a significant discussion point in the interviews: *my partner*; *my boyfriend* and *my girlfriend*; *my lover*.

6.1 *Partners*: several types of ambiguity

Although there was no appreciable difference in the number of times *my partner* was selected by gay and straight respondents to the questionnaire, it was noticeable during the interviews that the straight men had a lot more to say about this item than the gay men. This is largely due to the fact that for the straight interviewees, *my partner* carries more positive values than it does for the gay interviewees, who cite its usefulness largely in contexts where the concealment of their sexuality is deemed the best policy (see section 5.2 above).

For the straight men *my partner* suggested relationships that are variously based on commitment, longevity and permanence:

> you derive support from a partner not necessarily a lover or girlfriend . . .
> partner involves commitment
>
> (S2)

> you'd use partner if someone was thinking of staying with the actual
> person
>
> (S3)

Relevant to the temporal factor is the choice to co-habit and have children. Four out of six straight interviewees mention the impact of living together on their choice of lexical item. Both men who have children find *my partner* especially apposite. Interviewee S6 is explicit on both counts:

> in fact partner's much more applicable isn't it . . . especially now I
> have a child as well that's a reason not to use girlfriend it's like too sort
> of trivial it's kind of more permanent sounding I mean we've got a
> partnership . . . I suppose the word partner works quite well because
> when you move in together you are then teaming up you know joint
> resources it is a kind of partnership
>
> (S6)

The paradigmatic link with the word *partnership* is significant for the egalitarian and anti-sexist values that *my partner* carries for some straight men.

> I suppose you get a feeling that there is some kind of egalitarian rela
> tionship there you strive to have that it is a partnership rather than just
> a usual male female relationship
>
> (S1)

74

Similarly, another rejected the values associated with the institution which grounds the terms *my wife* and *my husband*:

> I'd still use it if we did get married I think it's really naff when people describe each other as husband and wife my wife like my car
>
> (S6)

Thus, for straight men with a critical angle on marriage, *my partner* is a potentially useful way of defusing (or disguising) that which is unacceptable about that institution. It thus has a promising future as a superordinate for both *live-in girlfriend* and *wife*.

The apparent formality of the term is mentioned by all the gay interviewees. This is not, however, simply linked to public discourse about intimacy. Rather, it describes the type and quality of the relationship, typically conceived of as:

> beyond the sexual
>
> (G1)

> not personal . . . not necessarily long-term, just more distanced
>
> (G6)

What is more, it is not associated with first-person referring. Rather, it is considered:

> a bit third party
>
> (G6)

> I might say his partner more than my partner
>
> (G2)

For the values or commitment and permanence in the relationship, gay men look to another item.

6.2 *Girlfriend, boyfriend* and the question of agency

Despite a common-sense coupling as a linked pair, the items *girlfriend* and *boyfriend* are not semantically symmetrical. While *boyfriend* will never be used by a man (gay or straight) to refer to a platonic friend who happens to be male, *girlfriend* (usually preceded by the indefinite article) is available to some women as a way of referring without sexual connotations to a female friend. Although the questionnaire results indicate an almost identical frequency of occurrence of *my girlfriend* and *my boyfriend* in the straight and gay 'scatter' of terms, the interviews suggest that the meanings that attach to one and the other are sufficiently different according to the variable of sexuality to complicate still further their transparency as a pair.

For straight men, the use of *my girlfriend* usually has a long personal as well as cultural history. Its associations with teenage romance are still fresh, even for an interviewee whose institutional leap into marriage is imminent:

> girlfriend is something you probably use when you're younger the reason why I probably still use it is cos that's the way I've termed it since I was you know sixteen seventeen eighteen with the same person someone actually pulled me up when I said girlfriend and said oh your fiancée
>
> (S1)

A much older interviewee justifies the use of *my girlfriend* on the grounds of clarity, although its teenage associations make him uncomfortable:

> I use my girlfriend it's a bit more explicit and more sexual I think than my friend it's also slightly more childish I mean kids of my children's age have boyfriends and girlfriends for a man of fifty-two to have a girl-friend sounds either a bit whimsical or regressive in some way so I use it if my kids need amplification or my partners sometimes who are not quite sure what I mean by my friend
>
> (S5)

Concomitant with the association of teenage heterosexual activity is an awareness that *my girlfriend* is redolent of gender-based inequality that sits unhappily in the value system of modern enlightened males:

> it's a fairly traditional one it doesn't have the same egalitarian meaning as my partner at face value it probably says you haven't got a relation-ship that's based on equality but because it is such a standard one you don't necessarily read too much into it
>
> (S1)

The straight male use of *my girlfriend* entails another dimension of meaning that is linked metaphorically to its 'immaturity'. Here, the early stage of a relationship itself constitutes a type of 'adolescence'. A number of inter-viewees made it clear that for them it was a transition word, one that would be used at the beginning only to be discarded if and when the relationship settled into a long-term commitment. For one interviewee (S4), the 'auto-matic choice' was now *my partner* as *my girlfriend* 'implies temporary'. For another, the switch from one to the other is almost predictable:

> the long-term relationship I would always refer to her as my partner the new one I would refer to as my girlfriend . . . it occurs it's hard to say but probably at the stage where you're going to move in together because to me the phrase partner has connotations of permanence whereas girlfriend is the sort of tentative stage
>
> (S2)

The element of meaning of *my girlfriend* that does enjoy general consensus amongst the straight men is its lack of ambiguity:

everyone knows exactly what you mean when you say a girlfriend

(S6)

it's a bit more explicit

(S5)

These are typical comments in which the romantic and sexual nature of the relationship is made clear.

Whereas for straight men *my girlfriend* was transitory, a skin to be shed once committedness, cohabitation and children became factors, for gay men *my boyfriend* carries the value, more than any other item, of a relationship that develops with time:

boyfriend is more of a relationship thing than partner I'd say you can say sexual partner without it being a boyfriend

(G1)

it does also in some contexts mean you're stressing your solidarity that you're together me and him . . . when you have a boyfriend you stay at home more settling down

(G4)

This difference is underlined still further by the fact that *my boyfriend* does not seem to suggest adolescence and immaturity for gay men. This gay interviewee confirms:

a previous partner who was fifteen years older I think I would probably have used boyfriend I don't think there's quite the same ageing process in gay men

(G2)

This is further endorsed by another gay interviewee:

I would call X Y's boyfriend and X is in his forties and Y is considerably younger so I don't have a strict age range for boyfriend

(G5)

With *boyfriend*, then, gay men have invested a lexical item with a value that highlights new quantitative (temporal) as well as qualitative (commitment) dimensions. Such an investment of lexical items with alternative meanings is a key strategy in the establishment of agency in language.

In gender studies, Butler has defined the term 'agency' as a subject's 'capacity for reflexive mediation' (Butler 1990: 143) in a culturally and socially specific configuration of knowledge, systems and procedures (what Foucault broadly termed a 'discourse' (see Fairclough 1992: 37–61 for a useful discussion of this term in Foucault's work)). In other words, agency refers to the subject's ability to resist being entirely formed by such configurations and to act upon them rather than being merely acted upon. A simple distinction between signifiers and signifieds enables us to trace the workings of agency in the distinctive gay use of *my boyfriend*. Agency here is affirmed principally by pressure exerted upon the *meaning*, the 'signified', of existing signifiers within hegemonic discourses rather than by the 'invention' of signifiers to represent new meanings.

Behind the apparently straightforward gay 'borrowing' of the signifier *boyfriend* from straight discourse, gay men are actively affirming an alternative set of sexual and romantic values and narratives for themselves. Moreover – and this is crucial – gay men are no longer excluding themselves from English by the creation of a parallel and – to outsiders – opaque linguistic universe as was the case with the relexicalisations of Polari (see section 4.2). Instead, they are colonising the lexical universe of 'straight' English itself in what is no doubt a reflection of their increasing self-confidence and sense of social identity. Note also the distinction between this 'colonisation' of lexis and the strategies of reappropriation noted above (4.2). There, subversive irony was directed (through lexis) at an unyielding social institution (marriage). Here, through *my boyfriend*, a fully redefined (indeed, 'revisited' (Pearce and Stacey 1995)) sexual and romantic narrative is claiming its right to social and linguistic space.

6.3 *Lovers* in public and private

Rejection of the term *my lover* is consistent across the group of straight interviewees while the gay interviewees are divided on the issue. The straight denial of the use of the term is particularly strong:

I'd never use that
(S1)

I wouldn't describe my partner to somebody else as being a lover
(S2)

The reasons given are twofold. First, it fronts the sexual aspect of a relationship to an excessive degree:

it suggests a very steamy relationship going on at the time . . . you need to be very confident to talk about sex to use it
(S1)

too sexual a term
(S5)

Second, *my lover* implies eternal triangles ('something triangular' (S3)) and deception:

it's like a kind of affair sort of thing something underhand about it you're cheating

(S6)

Some of the gay interviewees also subscribed to these attitudes. Use of the item was sometimes rejected:

I can't imagine the environment in which I'd use lover

(G2)

This was on the grounds that it fronted sex and carried clandestine associations ('slightly illicit' (G2)).

However, this picture was far from consistent across the gay group. Indeed, there were some very direct contradictions, particularly around the item's alleged 'steaminess' and its apparent suggestion of a lack of permanence. Thus, for this interviewee *my lover* was problematic:

too sexually connotated for my liking I think what I do with my partner sexually is between us not between anyone else so I think the expression my lover refers to someone you have sex with rather than somebody you love

(G6)

(Note here the conflation of two points: that sex between a couple is private while *my lover* drags it, unwelcome, into the public domain; that *my lover* suggests sex at the expense of love.) However, for another gay interviewee *my lover* encapsulates values that are highly prized, including, significantly, a reference to the sexual nature of the relationship which is not construed as either jealously private or removed from love:

it's very affectionate in terms of emotion . . . I want people to know I think lover emphasises that it's a bit more significant and permanent lover to me is not just a casual partner

(G5)

Another gay interviewee also associates it with positive values, explaining that it is:

stronger a deeper feeling kind of personal

(G3)

Significantly, he adds:

I don't see the personal thing stopping me saying it to people I don't know I kind of like that they get the message I'm not going to keep it sex behind closed doors

(G3)

Two possible explanations suggest themselves to me for the open disagreement amongst the gay interviewees about the meanings and values of *my lover*. In the first, the item is still at a formative stage of redefinition and re-appropriation by gay men. According to such an analysis, some of the gay respondents remain influenced by the negative values attached to the item in the straight lexicon, while others are in the process of reclaiming it by regenerating its connotations. This reading of the problem is essentially diachronic; with time, it suggests, the new gay colonisation of *my lover* will prevail across the whole of the gay community, much as *my boyfriend* seems to have done.

In the second explanation, which is essentially synchronic in nature, two parallel –indeed, incompatible – political projects for gay people are visible through the disagreement over *my lover*'s appropriateness. The first political project, which subscribes to the straight discomfort with the item, is an essentially assimilationist one in which gay people seek integration within the social and moral structures of straight society (see Sullivan 1995 as an example). According to this position, gay people (should) aspire to become accepted as capable of sustaining long-term, monogamous commitment according to the dominant heterosexual model. And, as such a model both excludes the possibility of multiple sexual partners within the couple and also upholds the distinction between public and private spheres, *my lover* is condemned by gay men, just as it is by straights, as suggesting infidelity and an unwelcome irruption of sex into public discourse.

The second political project, however, is one that challenges the entire value system predicated upon institutionalised heterosexuality (see Halperin 1995: 160–6). Refusing assimilation as a goal, it prefers strategies of contestation and subversion and uses *my lover* deliberately to front the sexual nature of gay relationships. In seeking to disturb the perceived prurience and sex phobia perpetuated by straight culture, gay people have identified key points of leverage in the issues of multiple partners and the naturalised dichotomy of public and private. In other words, in just those areas where the problems inherent in the use of *my lover* are located.

Caught up in the first flush of 1970s gay activism, Hocquenghem (1993 (1972)) noted early on how homosexual challenges to social acceptability went further than many other radical projects in this area: 'Revolutionary tradition maintains a clear distinction between the public and the private. The special characteristic of the homosexual intervention is to make what is private – sexuality's shameful little secret – intervene in public, in social organisation' (*ibid.*: 136). And in an example of a contemporary 'queer' reading of the public/private distinction, Sedgwick (1994) has underlined the way heterosexuality still arrogates the prerogative to determine the modalities of display and concealment:

> 'public' names the space where cross-sex couples *may*, whenever they feel like it, display affection freely, while same sex couples *must* always

conceal it; while 'privacy' . . . has historically been centered on the protection-from-scrutiny of the married, cross-sex couple, a scrutiny to which . . . same-sex relations on the other hand are unbendingly subject.

(Sedgwick 1994: 10)

Gay men possess an intimate inside knowledge of the operations of this discriminatory rule. For them, the private/public binarism that regulates sexual and romantic *display* always combines with the personally dangerous one of the secrecy/disclosure of their sexual *identity*.

In sum, for the straight interviewees *my lover* unquestionably overstepped the line between what is sayable in public and what is to be silenced. In contrast, for the gay interviewees, the circumscription of public and private spheres is problematised. Through this, a challenge is opened up to the strictures governing sex and sexuality's public speakability. For while the use of *my boyfriend* by a male speaker forces straight addressees to adjust their presumptions of heterosexuality about that speaker, the mention *my lover* by a man about another man also challenges what can and cannot be said about sexual intimacy in public.

7 CONCLUSION

In this chapter, I have explored the different attitudes and values that adhere to a particular group of lexical items according to the variable of sexuality. Issues relating to social change, to the problems of articulating difference, to agency in language and to the precarious nature of the public/private dichotomy have been helpful in understanding the ways in which distinct groups of speakers invest lexis with specific, shared and describable values.

Above all, my focus has been on the intimate experience of some key lexical items by a group of British gay men. I have found, as I anticipated from my own experience, that exclusion, discrimination and violence are pressures that other gay men are conscious of in their choice or avoidance of specific terms. But I have also found that many gay men today are equally aware of – and able to articulate – the importance of a choice of words for the elaboration of a distinct identity predicated upon same-sex object choice. In this connection, Cameron (1995) has noted that contemporary critical linguistics highlights the way the repetition of 'lexical, grammatical and interactional choices . . . contributes to the construction of a 'congealed' social and personal identity for the speaker' (*ibid.*: 17). She also draws attention to the fact that the psychosocial 'differences' that result from this linguistic fact weaken the premise of those who defend (or purport merely 'to describe') a 'common language'. The radical advocates of verbal difference argue, as she puts it:

that what liberals mean when they invoke the idea of a 'common' language is a language based on a massive repression of difference. The

intelligibility of this language depends on everyone accepting definitions which are presented as neutral and universal, but which covertly
represent the particular standpoint of straight white men from the
most privileged social classes.

(*ibid.*: 161)

I have sought to suggest that gay men in Britain today are using certain key
lexical items in ways that are distinct from their straight contemporaries.
Linguists and lexicographers alike – whatever their sexuality – should not
ignore this fact in their descriptions.

ACKNOWLEDGEMENT

I would like to thank Deborah Yuill for her support, encouragement and
criticism throughout the researching and writing of this paper.

REFERENCES

Béjoint, Henri (1983) 'On fieldwork in lexicography', in R.R.K. Hartmann (ed.)
Lexicography: Principles and Practice, London: Academic Press.
Butler, Judith (1990) *Gender Trouble*, New York and London: Routledge.
Cameron, Deborah (1985 1st edn) *Feminism and Linguistic Theory*, Basingstoke and
London: Macmillan.
—— (1995) *Verbal Hygiene*, London and New York: Routledge.
Cox, L. and Fay, R. (1994) 'Gayspeak, the Linguistic Fringe: Bona Polari, camp,
Queerspeak, and beyond', in S. Whittle (ed.) *The Margins of the City: Gay Men's
Urban Lives*, Aldershot: Arena.
Donovan, James M. (1992) 'Homosexual, gay, and lesbian: defining the words and
sampling the populations', in Henry L. Minton (ed.) *Gay and Lesbian Studies*,
Binghamton: Harrington Park Press.
Fairclough, Norman (1989) *Language and Power*, London and New York: Longman.
—— (1992) *Discourse and Social Change*, Cambridge: Polity Press.
Foucault, Michel (1971) *L'Ordre du discours*, Paris: Gallimard.
Halliday, M.A.K. (1978) 'Antilanguages', in *Language as Social Semiotic*, London and
New York: Edward Arnold, pp. 164–82.
Halperin, David M. (1995) *Saint Foucault: Towards a Gay Hagiography*, New York and
Oxford: Oxford University Press.
Hocquenghem, Guy (1993 (1972)) *Homosexual Desire* (trans. Daniella Dangoor),
Durham and London: Duke University Press.
Howard, Philip (1980) 'Love', in *Words Fail Me*, London: Corgi Books, pp. 88–95.
Kushner, Tony (1992) *Angels in America*, Part I: *Millennium Approaches*, London: Royal
National Theatre and Nick Hern Books.
Leap, William L. (1996) *Word's Out: Gay Men's English*, Minneapolis and London:
University of Minnesota Press.
Pearce, Lynne and Stacey, Jackie (eds) (1995) *Romance Revisited*, London: Lawrence
& Wishart.
Sedgwick, Eve Kosofsky (1994) *Tendencies*, London: Routledge.
Sullivan, Andrew (1995) *Virtually Normal: An Argument about Homosexuality*, London:
Picador.

Part II

NARRATIVES

4

THE ORGANISATION OF NARRATIVES OF DESIRE

A study of first-person erotic fantasies

Michael Hoey

1 INTRODUCTION

Because we live in a highly sexualised society, most of our fiction contains episodes that describe the sexual behaviour of its characters. Certain classes of fiction have achieved partial acceptance that have as their sole reason of existence the depiction of such behaviour, whether for erotic or romantic reasons; these include so-called top-shelf magazines such as *Mayfair* or *Men Only* and novel series such as those published by Mills & Boon. In this chapter, I report a preliminary investigation into the patterns of organisation of first-person narratives of desire and the way these patterns illuminate the construction and conception of sexual desire.

2 THE PROBLEM–SOLUTION PATTERN (AND RELATED PATTERNS)

Many narratives can be described in terms of culturally favoured patterns such as Problem–Solution and Goal–Achievement (see, for example, Hoey 1979/94, 1983/91, 1986; Jordan 1984; all based upon pioneering unpublished work by Winter 1976). The Problem–Solution pattern consists at its simplest of four or five parts: the Situation, the Problem, the Response and the Evaluation and/or Result. (Often the Evaluation and Result are merged as a single statement.) The Goal–Achievement pattern contains similar components: Situation, Goal, Means (of Achievement), and again Evaluation and/ or Result. The Situation is an optional element in the patterns and describes the background or context of a Problem or Goal. Importantly for our later discussion, the relationship holding between Situation and Problem or Goal is not a causal one except in so far as certain conditions in the reported world must pertain before certain problems can arise or goals can be formulated.

The Problem–Solution and Goal–Achievement patterns have been fully described elsewhere and it would not be appropriate to repeat that description here. A few salient features of the patterns need, however, to be mentioned if my subsequent discussion of erotic narrative is to be intelligible, which I will illustrate as far as is possible from the following extracts from a popular children's story. (Omitted material here and in subsequent examples is marked by three suspension marks, and all examples are numbered for ease of reference.)

(1)   Mr Nosey liked to know about everything that was going on. He was always poking his nose into other people's business . . . People did not like the way in which Mr Nosey would peek and pry into their affairs . . . The people of Tiddletown decided that Mr Nosey was becoming much too nosey, and so they held a meeting to discuss what to do about him. 'If only we could think of a way to stop him poking his nose into everything', said Mr Brush the painter. And then, a small smile spread over his face. 'Listen', he said, now grinning. 'I have a plan!' All his friends gathered round to listen to his plan.

    The following morning Mr Nosey was out walking along Tiddletown High Street when he heard somebody whistling behind one of the closed doors. 'I wonder what's going on here?' he thought to himself, and tiptoeing up to the door he quietly opened it and peeped in. 'SPLASH' went a very wet paint brush on the end of Mr Nosey's nose covering it with bright red paint . . . Poor Mr Nosey had to go straight home to try and remove the red paint, which was very difficult and rather painful . . . [The people of Tiddletown continue attacking his nose whenever he is nosey, until . . .] He was just about to peer out from behind the tree when it suddenly occurred to him that if he did something very nasty might happen to his nose. And so, he went on his way without being nosey. The Plan really had worked because after that Mr Nosey stopped being nosy and soon became very good friends with everybody in Tiddletown.

                (Roger Hargreaves, *Mr Nosey*, 1990)

The first point about Problem–Solution (and other) patterns is that problems and responses 'belong to' someone in the text (Hoey 1983/91; Jordan 1984). A Problem is always encoded as a Problem for someone; a Goal is always someone's Goal. So in the Mr Nosey story, Mr Nosey's nosiness is a Problem for the people of Tiddletown, their attacks on his nose are their Response to their Problem, and the final positive Result and Evaluation in the last sentence is a Positive Result for Tiddletown.

    Second, as a result of the previous point, patterns intertwine. So in the text above, Tiddletown's Response to their Problem creates a Problem for Mr Nosey, both an immediate one (his nose needs cleaning) and a longer-term one (he needs to avoid damage to his nose). Mr Nosey's Response to the bigger Problem is a Positive Result for Tiddletown and so on. As might be expected, this intertwining of patterns is of some importance to the description of erotic narrative.

A third important point about Problem–Solution (and related) patterns is that they may lodge inside each other. So in the Mr Nosey story, there is a Goal–Achievement pattern lodged inside the Problem–Solution one. The Goal is 'to stop him poking his nose into everything'; the Means of Achievement is 'the Plan'. Again we shall find this feature to be of significance to our description of erotic narratives.

A fourth point about such patterns is that they are characteristically reflected directly in the language of the text (Winter 1977; Hoey 1979/94). In the Mr Nosey extracts, Problem is signalled by *did not like* and *much too*, Response is signalled by *stop* and *do about*, and Positive Result/Positive Evaluation is signalled by *worked* and *stopped being nosey*. The embedded Goal is signalled by *to* followed by verb and the Means of Achievement by *way* and *plan*.

Fifth, and finally, the Evaluation and Result need not result in the end of the story. If they are positive, as in the Mr Nosey story, or extremely negative (death, penury, etc.), the story normally comes to a close, but if they are moderately negative (i.e. the Response has left the Problem unsolved or has resulted in a new Problem), then the pattern recycles and we expect a new Response to the Problem. The Mr Nosey story does not illustrate this feature, but anyone familiar with Alice in Wonderland will remember how Alice repeatedly eats and drinks magic substances in order to alter her size so that she can get through an interesting door, each time with unwanted Results often creating new Problems for her or changing the nature of her Goal. As we shall see, recycling occurs in erotic narratives also but under strikingly different circumstances.

3 THE EROTIC NARRATIVE

The Problem–Solution and Goal–Achievement patterns are regularly attested in, and help explain, fictional narratives, particularly of the thriller/mystery/adventure variety, but they will not accommodate the data provided by erotic narratives. To show why this is, it is convenient for a moment to consider what an erotic narrative structured in terms of Problem–Solution patterning would look like. Since such texts do not often occur, I have taken the risk of fabricating a few closely parallel examples. Consider, then, the following skeletal narrative using a Problem–Solution pattern:

(2)   I needed to make love. I made love with *x*. I then felt good.

Such a narrative is likely to be found highly offensive in that it encodes the other's body as a means to solving a Problem in the self. Furthermore, the Problem exists prior to the encounter with the other.

87

The Goal–Achievement pattern seems to encounter similar difficulties:

(3a)   I wanted to make love. I made love with x. I then felt good.

(3b)   I decided to make love. I made love with x. I then felt good.

In each case we have a text in which the other person is ancillary to the needs/intentions/interests of the self. If erotic narratives were always structured this way, they would be direct encodings of the transaction of prostitution, and intuition tells us that while such encodings undoubtedly will exist they are not characteristic of all erotic writing.

The problem with each of these patterns is that the Problem or Goal exists before the encounter with the other.

Consider now the following variants on the narratives just offered:

(4)   I found x terribly attractive. I needed to make love with x. I made love with x. I then felt good.

(5a)   I found x terribly attractive. I wanted to make love to x. I made love with x. I then felt good.

(5b)   I found x terribly attractive. I decided to make love to x. I made love with x. I then felt good.

Such narratives, though still intrinsically self-oriented, have been softened by the addition of a statement that appears to fulfil a Situation function but is in fact different from Situation as usually encountered. The versions with *needed* and *wanted* reflect the raw structure of some love stories as well as much pornography; the version with *decided* is associated with seduction narratives. The point is that the addition of the initial sentence has converted intuitively improbable narratives into narratives that are not intuitively unlikely.

The additional first sentence 'I found x terribly attractive' cannot however be treated as Situation because of the causal connections with the Problem or Goal. In normal Problem–Solution or Goal–Achievement patterns, it is the first Problem or Goal statement that gets the narrative pattern going; indeed, until such a statement is produced, there is no pattern. In the skeletal texts we are considering it would appear to be the 'I found x terribly attractive' statement that gets the pattern going, even if the exact status of that pattern remains unclear until the next sentence. In the light of that, let us consider an authentic erotic narrative (in this and subsequent examples, introductory non-narrative material, which in some cases conforms quite closely to true Situation, has been omitted for reasons of space):

(6)   Well, I took particular fancy to one male trainee who is younger than I . . . This guy was so sweet that I practically had to order him to call me by my first name rather than Ms. Blake. We really liked each other in a delightful sort of older sister/younger brother way . . .

I took the lead in our romance and *he* loved it! I'd give him an affectionate squeeze around the shoulders and I could feel him tremble. We gradually became more and more intimate, at my pace. And I do mean *intimate*, not just sexual – there's a *big* difference as you know! In bed, my seduction of him was motherly and nurturing, not sadistic, and he *really* cared about pleasing me. Our freedom to reverse roles and express our selves made intimacy soar. Anyway, we're still together even though I make twice the money he does.

(Cassie, from Friday 1991: 57–8)

Skeletally, this narrative conforms closely to my fabricated stories:

(7)   I took particular fancy to one male trainee. I took the lead in our romance and he loved it! We gradually became more and more intimate. Our freedom to reverse roles . . . made intimacy soar.

If we substitute *get close to* for *make love with* in story (5), we get the following:

(8)   I found *x* terribly attractive. I decided to get close to *x*. I got close to *x*. I then felt good.

This version closely resembles Cassie's story.

We have seen that the second, third and fourth sentences of texts (5a/b), (7) and (8) form a Goal–Achievement pattern. It would look as if we have a situation similar to that found for text (2), i.e. a Goal–Achievement pattern lodged within another pattern of a different type, and that the first sentence is the trigger of that pattern. The most natural characterisation of sentence 1 is Object of Desire. On the basis of this and other authentic texts I posit the following pattern:

Situation
Object of Desire
Desire Arousal
Attempt at Fulfilment
Evaluation and/or Result

Such a pattern is compatible with other recognised patterns. In many, perhaps most, circumstances, including the example above, Object of Desire and Desire Arousal merge into a single element; where they are separate, a causal relation inevitably connects the two elements. (Compare 'I took particular fancy to one male trainee' with 'One male trainee was attractive. I fancied him.')

Before we consider the data to see whether this putative pattern will account for other erotic narratives, there is one other variant of our skeletal pattern that it might be productive to consider – one which gives *x* a more active role.

89

(9) *x* needed/wanted/decided to make love (with me). I made love
     with *x*. We felt good.

From the point of view of *x*, this version is entirely explicable in the terms we
have already provided. Depending on which verb is used in the above encoding, then, the pattern is:

Problem/Goal for *x*
Response by narrator to Problem of *x*
          or
Means used by narrator to enable *x* to achieve Goal
Positive Evaluation by *x*

But this only accounts for one aspect of the narrative. What pattern will
account for the narrator's side of the story? There is no signal of Problem or
Goal nor even of Arousal of Desire (whatever real-world knowledge might
tell us). An authentic example of a narrative organised in such a way is the
following:

(10) Hearing a knock on my door I open it and standing there is a
      beautiful woman whom I have never seen before. She tells me that
      she wants me to fuck her, but only if I tie her up. She comes in and
      we strip one another, both thinking of what is to come and already
      getting excited. I get some rope nearby and we both go into the
      bedroom, and she lies down on the bed . . . I am getting a terrific
      hard-on as I tie her and she is about to have an orgasm. Finally
      when both of us can stand it no longer . . . I fuck her, getting and
      giving the best fuck that any man and woman can have.

                                        (Julius, from Friday 1980: 42)

Again a skeletal version of this is the following:

(11) Standing there is a beautiful woman. She tells that she wants me to
      fuck her. I fuck her, getting and giving the best fuck that any man
      and woman can have.

To account for such a text I suggest we need to posit a further pattern: the
Opportunity–Taking pattern, which has as its components:

Situation
Opportunity
Taking of Opportunity
Evaluation and/or Result

If we adopt this putative pattern of organisation, we can see that in the
skeletal version of Julius's tale we have in the first sentence a statement of
Situation that could have functioned as Object of Desire, had there been any
statement of Desire Arousal causally connected with it. The second of the

sentences is the trigger sentence, encoding an Opportunity for the narrator. In the third sentence, this Opportunity is taken, and in the separately presented final clause we are given a Positive Evaluation of the Taking. Once posited, it is not difficult to find examples of the Opportunity–Taking pattern in non-erotic writing. Some advertisements, for example, make clear use of it, usually embedded within one of the other patterns.

4 THE QUESTIONS AND THE DATA

I have posited two new patterns of organisation, Desire Arousal–Desire Fulfilment and Opportunity–Taking, which I claim may be associated with erotic narrative. Now the hypothesis has to be tested against a body of data. In particular the following questions require answers:

1 How many erotic narratives follow the patterns posited?
2 Is it apparent from the lexical expression of the Arousal of Desire and Opportunity components that an erotic narrative is under way?
3 How are Arousal of Desire and Opportunity signalled? Are the signals of the same kind as those associated with other patterns?

To tackle these questions, I began by examining narratives drawn from two books edited by Nancy Friday, *Men in Love. Men's Sexual Fantasies: The Triumph of Love over Rage* (1980) and *Women on Top* (1991). These books are anthologies of sexual narratives submitted to Nancy Friday as part of her research into the sexual imagination. Most of the narratives are fantasies though some are reports of experience; the great majority are written in the first person. All were submitted by non-professional writers for inclusion in Nancy Friday's books, which carry extensive and careful psychological comment. As such, they do not represent conscious attempts by the narrators to write erotically for an audience, though some contributors comment on their becoming aroused by their own writing. In so far, however, as they represent honest attempts on the part of the contributors to describe what it is that they find erotic, these narratives are reliable data for my purposes. Furthermore, they have the advantage that they represent untutored writing. Though there is no indication of the extent to which they have been subject to editorial interference, there is enough indication of variation to suggest that they have not been radically recast by the editor. The fantasies in *Men in Love* were submitted by men, those in *Women on Top* by women. All the writers in the sample were American; ages varied, though the women were characteristically younger than the men. Examples (6) and (10) were drawn from this set of data.

I discarded those fantasies that had either no or only a fragmentary narrative thread, and several fantasies from the male anthology were also passed over in favour of later narratives because they had apparently been submitted by women on behalf of their male partners. I likewise discarded all narratives of childhood sexual awakening, of which there were a number, since these are not in their content characteristic of erotic narratives in general, and I rejected any fantasies not involving members of the opposite sex, because I wanted to see whether male desire of female was differently expressed from female desire of male. I also wanted, as will appear below, to compare the relative frequency of the different patterns for each gender, and stories of same-sex attraction would have introduced another variable. I leave it to a subsequent study to investigate how the patterns characteristic of heterosexual erotic narratives relate to those of homosexual narratives.

Having eliminated unwanted data on the lines outlined, I then looked in detail at the first fifty narratives from each volume that met my criteria; this was to ensure an even coverage of writing by men and women. The next section describes the results of this investigation.

5 RESULTS OF INVESTIGATION INTO PATTERNS OF EROTIC NARRATIVES

Analysis of the first fifty non-fragmentary narratives in each of the two collections showed that they are indeed characteristically, though certainly not exclusively, structured around the two posited patterns of Arousal of Desire–Desire Fulfilment and Opportunity–Taking. Amongst the men, the distribution of patterns is shown in Table 4.1. (It should be remembered that stories quite often manifested more than one pattern; this explains the total percentage exceeding 100 per cent.)

It will be seen that among the men's narratives Opportunity was substantially the most common organisational starting point; almost a quarter began with or included an Arousal of Desire component, though nearly as many included a Goal or a Problem. Amongst the women, however, the picture was interestingly different in that the relative frequency of Opportunity–Taking and Desire Arousal–Fulfilment patterns is reversed as Table 4.2 shows. The women's narratives were, it will be seen, structured around Arousal of Desire, with instances of Opportunity–Taking patterns

Table 4.1

Opportunity–Taking	38%
Desire Arousal–Fulfilment	24%
Goal–Achievement	22%
Problem–Solution	20%
Other	14%

Table 4.2

Desire Arousal–Fulfilment	38%
Goal–Achievement	24%
Opportunity–Taking	22%
Problem–Solution	18%
Other	22%

being marginally less common than Goal–Achievement patterns; other patterns occurred with much the same frequency as in the men's narratives.

Tentatively one might see these results as supporting certain culturally endorsed stereotypical positions. Women tell stories that start with a positive reaction to another person, in that sense being other-centred; men are more inclined to tell stories that start with the opportunity for a sexual encounter, the person not being particularly relevant. Both sexes are equally likely, however, to tell a story with a self-oriented objective. It should be noted, though, that patterns may occur within patterns, and an Arousal of Desire may be followed by a Goal, as in our skeletal examples above. We need therefore to be cautious in interpreting the evidence.

Ignoring gender differences, it will be seen that the original hypothesis, that erotic narratives are characteristically organised as Opportunity–Taking or Desire Arousal–Desire Fulfilment patterns, has been supported. As the tables show, nearly two-thirds of narratives were organised in terms of either Desire Arousal–Fulfilment or Opportunity–Taking or both.

The analyses so far given are too simple. For a start, most erotic narratives manifest the intertwining of narrative patterns described for the Mr Nosey story. Looking again at example (10), we can see that the true structure is as follows:

Goal for woman
[*wants me to fuck her*]

Means of Achieving Goal
[*tells me*]   ⇒ Opportunity for narrator

Positive Result for woman   ⇐ Taking by narrator

Positive Evaluation by narrator of woman's achievement and narrator's Taking of Opportunity.

Likewise story (6) can be seen to have the following structure:

Desire Arousal for narrator
[*particular fancy*]

Attempt at Fulfilment by narrator   ⇒   Desire Arousal for 'trainee'
[*took the lead*]   [adoration]

Positive Result for narrator   ⇔   Attempt at Fulfilment
                                              by 'trainee'
[increasing intimacy]   [increasing intimacy]

Opportunities and Desire Arousals are always attributed to someone. The default position is that the narrator attributes Desire Arousal or Opportunity to her/himself, but, as the above example shows, such pattern-triggering elements can be attributed to someone else within the narrative. Once attribution is introduced, the possibility arises of there being the interplay of two narrative patterns, as we have seen operating in both the above texts, and we indeed regularly find such interplay. However, certain kinds of interplay are more likely to occur with one gender than the other.

We have seen an example of a woman attributing Desire Arousal to a man. Within the fifty men's narratives, however, only two of the narratives explicitly encodes the attribution to a woman. The following example is one of them and also shows the interaction of both the patterns we have associated with erotic narrative – the Desire Arousal–Fulfilment and Opportunity–Taking patterns:

(12)   Even in the darkness of the movie house, I became aware that my wife would go into a kind of trance whenever Mr Newman was dominating the action or was the centre of attention. When we got home, we had a few drinks, and we talked. My wife could not stop discussing how well Mr Newman had played his role. Seeing her excitement and how stimulated she was becoming just remembering the film, I took it upon myself to pretend to be Paul Newman in our bedroom. I tried to stand the way he did in the movie; and I spoke to my wife, using some of the phrases we had just heard him use. I even encouraged her to call me 'Paul'. Between my (amateur) acting ability and my wife's (very strong) fantasies, I was a box office smash hit. The night ended early the next morning – sunrise, as a matter of fact – with two of the world's most sexually satisfied people.

                                              (Murray, in Friday 1980: 68)

Here the patterns are:

Object of Desire
[Paul Newman]

Desire Arousal for wife   ⇒   Opportunity for Murray
[excitement at Paul Newman]   [wife's stimulation]

Attempt at Fulfilment by wife   ⇐ Taking of Opportunity by Murray
[implicit in love-making]   [acting like Paul Newman]

Positive Evaluation of Attempt   + Positive Evaluation of Taking
[*two of the world's most sexually satisfied people*]

Although this interlocking of patterns is quite characteristic, the explicit spelling out of the Desire Arousal element for the woman is unusual. As noted there are only two pattern-triggers attributed to someone other than the narrator in all the fifty examples of men's writing (i.e. a mere 4 per cent). (The second example in my corpus explicitly spelt out that a woman was taking an Opportunity.) In every other case, the Desire Arousal or Opportunity for the woman was left implicit, by which I mean that the reader is left to infer Desire Arousal to make sense of the text.

This failure of the men to assign explicit markers of Desire Arousal or Opportunity to the women in their narratives contrasts with the women's sexual narratives, where seven (14 per cent) of them attribute Desire Arousal or Opportunity to the man. (Attribution of the triggers of Problems, Goals and Gaps in Knowledge, incidentally, was about equal for both groups.) We have already seen one such example (6), but it has to be said that this was not entirely typical, with its emphasis on the woman's use of her power. If we examine one of the other examples of other-attributed Desire Arousal, we will see another context in which women might favour this text-organisational possibility more than men:

(13)   I am very large-breasted (42E) and for most of my life this has bothered me. My clothes never fit right, etc. As I've become older, it has been to my advantage, as many men are turned on by big tits, and believe me, I often notice them looking! My new boss is also aroused by my titties and that turns me on tremendously . . . Because he has been so obviously interested, I wear very low-cut tops and bend over next to him while he is sitting down. I press up against his back when I can, etc., and believe me, he looks! His wife is also in the office, so he probably won't try anything, but since he stares at my titties all day, I am in a constant state of arousal . . . I can't stop fantasising about going into his office where he is playing with his big prick (I've checked it out and through his pants it looks to be a nice size!). Since I have no underwear on, I climb onto that beautiful tool and we fuck right there in his chair while he sucks my titties. I can hardly stand to be around this man. I have a constant desire to grab his cock and work him up, but I can't because I adore his wife. If he ever tries to touch a tittie, believe me, I won't stop him. I rush home from work every day and masturbate myself into two or three deliciously wonderful orgasms.

(Toby, in Friday 1991: 174)

This text is only briefly narrative:

(14)   going into his office
        he is playing with his big prick
        I climb onto that beautiful tool
        we fuck right there

and this is organised as Situation → Opportunity → Taking → Positive Result. But the larger pattern of which (14) is only a small part is organised around Desire Arousal, for which the above mini-narrative becomes the Desire Fulfilment in fantasy and the last sentence of the whole passage becomes the Desire Fulfilment in actuality.

There is nothing unusual about one pattern being lodged inside another nor is the embedding of narrative inside non-narrative in the least out of the ordinary. The Desire Arousal in this text, however, takes a more complex form than the fabricated examples given earlier might have suggested. In those examples the pattern was:

I saw x. I wanted to make love with x

where the wanting to make love is the direct consequence of those qualities of x apparent to the eyes. In Toby's text, however, we have two interlocking variants of this:

(15)   I showed myself to y. y wanted to make love with me.

(16)   I saw that y was aroused by me. I wanted to make love with y.

Both are clear examples of Desire Arousal – they do not require us to posit further patterns of organisation – and as before they are causally connected. There are however significant differences between these possibilities and the ones we were considering earlier. To begin with, in the latter case, we have an encoding of a Desire Arousal pattern that is dependent upon a prior (reciprocal) pattern.

The other pattern, (15), is perhaps of more interest in that the causal connection involves agency by the desired. Toby makes herself into the Object of Desire. Indeed the addition of a purpose clause would convert it into a Goal–Achievement pattern:

(17)   I showed myself to y in order to arouse y. As a result y wanted to make love to me.

I have noted elsewhere that related patterns often have indistinct borderlines (Hoey 1986) and the fabrications (15) and (17) (and Toby's original) appear to exist on that borderline between two patterns.

Why should this pattern occur with noticeable frequency in the women's data and not in the men's? The answer appears to lie in another area of culturally endorsed sexual stereotyping. Don Juan is the archetypal male seducer; there is perhaps no equivalent female archetype. As Spender (1985) has forcefully pointed out, the vocabulary of English licences male seducers but castigates the female equivalent. On the other hand, that same vocabulary allows us to refer to a woman as a 'tease' (institutionalised in the work and word *striptease*) or a 'flirt', both terms being only weakly pejorative. In narrative terms, seduction is about achieving Desire Arousal for the other in order to achieve Desire Fulfilment for oneself, whereas flirting is about Desire Arousal in the other with no further Goal in mind. Toby has fallen in with the stereotype in that the main focus of her text is on teasing not seducing.

I referred in several places to the explicit signalling of Desire–Arousal or Opportunity, but as yet I have given no systematic answer to the question: How are these patterns recognised? With regard to the Opportunity–Taking pattern there appears to be no large characteristic signalling vocabulary for Opportunity. Instead what marks out an Opportunity statement is that it encodes an encounter with something that has an unambiguous purpose. Consider, for example, the following:

(18)   The door was open. So she peeped in.

        (Goldilocks and the 3 Bears)

(19)   Then God opened her eyes and she saw a well of water. So she went and filled the skin with water and gave the boy a drink.

        (Genesis 21: 19)

A door's function is to offer access on some occasions and to bar access on others. An open door has therefore the unambiguous function of offering access. A well of water is a store of water intended for drinking. The Opportunity–Taking in each case describes the logical consequence of the encounter: the making use of the object in accordance with its purpose. This will not describe all such cases; it is a common feature of thrillers for the hero(ine) to make use of an object in ways different from that originally intended for it, but, importantly, such Opportunity–Taking structures are always embedded within larger Problem–Solution structures. When Opportunity–Taking occurs on its own, or as the outer structure, the Opportunity always involves an object with a purpose and the Taking the fulfilment of that purpose.

With regard to the Desire Arousal pattern, there is more to say in that this pattern has signals very like those identified for Problem–Solution patterns and their like. Consider the following statement of Object of Desire and Desire Arousal:

(20)   The man in my fantasy is a real person, with whom I have a friendly, working relationship. He is a few years older than I am, a professional, large-framed, and has somewhat of a potbelly. He is

definitely not the Romeo type, and is not flirty or aggressive with women. He doesn't radiate sex appeal, like some men, so not all women are drawn to him like a magnet. Except me. Ever since I met him, I have been drawn to him physically and emotionally. He is extremely sexy to me, with his shy, boyish charm and his big brown eyes . . . I still crave him, and desire him every time I see him.

(Mary, from Friday 1991: 58–9, slightly reordered)

There are a number of words here that either explicitly or ambiguously have the function of conveying Desire Arousal – *sex appeal, drawn to, sexy, crave, desire*. I would suggest that these items are authentic signals of the Desire Arousal pattern in much the same way that items like *problem, difficulty*, and *need* are signals of the Problem–Solution pattern. *Crave, desire* and *appeal* are used in non-sexual variants of the pattern, as in for example narratives concerned with food or consumer goods; interestingly *sexy* has recently broadened out in the same way. Other signals of Desire Arousal found in my corpus include the following: *take a fancy to, attracted (to), turned on (by), stimulated, fascinated (by), hunger, lust, excited (by), digs, appealing, distracted (by)*, and of course *erotic*. With regard to the signal *hunger*, Patthey-Chavez *et al.* (1996) note in their study of erotic fiction for women that '[One] group of domination metaphors is one related to food, hunger and eating. Women become the food consumed by men and in so doing they satisfy a basic hunger. Both men and women *hunger* for sex' (Patthey-Chavez *et al.* 1996: 91). Support for the view that these are true pattern signals comes from the fact that one of these items, *desire*, is also associated with the pattern of Goal–Achievement. Conversely *need*, normally associated with Problem–Solution, is an obvious alternative to *crave* in the context above. It has been noticed before that signals of patterns often cross pattern boundaries (Hoey 1986); *answer*, for example, may signal the Response to a Problem, the Means of Achieving a Goal, or the Filling of a Gap in Knowledge.

But the passage above also points to another aspect of the openings of Desire–Arousal narratives. Mary meticulously spells out that her fantasy man does not conform to the stereotype of Object of Desire. This alerts us to the fact that there is such a stereotype. Here are two examples from the women's corpus:

(21)   He is gorgeous as most construction workers seem to be, golden tan, defined muscles, cute-cute ass, golden curly hair, strong rugged face.

(Liz, from Friday 1991: 66)

(22)   He's physically very appealing. Late 30's. Very hairy. With hair all over his chest, back, neck. Thick beard. Fantastic intense eyes with wrinkles around the eyes where he squints in the sun. He starts

taking his shirt off, boots, jeans; under his jeans he wears cutoffs. He's very brown, not Mr Universe but a very good-looking body, large muscular legs, very powerful arms, his hands are especially beautiful.

(Sue, from Friday 1991: 75)

It will be seen from the above, which are entirely representative, that certain aspects of the descriptions seem to identify them as being Objects of Desire. Descriptions in general may serve to allow identification, offer character detail or motivate action. But the descriptions just given focus on features that would only permit identification in unusual circumstances and they offer no clue as to character; they also refer to stereotypical features of attractive masculinity such as tan, hairiness and muscularity. Furthermore, the descriptions are interwoven with positive evaluations: *gorgeous, fantastic,* etc. These are the items that set up the causal link between the Object of Desire and Desire Arousal and they are entirely characteristic of Object of Desire descriptions.

The same points may be made about the men's data. The following are adequately representative:

(23) Suddenly I see a beautiful woman lying face down on a towel behind a sand dune, out of the wind. She's wearing a very brief two-piece suit with practically nothing but a G-string over her ass . . . When she raises herself up, I realise she has unfastened the top of her suit so she can tan evenly, and I can see all of her beautiful breasts. They're big with rosy-brown tits surrounded by pink dimpled circles.

(Burt, from Friday 1980: 43)

(24) Samantha was a receptionist for another law firm in the building. She was my type – slim hipped with well shaped legs and ass, with small breasts and supersensitive nipples.

(Miguel, from Friday 1980: 71)

As before it will be noticed that the descriptions are not designed to allow ready recognition of the person described nor do they provide character detail. We have focus on breasts, nipples, legs and the 'ass'. As before the description is liberally sprinkled with evaluative terms – *beautiful, my type, well shaped* – which directly connect with the Desire Arousal.

Once we recognise that these are the characteristic signals of Desire Arousal–Fulfilment, we can also identify a final variant of the pattern – the auto-erotic narrative, an example of which follows. Since, however, there are a number of features of this text worthy of comment and it will serve as an appropriate demonstration of the way the various elements of the description interact, I will quote a fuller version of the narrative than I have previously; individual sentences are numbered for ease of reference.

99

(25)   (1) I fantasise that I am in my room with my curtains pulled open for a good view . . . (2) As I begin to undress to get ready for bed, I slowly pull off my skirt to reveal my smooth legs and lace panties. (3) Taking my time, I unbutton my blouse to reveal my large tits as I watch myself in the mirror. (4) My stomach is very flat because I spent years in a ballet company; its snow-white skin is as smooth as satin and as soft as velvet.

(5) Slowly my hands caress my stomach up and down. (6) I play with my belly button. (7) It is so deep and soft. (8) Gently my hand moves up to find my breast. (9) I feel the lace of my bra beneath my fingers, my hands search for the clasp, and soon it falls onto the floor. (10) My nipples are big and pink, not yet erect. (11) I lick my fingers and squeeze a nipple between my thumb and forefinger . . . (12) I can feel the presence of a man watching me outside my window . . . (13) I dream of feeling a man inside me as my middle finger enters my moist heaven.

(14) Just as I'm about to climax, a man enters my room, the handsome man from the window. (15) He has an intense look that I can feel down in my soul. (16) He is slightly dirty and sweaty from labour, but he looks so good. (17) His muscles are bulging. (18) He moves closely behind me. (19) He gets down on his knees behind me. (20) He pulls off his shirt so that I can see that his nipples are as hard as mine. (21) He pushes them against my back as he begins to fondle my tits. (22) His hands are so big and so strong. (23) I can't help but breathe quickly, he excites me beyond belief.

(24) My hands unfasten his jeans, and I can see his cock, not long but thick, the way that feels good between my hands. (25) We fall together onto the floor . . . (26) Then I put my hands back on his dick and glide it into my pussy.

(27) He feels so strong. (28) I can feel his heart beating throughout his body. (29) My fingers start to tingle. (30) He is trembling like a child. (31) Suddenly, I feel him as he reaches orgasm. (32) I am filled with delight.

(33) He squeezes me next to him, and kisses my face. (34) His lips soon find my tits. (35) He licks them with tenderness. (36) I can feel him suck on my nipples, and with all the excitement I push his shoulders down hard and raise my hips . . . [She describes her own orgasm.] (37) I'll never forget our experience, and always from then on I will leave my curtains open and do a special dance just for him.

(Faith, in Friday 1991: 180–1)

It will be seen that this passage has many of the features associated with male erotic narratives. There is the attention to the same body features:

smooth legs, large tits, nipples – big and pink. There is also the evaluation, albeit more muted: *soft and smooth*, both of which are objective observations but have positive connotations. The difference of course is that here the Object of Desire is the narrator's own body. (Interestingly no equivalent text to this was found in the men's data.)

This text has features in common with 'tease' story (13), where the narrator described her big breasts and nipples and evaluated them in terms of men's reactions to them. Indeed although no man is mentioned until sentence (14), sentence (1) makes it clear that in addition to the Desire Self-Arousal there is also an intention to arouse desire in another. The difference lies in the fact that there is no particular man in mind – the intention is to arouse desire in any other. A feature of many of the narratives in both the women's and the men's corpus is the assumption that any man or woman is sexy – as long as they are beautiful, cute, etc. All I can say is that this feature of the fantasy narratives does not correspond with my own experience of life.

Another feature in this narrative worthy of comment occurs in sentences (30)–(32). Here we have a Positive Evaluation by the first-person narrator of the Positive Result for the other person of his Attempt to fulfil his own Desire. This occurs sporadically in a number of narratives, by both women and men; one of the male narratives sets up as a Goal the giving of pleasure to the woman and finishes when that Goal is achieved. Perhaps because of the limitations of the first-person narrative very few of the narratives interweave Positive Evaluations by both parties of the other's satisfaction.

The final feature on which I wish to comment is sentence (37). Whereas such patterns as Problem–Solution and Goal–Achievement recycle when the Response, Means of Achievement, etc. is unsuccessful, here we have the hint of a recycling because the Fulfilment of Desire has been *successful*, though the recycling is deferred beyond the boundaries of the narrative. Elsewhere this hint becomes explicit and the recycling is immediate. The pattern in such cases is thus:

(26)   I found x terribly attractive. I made love with x. That felt good. So
        I made love with x again. That felt good, etc.

Such narratives are common and it is only the exigencies of space that prevent me from illustrating this pattern.

6 CONCLUSIONS, CAVEATS AND COMMENTS

A case has been made in this chapter that erotic narratives are organised according to regular principles that are both compatible with and slightly separate from those previously identified as implicated in the organisation of narrative. Analyses of a variety of narratives have revealed a characteristic signalling of the patterns, the interaction of attributed patterns and recycling, albeit under different conditions from those previously observed.

The analysis presented in this paper must however be approached cautiously. The data are limited and are drawn entirely from two collections of fantasies edited by Nancy Friday. The collections are far from unordered; the editor has played a central role in selecting and grouping the narratives according to theme. Furthermore, the two collections were published over a decade apart, and sexual attitudes amongst men may have changed in the interim. The average age of the contributors to the men's volume is higher than that of the women's, which may have the effect of widening the gap further.

Finally, the contributors to both volumes were honestly expressing their needs and desires; they were not conscious of narrating for its own sake and their immediate audience was only Nancy Friday not the wider public. That may give their narrations a particular interest for a linguist – and incidentally, and importantly, absolves them of personal blame for any ethical problems their narratives may give rise to, in that these are intended as confessions not entertainments. However, but it also raises questions about the direct applicability of the descriptive approach I have outlined to data of a more self-conscious kind, e.g. to erotic episodes in novels not primarily (or not only) erotic in intention on the one hand and to deliberately and professionally produced erotic writing on the other.

Preliminary examination of data of the kind just described does however suggest that the system of description outlined in this chapter has applicability. One example proves nothing, but the following brief extract, from a professionally written story in a collection of erotica written by and for women, illustrates both the Opportunity–Taking and the Desire Arousal patterns:

(27)   'Kiss my ass,' Claudia whispered to him. 'It's beautiful.'
        'It is', Al agreed. 'But I've never been a "butt boy".'
        'You will be,' Claudia said. 'Starting tonight.' She drew herself
        onto her knees like a lace-clad kitten. She cupped one warm, firm
        globe in her hand and traced a feathery circle onto the skin. It felt
        very, very nice indeed. 'Come on, kiss it,' Claudia told Al.
        The commanding, yet gentle tone of Claudia's surprised even
        her. Al's eyes were glazed with lust as he listened. He seemed
        almost hypnotized, and did just what she said.

                                                        (Tavel 1992: 180)

This text combines both erotic writing patterns. The request/command in the first sentence represents a clear Opportunity, reiterated further down; the last sentence reports the beginning of the Taking. The second sentence offers her 'ass' as Object of Desire (*beautiful*), which the penultimate sentence shows has caused Desire Arousal (*lust*).

Just as importantly, examination of non-erotic data suggests that the patterns introduced in this chapter have applicability there also. Advertisements in particular regularly use Opportunity–Taking and Desire Arousal–

Desire Fulfilment patterns, perhaps hinting at the commodification of sex on the one hand and the eroticisation of selling on the other. Notoriously, of course, advertisements sometimes seek to create an Object of Sexual Desire in order to encourage a displaced Desire Fulfilment in the purchase of the product or service advertised.

It is my hope that this study of the characteristic patterns of a neglected kind of narrative (neglected, that is, by linguists!) will arouse a desire in my readers to investigate other kinds of narrative; the opportunities are all around us if only our eyes could be opened.

And at that point the chapter would normally finish. The hints as to future research combined with my contrived use of key words in the paper clearly mark the previous paragraph as the end. But, for better or worse, sexual data have a different status from other kinds of data and, as Fairclough (1989) has argued, the discourse analyst has a duty to engage with the societal implications of her or his study. In the final page of this chapter therefore I wish to reflect upon the wider ethical implications of the patterns I have found to be characteristic of erotic narratives.

I note, first, that narratives of Desire Arousal–Fulfilment contain within them an ethical puzzle. It was remarked earlier that Problem–Solution patterns and Goal–Achievement patterns such as were illustrated in my fabricated examples (2), (3a) and (3b) encoded narratives of abuse; a narrative about a visit to a brothel would have just such structures. I also noted that if one added a statement of Object of Desire which can be deemed to be causally connected with the statement of need or want, it appeared to make the narratives more acceptable. The puzzle, though, is this: the Problem–Solution and Goal–Achievement patterns are still there lodged within the larger Desire Arousal patterns. It is as if the inclusion of an Object of Desire statement licenses a narrative in which the other person's body may be used for the satisfaction of self. In other words, all it needs to make a narrative of abuse acceptable is a statement of desire aroused. This of course ties in with the old excuse for seduction and even rape that blames the beauty, desirability, dress or behaviour of the injured party for their own injury; the crude words 'She was asking for it' would be the sinister side of the Desire Arousal–Fulfilment pattern.

Interestingly, however, this pattern is more closely associated with the women's narratives than with the men's, though it was of course common in both corpora, and few of the narratives from either corpus depict the other person as unwilling. In these cases the licence for selfishness appears to correspond with the notion of desire as uncontrollable, reflected also in our metaphorical system – they *fell* in love, he was *madly* in love, she was *maddened* with desire, he was *insanely* jealous, she was *crazed* with lust (see Lakoff and Johnson 1980). Patthey-Chavez *et al.* (1996) comment of erotic fiction that characters are transformed by desire as desire enters them and takes them over. Thus once the Object of Desire has acted upon the narrator, he or she has a problem or a need that requires their action; they are in some sense not in control of the causal chain that leads to the use of the other.

The picture is little different with Opportunity–Taking. We have seen that Opportunity is signalled by the mention of something with an un-ambiguous purpose, and the implications of this are clear for Opportunity-triggered erotic narratives. The beautiful woman or the handsome man are objects with a purpose and that purpose is fulfilled when the Opportunity is taken. It may not be news to women that many men think of them as sex objects, i.e. objects for the purpose of sex, but my analysis of men's erotic narratives confirms the belief (though such narratives were of course far from absent from the women's corpus also).

Not all erotic narrative is as I have characterised it. As already noted a number of narratives in the corpora are concerned with making oneself available for the satisfaction of the other. Out of the pleasure that such narrators take in describing the pleasure of the other comes pleasure for the reader also. In this author's opinion, these texts are the most truly erotic.

ACKNOWLEDGEMENT

During the preparation of this chapter I had the good fortune to supervise Lesley Foulds in an undergraduate dissertation on the narrative structures of Mills & Boon novels. I had a number of illuminating discussions with her about the operation of the patterns ascribed in this chapter. Both these dis-cussions and the resulting dissertation helped me clarify my views. While I take responsibility for the patterns proposed and the data analysed here, my argument has definitely benefited from her work. Those who doubt the reality or the value of connection between research and teaching: please note.

REFERENCES

Fairclough, N. (1989) *Language and Power*, London: Longman.
Friday, Nancy (1980) *Men in Love. Men's Sexual Fantasies: The Triumph of Love over Rage*, London: Arrow Books.
—— (1991) *Women on Top*, London: Hutchinson.
Hargreaves, Roger (1990) *Mr Nosey*, Manchester: World International.
Hoey, Michael (1979) *Signalling in Discourse*, Discourse Analysis Monographs No 6, Birmingham: English Language Research, University of Birmingham; abridged as 'Signalling in discourse: a functional analysis of a common discourse pattern in written and spoken English', in Malcolm Coulthard (ed.) (1994) *Advances in Written Text Analysis*, London: Routledge, pp. 26–45.
—— (1983) *On the Surface of Discourse*, London: George Allen & Unwin, re-printed (1991) by the Department of English Studies, University of Nottingham, Nottingham.
—— (1986) 'Overlapping patterns of discourse organization and their implications for clause-relational analysis of Problem–Solution texts', in C.R. Cooper and S. Greenbaum (eds) *Studying Writing: Linguistic Approaches*, Written Communication

Annual: An International Survey of Research and Theory, vol. 1, London: Sage, pp. 187–214.

Jordan, Michael P. (1984) *Rhetoric of Everyday English Texts*, London: George Allen & Unwin.

Lakoff, G. and Johnson, M. (1980) *Metaphors We Live By*, Chicago: University of Chicago Press.

Patthey-Chavez, G.G., Clare, Lindsay and Youmans, Madeleine (1996) 'Watery passion: the struggle between hegemony and sexual liberation in erotic fiction for women', *Discourse & Society* 7(1): 77–106.

Spender, Dale (1985) *Man Made Language*, London: Routledge & Kegan Paul.

Tavel, Catherine (1992) 'Claudia's Cheeks', in Susie Bright and Joani Blank. *Herotica 2: A Collection of Women's Erotic Fiction*, Harmondsworth: Plume, Penguin.

Winter, Eugene O. (1976) 'Fundamentals of information structure: pilot manual for further development according to student need', mimeo Hatfield Polytechnic.

—— (1977) 'A clause relational approach to English texts: a study of some predictive lexical items in written discourse', *Instructional Science* 6(1): 1–92.

5

'AN EXPLOSION DEEP INSIDE HER'
Women's desire and popular romance fiction

Mary M. Talbot

1 INTRODUCTION

It is something of an understatement to say that the bulk of romance fiction read by women is not held in high regard. The genre is judged to be a legitimate target for ridicule by the non-romance-reading public, with equal quantities of scorn heaped on romance readers themselves. A frequent and familiar criticism, particularly of publications at the bottom end of the market, is that 'they are all the same'. The fact that the genre is as varied as any other, and has a very respectable parentage, tends to be overlooked. Among the predecessors of modern romances are some literary classics from the eighteenth and nineteenth centuries: Samuel Richardson's *Pamela*, Jane Austen's *Pride and Prejudice*, Emily Brontë's *Wuthering Heights*, and Charlotte Brontë's *Jane Eyre*.

I am not intending to echo this kind of disparagement. Nor am I interested in establishing the legitimacy of some romance fiction at the expense of all the rest (as, for example, Q.D. Leavis did in the 1930s in *Fiction and the Reading Public*, in which she disparaged the popular romances of the period written by people like Ethel M. Dell, in contrast with the 'legitimate' romances of D.H. Lawrence).

What I am interested in is the evident appeal of the type of publication produced by the British publishers, Mills & Boon®.[1] Selling well over 180 million copies a year worldwide, Mills & Boon has become something of a byword for women's popular romance fiction. Of all contemporary romance writing, novels published by Mills & Boon are probably the most readily dismissed by non-readers. It is true that the novels are highly formulaic compared with other publications selling in anything like the same enormous quantities and readers do have firm expectations of the romance genre, as Janice Radway's ethnographic work has shown (Radway 1987). A woman initially feels hostile towards a man; circumstances force them together and finally she realizes she loves him. Even these books, however, are nowhere near as formulaic as their detractors inevitably assume. It has been said, for example, that the 'first kiss' has to occur by the third page. This is simply not the case.

Mills & Boon romances change with the times. In particular, they keep in step with shifts in taboo. Contemporary writers of romance fiction for Mills & Boon are under a good deal less pressure to be indirect in dealing with the physical and the erotic than they would have been ten or fifteen years ago. The heroine's sexual arousal, if mentioned at all, used to require a good deal of euphemism and circumlocution. In contemporary Mills & Boon, symptoms of her arousal are frequent (erect nipples and dilating pupils, in particular). Interestingly, this is not necessarily the case in translation where different cultural expectations come into play. The practical outcome is frequently a novel which is considerably shorter than the original English text (Paizis 1995).

In this chapter, I attend to textual representations in the popular romance fiction published by Mills & Boon. I examine the representation of women's desire in two recent romances (*No Guarantees* (1990) by Robyn Donald and *Passionate Awakening* (1990) by Diana Hamilton). These were chosen at random. By looking at representations of men as objects of desire, and at representations of the heroines' responses to them, I show that women's desire is depicted as essentially reactive in nature. Women are presented in perpetual, self-defeating struggles for self-control in their attempts to suppress the irresistible attraction of the forceful male. My investigation of these textual representations centres on detailed analysis of a single long passage, in which I examine the distribution of process types, narrative points of view, and encoding of the heroine's erotic responses. I conclude with speculations about the pleasure-providing function of romance fiction in women's lives and its socially reproductive function.

2 THE OBJECT OF DESIRE: REPRESENTATIONS OF THE ROMANCE HERO

Romance fiction is full of detailed descriptions of the hero. Both heroes of the two sample texts I have chosen to look at are property owners with limitless capital. And their prowess does not end there. Not only do they own the world (or at least a substantial part of the local surroundings), they are physically perfect, powerful and dominating. They are embodiments of hegemonic masculinity, presented as desirable, highly eroticised and utterly irresistible. The 'splendid physical presence' of the male protagonist in *No Guarantees*, for example, is not all down to his physical beauty. We are told that:

> it was *not* Quinn's looks nor the lean power and grace of his body that made him so blatantly attractive. What impinged immediately on any

woman was the aura of male sexuality combined with a bone-deep, understated power based on character and intelligence.

(Donald 1990: 49, my emphasis)

Despite the negation, however, physical power *is* very important. Aggression, muscular build and great physical strength are the quintessentially masculine attributes in these stories. They are major preoccupations and a good deal of story space is given over to their display. The muscular strength of the character Quinn, described above, for instance, is needed to repair storm damage to a culvert on the heroine's property. The heroine, a young widow called Camilla, has inherited a run-down dairy farm from her late husband. Unable to pay for necessary repairs, she has unwillingly accepted Quinn's help. She is terrified of him because he is angry:

> She had known that he was strong, but she hadn't realised that he possessed this kind of power and brute, raw force. Yet in spite of the disciplined ferocity with which the stones were set in place, he moved gracefully, with a feral flexibility that kept her well away from him.
>
> (*ibid.*: 87)

Sometimes aggression and muscularity are simply physical attributes ('that aggressive profile . . . the too-close muscular thighs' (*Passionate Awakening*, Hamilton 1990: 61)). Both stories contain scenes of aggression in which the hero intimidates the heroine. It is his sexual forcefulness, sometimes outright aggression, that precipitates all the erotic passages. In narrative terms this is a necessity, since the heroine is not fully aware of her desire, and even if she were she could not act on it. Any yearnings she feels must be suppressed. Incidentally, the aggressively profiled hero above has the improbable name of Luke Derringer, worthy of a character in a boys' action story, a derringer being a handgun.

In an earlier study of Mills & Boon romance fiction (Talbot 1994, 1995), I focused on a story called *No Gentleman* by Kate Walker (1992). Among other things, I examined a passage presenting the first meeting between the protagonists, at a costume ball. The passage contained a detailed visual allusion to the Regency romance hero. This allusion was made possible by the costume ball: the hero went to the ball as 'Mr Darcy', the allusion being to the key male figure in *Pride and Prejudice*; the heroine went in an Empress-line dress, as worn by Elizabeth Bennet, the female protagonist in the same novel. This passage, which introduces the Mills & Boon hero, provides a list of the items of clothing he is wearing. These are collocated with details about their colour and fabric, their texture and cut. In this itemisation, the hero's physique is revealed. In the process we are involved in both a fashion discourse and a discourse of sexuality, in which gender difference is maximised. Part of the eroticised difference comes from the details of 'feminine' clothing (velvet, quantities of lace, etc.) set against his masculine face and physique.

This eroticised contrast – feminine fabrics and textures, masculine figure and features – make him the epitome of the Regency romance hero.

The sample texts I have chosen this time do not contain allusions to the Mills & Boon subgenre of Regency romance. The eroticised difference is still present, but it is encoded in other ways. The masculine aggression, muscularity and physical strength that we have already observed are contrasted, with varying degrees of explicitness, to feminine passivity, flaccidity and weakness. The following passage is taken from an auction scene in *No Guarantees*, in which Quinn jokingly reassures Camilla that if she starts bidding rashly he will clap a hand over her mouth. His strength to overpower her is presented as erotic:

> Her glance fell to his hands. Lean-fingered, tanned, they were more than capable of physically silencing her. She had a momentary vision of them, dark and strong against the transparent pallor of her skin, and swallowed, appalled at the flicker of forbidden excitement it aroused in her.

> (Donald 1990: 22)

This eroticised power is located in this instance in the character's hands. In the next section below, I present a longer passage, this time from *Passionate Awakening*, in which the hero's power over the heroine is eroticised.

The passage above also illustrates another frequently used device. There is a visual contrast of the woman's 'transparent pallor' and the darker, tanned skin of the man's hands. Eroticisation in Mills & Boon depends on the maximization of gender difference. In addition to the dichotomies I have already indicated, the eroticised difference between male and female is often encoded in skin tone. As far as I know, however, both protagonists are always white.

3 THE HEROINE'S RESPONSES

The female protagonist of popular romance fiction is almost always a woman tormented. She is beset by urges she can barely control. She is sexually aroused by the attentions of a man who is the epitome of masculinity, as described above. But, for one reason or another, she always dislikes him initially, so these attentions are unwanted, throwing her into an agonising state of confusion and conflicting emotions.

Some kind of prohibition is always in place, inhibiting the heroine's response to the sexual male. Consequently, her responses disturb her greatly. In the *No Guarantees* auction scene extract above, for example, Camilla is 'appalled at the flicker of forbidden excitement' she feels. The prohibition, or barrier, to the heroines' responses in the two novels is, as it happens, very similar. In Camilla's case, her late husband had been involved in some form of feud with the hero, prejudicing her view of him. This feud turns out to have been one-sided and petty – a sign, incidentally, that her late husband was an unworthy partner for her. He is also revealed to have been a sexually unsuitable partner. Although widowed, Camilla 'had never known what it was like to desire a man. The caresses she had known from Dave seemed perfunctory, a casual fulfilling of an inconvenient need' (Donald 1990: 60). This means that, despite having been married, she is still emotionally virginal: 'Nothing in her marriage had prepared her for the primitive impulses that coursed through her body' (*ibid.*). In *Passionate Awakening*, the heroine's initial negative feelings for the hero are established in a similar fashion, being based upon her (unsuitable) fiancé's dislike of him.

Another characteristic of the Mills & Boon romance, as striking as the fraught condition of the heroine, is the way it is intensively *focalised* through her. That is, the story is presented to us exclusively from her perspective; we are never in any doubt about her emotional state at any moment: her anxieties, frayed nerves and feelings are very much in evidence. Elsewhere, I have made use of a distinction between omniscient (authorial) narration and focalised (character) narration (Talbot 1995). In Mills & Boon novels, however, the narration is virtually always focalised through the central character; there is no distinct, independent narrative voice[2]. We are given the heroine's point of view throughout, both perceptually, through her senses, and cognitively, as an interpreter of what is going on. I refer to these below as sensory and interpretive points of view.

We receive the character's world through her eyes and ears, and through her opinions. The only exception is when we are given descriptions of the heroine's outward appearance, notably details about the colour of her hair, eyes and complexion. Occasionally, writers contrive to present these from the heroine's viewpoint too, with the help of such devices as mirrors in the hallway. There is such a device in *No Guarantees*. Two substantial paragraphs provide us with all the details, beginning as follows:

> Gazing disparagingly at her reflection, she sighed. Oh, the jacket and trousers suited her long legs and wide shoulders, but they were hardly glamorous . . .
>
> Dispassionately she itemised her looks: palest grey eyes set slantwise in thick, straight black lashes; a cap of straight black hair . . .
>
> (Donald 1990: 9)

In my study of *No Gentleman*, I pinpointed in a single passage the two characteristics outlined above: intensive focalisation through the heroine and her struggles to control her inadvertent responses. I did this by examining the way these characteristics were encoded in the verbs assigned to the protagonists, identifying the types of process each of the verbs represented. Examples of different process types in verbs are *catch* (an action process), *realise* (a mental process) and *say* (a verbal process). This framework is basically Hallidayan (Halliday 1985) and is widely used in critical linguistics (e.g. Fowler *et al.* 1979; Kress and Hodge 1979).

In the *No Gentleman* study, I found a preponderence of mental processes with the heroine as their grammatical subject, reflecting the close focalisation through her. The mental-process verb *knew* in the following is just one example: 'He was just playing with her, she knew that.' There were exceptions to this, but these still seemed to be representing mental states indirectly; either metaphorically or in the description of a symptom. For example, the verb *quickened* in the following is representing an action process, but it is being used in a description of inner turmoil: 'her pulse-rate quickened disturbingly in response to the light pressure of his fingers on hers'. The hero by contrast was the grammatical subject of action-process verbs, all of which functioned as the cause of the heroine's discomfiture: e.g. 'to Anna's astonishment and complete consternation, he performed a low, elaborate bow over her hand'. (For details of the distribution of process types in the passage, see Talbot 1995: 84.)

4 'AN EXPLOSION DEEP INSIDE HER': A SAMPLE PASSAGE FROM *PASSIONATE AWAKENING*

In *Passionate Awakening*, the focalisation through the heroine is equally intense and a large proportion of the text is taken up with her inadvertent responses to the hero's appearance and actions. These uncontrollable responses are encoded a little differently, however, being altogether more 'physical' than in the heroine's response in *No Gentleman*.

4.1 The text

The following passage, taken from the end of chapter 1, depicts the first major private encounter between the protagonists. Not surprisingly, it contains most of the heroine's responses to the desirable male that occur in the chapter. He has come into the garden to speak to her. She is in the process of taking down the washing, which has prompted him to make a witticism alluding to the 'four and twenty blackbirds' nursery rhyme. (The sentences are numbered for ease of reference.)

> (1) He had moved into her line of vision now, and the startlingly blue eyes seemed even more vivid out here, the thick hair darker, with a sheen like a raven's wing. (2) And his mouth was teasing, softer than she remembered it, and she closed her eyes because looking at him completed a chemical reaction that sparked off an explosion deep inside her.
>
> (3) 'And of course you won't be the maid much longer,' he remarked, his voice as dry as dust. (4) 'You'll be queening it in the parlour. (5) Do you like bread and honey – or do your tastes run more to caviar?'

(6) 'Are you trying to say something?' she rasped, gathering up the last of the towels. (7) The allusion wasn't lost on her and she could cheerfully have hit him.

(8) 'Maybe.' (9) A strongly defined dark eyebrow tilted upwards and the sensually wide mouth curled, revealing white, even teeth. (10) 'Or maybe I'm wondering why a woman like you should be marrying a man like Cousin Norman. (11) Security, is it?'

(12) She dragged in a sharp shallow breath, her heart pattering wildly under her breastbone. (13) He had moved in front of her, blocking the path, and to get past him she would have had to step on to Norman's neat rows of french beans. (14) Her arms tightened around the bundle of towels. (15) They smelt of fresh air and sunshine and, faintly, of fabric conditioner, and yet did nothing to mask the raw scent of masculine sexuality which this man seemed to exude from every pore.

(16) 'I find that remark thoroughly objectionable.' (17) Her chin came up and her narrowed eyes glittered darkly, although she did manage to keep her voice coolly dismissive, masking her anger.

(18) Infuriatingly, he chuckled. (19) 'Cut the haughty act, Annie.' (20) And he moved closer, crowding her, making her stomach churn, and a strong tanned hand moved, lean fingers cupping her chin, setting her skin on fire, making her flesh pulse with unbearable sensation.

(21) She jerked her head back savagely, sending silky Titian strands flying about her head, bright colour to balance the hectic scarlet that stained her cheekbones, darkening her eyes to jet. (22) But, effortlessly, his fingers tightened, calmly stilling her frantic movements, holding her head rigid.

(23) Stingingly, she was aware of the imprint of his fingers, of the slow, hypnotic movement of his thumb, moving with erotic lightness against her cheekbone, feathering her skin with searing sensation. (24) Blindly, she closed her eyes, fighting to control the force of the feelings he was so heedlessly creating within her. (25) She was shamingly aware of the way her lips were quivering, as if in invitation, and was unable to do anything about it.

(26) 'You are a beautiful woman,' he imparted, a wry note in his husky voice. (27) 'But you lack that vibrancy, the glow that marks a woman in love.' (28) His fingers tightened fractionally, making her eyes fly open, his own holding her unwilling gaze with aquamarine intensity. (29) 'You're not in love with Norman and yet you've agreed to marry him. (30) Don't blame me if I draw my own conclusions.'

(31) She almost spat at him then, but his next words, softly spoken but impregnated with deadly meaning, shocked her into total immobility.

(32) 'You're far more sexually aware of me than you are of him. (33)

And don't deny it,' he warned silkily, 'or I might be tempted to prove it.'

(34) Then he smiled, very slow, very sure of himself. (35) 'There's a pretty potent brand of chemistry between us – immediate and undeniable. (36) And you know it. (37) I saw the recognition in your eyes the first time we met, outside Monk's Hall. (38) You panicked then and you're panicking now.'

(Hamilton 1990: 25–7)

So the first chapter ends. In the following subsections, I examine the distribution of process types, focalisation, and encoding of the heroine's erotic responses.

4.2 Process types

As in the passage I examined from *No Gentleman*, the hero in the above extract from *Passionate Awakening* is the grammatical subject of a large number of action-process verbs (25 out of the 33 verbs assigned to him in all). In contrast with the passage previously examined, so is the heroine (25 out of 32 in all).[3] The action-process verbs are listed in Table 5.1. Included in the table are six noun phrases and a prepositional phrase which contribute to the encoding of action processes in the passage. I will return to three of the five in Annie's column when I go on to the encoding of her erotic responses.

Processes other than the action type are relatively infrequent in this passage. Luke is the grammatical subject of two behavioural-process verbs (*chuckled* and *smiled*) and three verbal-process verbs (*remarked, imparted* and *warned*). Annie is the grammatical subject of a behavioural-process verb (*looking at*), a verbal-process verb (*rasped*) and a mental-process verb (*remembered*). The few other remaining verbs are relational (five attributive occurrences of *seemed* and *was*).

The passage examined is an 'action' scene, containing predominantly action processes. It presents the protagonists in conflict; they are engaged in a struggle. Annie is rather like a spirited young horse, especially in (21). It is almost as if the protagonists were doing battle (see Walter Nash's comments on sex scenes in romances: he compares them with 'action' sequences in men's genre fiction (Nash 1990: 140–5)).

4.3 Focalisation

The narration in the passage is focalised through Annie. Throughout most Mills & Boon novels, including this one, the overt signalling of focalisation is achieved very straightforwardly through use of mental-process verbs (the predictable regularity of verbs like *thought, realised, knew, decided, hoped* and related constructions like *was aware*). Given, however, that this particular

113

Table 5.1 Distribution of action processes in the narration

Sentence	Luke Derringer	Annie Moss
(1)	had moved	
(2)		closed
		a chemical reaction
		an explosion
(6)		gathering up
(7)		could ... have hit
(9)	tilted	
	curled	
	revealing	
(12)		dragged in
		pattering
(13)	had moved	
	blocking	to get (past)
		would have had to step
(14)		tightened
(15)	to exude	
(17)		came up
		glittered
		did manage to keep
		masking
(20)	moved	
	crowding	
	making	churn
	moved	
	cupping	
	setting	on fire
	making	pulse
(21)		jerked
		sending
		flying
(22)	tightened	
	stilling	her frantic movements
	holding	
(23)	the imprint	
	slow, hypnotic movement	
	moving	
	feathering	
(24)		closed
		fighting
		to control
	was ... creating	
(25)		were quivering
		to do
(28)	tightened	
	making	fly open
	holding	
(31)		spat
	shocked	total immobility

passage is an action scene, focalisation is achieved less through Annie's reported thoughts than through her senses.

Angle of perception plays a part in this, as in (1), where the hero's activity is presented as a movement into Annie's perceptual field; the narration gives us her interpretations of events. Listed in Table 5.2 are elements in the passage presenting her sensory and interpretive points of view. The distinction here is between processes of perception (sight, hearing, touch: the operations of Annie's nervous system) and cognition. Note also that there are three reported thoughts in the passage. In them she is registering sensations; they could therefore be said to fall between these categories. The reported thoughts use the mental-process verb *remembered* in 'she remembered [his mouth]' and the relational verb *was* with a mental-state *aware* as an attribute: 'she was aware of the imprint of his fingers . . . she was shamingly aware of the way her lips were quivering'.

Table 5.2 Focalisation: sensory and interpretive points of view

Sentence	Sensory	Interpretive
(1)	he had moved into her line of vision the startlingly blue eyes seemed [to her]	
(2)	she closed her eyes looking at him *explosion deep inside her*	she remembered [his mouth]
(7)		The allusion wasn't lost on her could . . . have hit him
(12)	*She dragged in a sharp shallow breath, her heart pattering wildly under her breastbone*	
(15)	They [towels in her arms] smelt of . . . this man seemed [to her] to exude	
(18)		Infuriatingly
(20)	*her stomach churn her skin on fire her flesh pulse with unbearable sensation*	
(23)	hypnotic movement of his thumb *erotic lightness against her cheekbone searing sensation*	she was aware of . . . his fingers
(24)	Blindly, she closed her eyes feelings	
(25)		She was shamingly aware her lips were quivering, as if in invitation
(31)		his next words, . . . impregnated with deadly meaning

Through the intense sensory focalisation in this passage, we are party to activity going on inside Annie's body which only she can possibly be aware of. Her breathing difficulty and accelerated heart rate (12) might possibly be visible to an attentive observer. An outside observer would certainly be able see her blushing in (21) ('the hectic scarlet that stained her cheekbones') and might also be aware of her churning stomach (20). But even the most attentive observer could not perceive the more intimate details: the 'explosion deep inside her' (2) or the 'searing sensation' (23) produced by the movement of his thumb on her cheek. These representations of erotic responses to the hero are in italics in Table 5.2. They are examined more closely in the next section.

4.4 Encoding of responses

A large proportion of the text is taken up with Annie's inadvertent responses to Luke's appearance, actions and utterances. They can be viewed as cause and effect pairs: 'this happens which makes that happen'. In order to look at these cause–effect pairs, I have isolated the sentences in the passage containing them. Table 5.3 shows some of them (see the Appendix for the full list). The causal relationship is made explicit in (20) and (28) with three uses of the verb *make* (in the sense of *cause to*). The action processes in Annie's responses are in italics.

Some of the action processes are encoding physiological activities: heartbeat, pulse, the stomach's movement. There are clearly various metaphors in operation too, representing her body's involuntary responses. They involve chemistry and combustion. In (2) we have chemistry and combustion in combination, in a sentence which seems to mimic the chain reaction it refers to. These metaphors for the heroine's involuntary responses firmly establish them as physical, uncontrollable and dangerous. Her desire is represented as fundamentally reactive; it emerges in response to action on the part of the hero.

The heroine's early responses to the desirable hero in *No Guarantees* are far less fevered than the ones we have just looked at. The exposition concentrates on establishing her status as a widow, so there are fewer representations of the heroine's desire in the first chapter. I have already mentioned her 'flicker of forbidden excitement', which occurred in chapter 1. There is also one metaphor for the erotic, in the weaker form of simile: 'His hands rested a moment on her shoulders. A tingle, like a charge of electricity, sizzled through her' (Donald 1990: 18). It may be improper for a widow to succumb to lust in chapter 1. She makes up for it later, however.

In these novels, as in all Mills & Boon, the woman is barely in control of herself. Moreover, it is the man who knows what is going on, not her. At the end of the first chapter of *Passionate Awakening*, the hero articulates the repeated chemistry metaphor (seen in sentence (2)) in the passage:

Table 5.3 Some Cause–Effect Pairs

Sentence	Cause	Effect
(2)	looking at him	
		completed *a chemical reaction* that sparked off *an explosion* deep inside her.
[...]		
(9)	A strongly defined dark eyebrow titled upwards and the sensually wide mouth curled, revealing white, even teeth.	
(10)	'Or maybe I'm wondering why a woman like you should be marrying a man like Cousin Norman.	
(11)	Security, is it?'	
(12)		She *dragged in* a sharp shallow breath, her heart *pattering* wildly under her breastbone.
[...]		
(20)	And he moved closer, crowding her,	
		making her stomach *churn,*
	and a strong tanned hand moved, lean fingers cupping her chin,	
		setting her skin *on fire*, making her flesh *pulse* with unbearable sensation.
(23)	... the slow, hypnotic movement of his thumb, moving with erotic lightness against her cheekbone, feathering her skin	
		with searing sensation.
(28)	His fingers tightened fractionally,	
		making her eyes *fly open*

There's a pretty potent brand of chemistry between us – immediate and undeniable. And you know it. I saw the recognition in your eyes the first time we met . . . You panicked then and you're panicking now.

(Hamilton 1990: 27)

His diagnostic observation is the first stage of the heroine's education. Similar diagnostic comments, emanating from the objects of desire themselves, can be found in most Mills & Boon. They are always right. In Mills & Boon, men are always knowledgeable about women's desire. The hero's task is to teach the heroine what she secretly knows but will not admit to herself. In the course of the narrative in *Passionate Awakening*, Annie learns to face up to the truth: her desire for the intimidating hero is something to come to terms with and accept. Similarly, in both *No Guarantees* and *No Gentleman* the heroine learns that she has misinterpreted the desirable male's actions – and her own feelings – and thanks to his guidance and wisdom realises that she has wanted him all along. Relationships between men and women are presented in terms of the naturally predatory male's intimidation and ultimate conquest of the naturally resistant (but secretly desiring) female.

5 CONCLUSION: READING ROMANCES

I have been pointing to generic features of Mills & Boon romances. The narrative is intensively focalised through the heroine. At the outset, we have a bad impression of the hero because she initially dislikes him. As we have just seen, she tries to repress her desire for him, but he sees through her futile attempts. Diagnostic comments like the one above, from the object of desire himself, are very common. Other generic features are the eroticisation of difference and eroticisation of the struggle between the protagonists. There are differences between the stories, however, such as the pacing of erotic intensity in the two I have looked at. I think it is unacceptably dismissive simply to assume they are all identical. The more of them I read, the less confident I am about easy generalisations. There are even occasional exceptions to the focalisation, emphasised dangerousness of the hero and vulnerability of the heroine (I have come across one, namely Catherine Spencer's *The Loving Touch* (1990), a novel in which both characters are hospital physicians).

Romance is a traditional source of erotic material for heterosexual women. In societies in which women's sexual fantasies are not widely affirmed, and certainly not approved of, Mills & Boon romances fill a vacuum. They provide something for which feminism has so far had little to offer; namely a celebration of women's heterosexual desire (for discussion of this problem for feminism, see Hollway 1995). Romance fiction does not offer an emancipatory discourse, of course. It offers women participation in successful heterosexuality and a kind of triumph for femininity – and all without transgressing society's expectations concerning gender identity. Put simply, women can achieve what they want, sexually and otherwise, through their 'natural' (that is to say, naturalised) femininity, without having to subvert it. Your secret desires can be satisfied without even having to ask, which would of course be most unfeminine. Some ruthless, dominant male will descend upon you and force you to admit your desire. It is simply a matter of waiting to be swept off your feet (see Nancy Friday on the 'Swept Away Phenomenon' in real life and its casualties, particularly in terms of unwanted pregnancies (Friday 1991: 35–42)).

In romances, the exaggerated male activity and female passivity certainly seems larger than life. But it is also visible in non-fictional courtship narratives – at least, in one study of married couples' own accounts of their courtships (Silberstein 1988). In this study, the women's stories centred on 'the need to decide – to react' (*ibid.*: 139), while the men's were narratives of orchestration and conquest.

If an actual reader derives pleasure from the eroticised characters and their interaction in *No Guarantees* and *Passionate Awakening*, she does so only by going along with the way they are represented. In particular, to be the vicarious recipient of the hero's attentions and experiencer of desire, she has to accept a feminine subject position congruent with that of the focalised character. This acceptance may, of course, be fleeting. She may use such fiction to refresh herself and return unscathed, so to speak, and invigorated from the fantasy world supplied by fiction. The feminine subject position offered may, however, correspond rather closely with her subjectivity as female in her own life. If it does, then the fantasy eroticism will, apart from anything else, reinforce her perception of possible real relationships and her sense that her gendered identity is 'natural'. Her emotional/sexual dependency is presented as a natural and even desirable element of femininity.

Hence, we cannot make grand claims about the baleful effects of reading romance fiction, on the basis of their content alone. We can, however, comment on their conservatism, and the possible consequences for some readers of repeated doses of Mills & Boon's variety of fantasy eroticism. Hegemonic masculinity is presented as desirable, indeed irresistible. In Mills & Boon, women desire the men who intimidate them. Apparently problematic relationships are reinterpreted as good ones. Men do not need to change. Women just have to learn how to understand them.

In conclusion, we might consider this conservatism in the light of the popular conception of romance fiction as something to be despised. Ethnographers of romance have shown that romance readers know their reading material is disparaged by the world at large; some of them are sufficiently embarrassed about it to offer justifications (Owen 1990; Radway 1987). The sexual fantasies millions of women read offer them dominant, oppressive forms of masculinity as objects of desire. One might think that this would be met with approval. Instead they are scorned for it.

NOTES

1 Mills & Boon has been a publishing house since 1908, although it has not always specialised in romance fiction. In 1972, it merged with Harlequin, a similar, North American romance publisher. It has been controlled by a Canadian communication conglomerate, Torstar Corporation, since the mid-1970s.

2 The distinction between focalisation and narration originates in Gérard Genette 1972. It is now in general currency in studies on narrative (see Genette 1980 or Rimmon-Kenan 1989).

3 Some of them could probably be analysed differently, however. There is a good deal of overlap between material and behavioural processes: the verbs in *Her narrowed eyes glittered darkly* and *her lips were quivering* could equally be behavioural processes. They satisfy the grammatical criteria for either kind of process.

REFERENCES

Donald, R. (1990) *No Guarantees*, Richmond, Surrey: Mills & Boon.

Fowler, R., Hodge, R., Kress, G. and Trew, T. (1979) *Language and Control*, London: Routledge & Kegan Paul.

Friday, N. (1991) *Women on Top*, London: Hutchinson.

Genette, G. (1972) *Figures III*, Paris: Seuil.

—— (1980) *Narrative Discourse*, Ithaca, NY: Cornell University Press.

Halliday, M.A.K. (1985) *An Introduction to Functional Grammar*, London: Edward Arnold.

Hamilton, D. (1990) *Passionate Awakening*, Richmond, Surrey: Mills & Boon.

Hollway, W. (1995) 'Feminist discourses and women's heterosexual desire', in S. Wilkinson and C. Kitzinger (eds) *Feminism and Discourse*, London: Sage, pp. 86–105.

Kress, G. and Hodge, R. (1979) *Language as Ideology*, London: Routledge & Kegan Paul.

Nash, W. (1990) *Language in Popular Fiction*, London: Routledge.

Owen, M. (1990) 'Women's reading of popular romantic fiction: a case study in the mass media. A key to the ideology of women', unpublished Ph.D. dissertation, University of Liverpool.

Paizis, G. (1995) 'The romantic novel – translation, realism and myth', unpublished paper presented at 'Romance and Roses', a conference on Mills & Boon romance, University of Liverpool.

Radway, J. (1987) *Reading the Romance*, London: Verso.

Rimmon-Kenan, S. (1989 (1983)) *Narrative Fiction*, London: Routledge.

Silberstein, S. (1988) 'Ideology as process: Gender ideology in courtship narratives', in A.D. Todd and S. Fisher (eds) *Gender and Discourse: The Power of Talk*, vol. XXX: *Advances in Discourse Processes*, Norwood, NJ: Ablex, pp. 125–49.

Spencer, Catherine (1990) *The Loving Touch*, Richmond, Surrey: Mills & Boon.

Talbot, M.M. (1994) 'Almost uncontrollable urges in women's popular fiction', unpublished paper presented at 'Our Own and Others' Voices', 17th Annual Conference of the Organization for the Study of Communication, Language and Gender, Florida.

—— (1995) *Fictions at Work: Language and Social Practice in Fiction*, London: Longman.

Walker, K. (1992) *No Gentleman*, Richmond, Surrey: Mills & Boon.

APPENDIX: CAUSE–EFFECT PAIRS

Sentence	Cause	Effect
(2)	looking at him	completed a chemical reaction that sparked off an explosion deep inside her.
[. . .]		
(9)	A strongly defined dark eyebrow tilted upwards and the sensually wide mouth curled, revealing white, even teeth.	
(10)	'Or maybe I'm wondering why a woman like you should be marrying a man like Cousin Norman.	
(11)	Security, is it?'	
(12)		She dragged in a sharp shallow breath, her heart pattering wildly under her breastbone.
[. . .]		
(20)	And he moved closer, crowding her,	making her stomach churn,
	and a strong tanned hand moved, lean fingers cupping her chin,	setting her skin on fire, making her flesh pulse with unbearable sensation.
(21)		She jerked her head back savagely,
[. . .]		
(22)	But, effortlessly, his fingers tightened,	calmly stilling her frantic movements, holding her head rigid.
(23)		Stingingly, she was aware of the imprint of his fingers,
	of the slow, hypnotic movement of his thumb, moving with erotic lightness against her cheekbone, feathering her skin	with searing sensation.
(24)		Blindly, she closed her eyes, fighting to control the force of the feelings he was so heedlessly creating within her.
(25)		She was shamingly aware of the way her lips were quivering, as if in invitation, and was unable to do anything about it.
[. . .]		

Sentence	Cause	Effect
(28)	His fingers tightened fractionally,	
		making her eyes fly open,
	his own holding	
		her unwilling gaze
[. . .]		
(29)	'You're not in love with Norman and yet you've agreed to marry him.	
(30)	Don't blame me if I draw my own conclusions.'	
(31)		She almost spat at him then, but
	his next words, softly spoken but impregnated with deadly meaning,	
		shocked her into total immobility.

6

'YOU WOULD IF YOU LOVED ME'

Language and desire in the teen novel

Murray Knowles

His father, having repaired to the pub for refreshment after beating up his family, learned about the theft of the motorbike from the top of Fiddler's Creek. He went home and woke Penn up, threatening him drunkenly and loudly.

(Peyton 1970: 153)

'I'm not having this staying-in-bed business', said Maurice. He stepped forward and snatched the bedclothes off. Naked, Nick [Maurice's son] grabbed at his coverings and yelled. 'Fuck off!'

(Prince 1986: 109)

Sybil Davison has a genius I.Q. and has been laid by at least six different guys.

(Blume 1986: 5)

1 INTRODUCTION

One of the most significant developments in children's fiction in the last thirty years has been the publication of books focusing on what were previously taboo subjects. Often referred to as 'realistic fiction', this genre, aimed at the teenage reader, professes to 'tell it as it is'. Thus, families are no longer regarded as sacrosanct and sex and violence are no longer topics to be avoided. The three extracts above illustrate well the departure from the cosy, middle-class world of Enid Blyton.

In Knowles and Malmkjaer (1996: 141–2), we point out how the relatively new genre of realistic fiction has its roots in the United States in the late 1960s and the 1970s with writers such as Judy Blume, Betsy Byars, Robert Cormier, S.E. Hinton and Paul Zindel. All of these writers are still very popular and Robert Cormier, the main focus of this chapter, one of the most popular of all. As the genre became established, the sexual content of the narratives became more and more explicit. Judy Blume's *Forever* (1975) contained the first full description of an adolescent heterosexual encounter while, three years previously, Isabelle Holland's *The Man Without a Face* featured a homosexual relationship. Sexuality had, by the later 1970s, become a major theme of the realistic adolescent novel.

123

Realism should be seen as multi-faceted (see Egoff 1981: 60–3) and at its best the genre treats issues with sensitivity and compassion. Certainly sexuality is an issue for young people struggling through adolescence and it is right, therefore, that authors pay attention to the personal intensity of that struggle. What is of particular interest in the representation of adolescent sexual desire is not only the linguistic strategies used by authors to describe sexual encounters between characters but also those strategies by which they allow their characters to think and talk about sex. In this chapter I am concerned with the language of sexual desire as articulated in the thoughts of a physically unattractive male adolescent.

In attempting to unravel characters' views of the world and points of view encoded in text, the description of collocation and transitivity are complementary. Vocabulary choices are important because 'Words . . . are selected from a determinate set for the situation at hand and have been previously shaped by the community or by those parts of it to which the speaker (or writer) belongs' (Montgomery 1986: 176). It is the words selected by the author that the reader receives. It is these words that name and describe participants in certain ways, including what they do and say to each other and what they feel about each other. Certain verbal and nominal groups are selected in preference to others and we might ask ourselves why. For example, in the extract upon which this chapter focuses (see clause complex (12) in the text on p. 131) Cormier selects specific lexical items when referring to the main character's father. He represents him as someone who can be 'half drunk and wobbly' and who has 'greasy' dollar bills. This lexical selection allows the writer to present a reductive linguistic portrait of the character, which raises the question of the view of the world that an author wishes to give his/her implied reader (that is, the reader the author has in mind when they construct the text; see Chatman 1978: 151). Equally, the question arises of what view of the world the real reader constructs as he or she actually reads the text. In the example mentioned, a reader does not have to have a drunken father to decode the text. A reader's own world knowledge allows them to interact with the writer and 'out of this interaction of authors and readers the meaning of what is written emerges' (Musgrave 1985: 4).

I adopt a Hallidayan framework for the analysis of transitivity – the verbal system determining the representation of 'who does what and to whom'. In addition, where appropriate I shall refer to the concept of *boulomaic* modality. This system of modality is closely related to deontic modality, and as Simpson (1993: 48) tells us, it 'is extensively grammaticized in English in expressions of "desire". Modal lexical verbs, indicating the wishes and desires of the speaker, are central in the boulomaic system.' He gives examples such as *hope, wish* and *regret* (see also Perkins 1983).

In the vast range of titles for teenagers that have accumulated over the last quarter of a century there is considerable variation in literary quality.

At their most positive the books provide entertaining narratives in which the main characters emerge from the crisis having attained some degree of maturity and with the book concluding on a hopeful note. Others, however, seem to portray their main characters in terms of utter hopelessness. One of the best known of teenage children's writers is Robert Cormier whose *The Chocolate War* was first published in 1975 (page references are to the 1992 edition). This book falls into the latter of the two categories noted above.

At one stage in the narrative Cormier presents a minor character called Tubs Caspar. Minor he may be, but the descriptive focus is such that the overwhelming feeling that this is a tale of hopelessness is powerfully re-inforced. The description of Tubs selling boxes of chocolates allegedly for school funds starts with a straightforward account of his physical actions. However, it soon becomes apparent to the reader that we are not just having the actions and thoughts of the boy described for us. We are, as readers, in some sense inside his mind. The Tubs Caspar passage is presented and analysed in section 3.

2 COLLOCATION AND TRANSITIVITY

In concentrating on a linguistic description of the encoding of desire in a section of Robert Cormier's *The Chocolate War* I shall be concentrating mainly, though not entirely, on significant lexical patterning, particularly collocation, and the different ways in which experiences are encoded in language by the choices made from the system of transitivity. The linguistic representation by writers of how adolescents *are, think, feel* and *behave* in the emotional intensity of their teenage years is of interest when it comes to comparing the reality of those fictional thoughts, feelings and actions with what goes on in the real world. The passage I shall be discussing below is, in fact, an account of one boy's experiences of the world around him and the frustration he is going through because of those experiences. We, as readers, are in his mind, seeing the world from his point of view. I summarise the salient features of the appropriate linguistic frameworks below.

2.1 Collocation

The notion of collocation is derived from Firth (1957a; 1957b) and since then has been further refined and developed by, among others, Halliday (1966) and Sinclair (1966; 1987; 1991). The notion relates to the tendency of certain words to appear close to certain other words or to 'the company words keep' (see Carter 1992: 36). In carrying out a collocational analysis, sets of concordance lines in which the word under consideration – known as the nodal item or 'node' – is displayed in centre position provide the main analytic tool. It is also worth noting how some words tend to evoke certain associations. Louw (1993: 158), quoting personal communication with Sinclair in 1988, has named these associations 'semantic prosodies'. Thus, for example, Louw shows how the phrasal verb *set in* tends to occur in the context of words referring to unpleasant things such as death, as in the clause 'rigor mortis had *set in*'.

Collocation enables writers to encourage certain reader reactions to, and associations between, characters, situations and feelings in the fictional worlds of realistic novels. Consider the concordance lines (Table 6.1) taken from my selected text dealing with the frustrations of adolescent male sexual desire. The main character in the text is Tubs Caspar, and the item *Tubs* or the pronominal *he* – when that item refers to the boy – provide the nodal items. It is not necessary to carry out a detailed linguistic analysis at this stage. That will come later after I present the text in its entirety. What is important at this point is the fact that these concordance lines exemplify the usefulness of collocation in critical linguistic description for establishing the profile of significant lexical items, here the collocates of the nodal items *Tubs* and *he*. For example, there are lexical items which form a set ascribing physical features: *short* (line 1), *fat* (1), *overweight* (8). The boy is presented to the reader as physically unattractive. *Weight* (12) and *bulge* (13), while not modifiers of the nodal items, add to this representation by occurring in their vicinity. *Short* and *fat*, in particular, when they occur together in English carry a particular connotation of unattractiveness. The semantic prosody is negative. This is important, as we shall see when I consider in more detail the linguistic manifestation of sexual desire in the text as a whole. There is also a set of collocates which ascribe emotion to Tubs: *desperate* (2, 14), *need* (2, 14, 36), *hate* (19), *worry* (35). The boy is not only physically unattractive but he also appears to be in an extreme emotional state.

The notion of emotional pressure is further heightened in the verbal groups functioning as predicators with *Tubs* or *he* as subject by the use of *had to* (11, 20, 21, 23). The boy has no choice. And, whatever it is that has subjected him to such compulsion, it has to be done *furtively* (11). We realise from line 5 that a girl is involved and the occurrence of *sneak out* (21) ascribes responsibility to her for Tubs's mental state. She is obviously not approved of by Tubs's mother, but she is the focus of the boy's sexual desire as the occurrence of the items *rubbed against* (25), *brushed against* (27, just outside the printed range), *hardening* (29) and *under her sweater* (37) confirm.

Other verbal groups are also important in the representation of the boy. There are ten instances (4, 7, 19, 24, 25, 28, 31, 32, 33, 35) where Tubs is the subject of 'thinking' verbs. Much of what is important in the boy's world appears to be going on in his head. There is little physical action ascribed to Tubs and where it is it usually extends the image of compulsion, of the boy not being in control. In lines 1 and 2, Tubs is not even in control of his own movements and in line 12, where he is, it is in order to ease his *burden*.

An exercise such as that carried out above can show how the language of parts of a text which deal with a main character, a situation and a mental state may lead the reader to form an impression of that character (and indeed of the other characters referred to such as Tubs's parents and the girl) and to evaluate his actions and emotions. Thus, the seemingly negative world of Tubs Caspar as represented by Robert Cormier might well be negative because of his sexual frustration and the hint of Rita's sexual manipulation which fuels it.

2.2 Transitivity

Halliday's description of the system of transitivity is based on the clause and its aspect of meaning as representation. In other words, how the clause presents the processes which take place in the world, the participants in them and the circumstances attendant upon them. Essentially this concerns 'who does what to whom, when and how' or as Halliday (1994: 107) puts it: 'Our most powerful impression of experience is that it consists of "goings-on" – happening, doing, sensing, meaning, and being and becoming.' Halliday (1994, chapter 7) provides a detailed classification and description of the different types of process and their participants. Halliday himself used the transitivity model in his analysis of William Golding's *The Inheritors* in 1971 and several others in the field have adapted the framework for their own work in language and literature (see, for example, Leech and Short 1981; Kennedy 1982; Hasan 1985; Toolan 1990; Montgomery 1993; Simpson 1993; Knowles and Malmkjaer, 1996).

In this chapter I am concerned with Material (doing), Mental (sensing), Verbal (saying) and Relational (being) processes. I use a much simplified variant of Halliday's framework, as follows.

Material: these are processes of *doing* and they are realised by verbs of action as in *Sarah shot the dog behind the shed*. Here, *Sarah* is the Actor, *the dog* is the Affected (also known as the Goal), *shot* realises the Material process and *behind the shed* the Circumstance.

Mental: these are processes of *sensing* and *perceiving* (see, hear, etc.), *cognition* (know, understand, etc.) and *affection* (love, hate, etc.) as in *Sarah liked the dog*. Here *Sarah* is the Senser, *the dog* is the Phenomenon, and *liked* realises the Mental process (Affective).

Verbal: these are processes of *saying* and *communicating* as in *Sarah announced her decision to the world*. Here *Sarah* is the Sayer, *the world* is the Recipient, *announced* realises the Verbal process and *her decision* is classified as the Verbiage.

Relational: these are processes of *being* and can involve the ascription of an attribute to some entity as in *Sarah is very cruel*. Here *Sarah* is the Carrier, *very cruel* the Attribute and *is* realises the Relational process (Attributive).

127

Table 6.1

				n
1	The short fat legs of	Tubs Caspar	carried him through the
2	desperate need for money that sent	Tubs	scurrying around town like a mad
3	home and was always driving around.	Tubs's	left arm began to ache from the we
4	soon as possible When would that be?	Tubs	didn't know. Money, money, mone
5	beautiful She was so beautiful that she made	Tubs	all shaky inside, like an earthquake
6	tax. 'Hon –' she never called him	Tubs	'that's what I want most in all the
7	$18.95 plus 3 per cent sales tax which	Tubs Caspar	figured out would make a grand tot
8	happy all at the same time. Him–	He'd	forty pounds overweight
9	in what was for him record time.	he	have made better time if one of his
10	flat but definitely beyond repair and	He	didn't have money to buy a new on
11	at doors and ringing doorbells.	he	also had to do it furtively, afraid th
12	from the weight of the chocolates and	He	shifted his burden to his other arm,
13	the reassuring bulge of his wallet.	He	had already sold three boxes – six
14	but that wasn't enough, of course.	He	was still desperate. He needed a hel
15	enough of course. He was still desperate.	He	needed a hell of a lot more by tonig
16	any chocolates at the last six houses	he'd	visited. He had saved every cent he
17	at the last six houses he'd visited.	He	had saved every cent he could from
18	he'd visited. He had saved every cent	he	could from his allowance and had
19	arrived home half drunk and wobbly.	He	hated doing that – stealing from
20	his parents hated her for some reason.	He	had to sneak out to meet her. He ha
21	He had to sneak out to meet her.	He	had to make phone calls from Ossi
22	an earthquake going on. At night	he	could have one without even touchi
23	now her birthday was tomorrow and	he	had to buy her the present she want

24 tax amounting to fifty seven cents.	He	knew that he didn't have to buy her
25 The first time she rubbed against him	he	thought it was an accident and he
26 he thought it was an accident and	he	pulled away apologetic, leaving a
27 against him again. That was the night	he'd	bought her the earrings – he knew
28 night he'd bought her the earrings –	he	knew it wasn't an accident. He'd fe
29 – he knew it wasn't an accident.	He'd	felt himself hardening and was
30 of, she'd bring the sandwiches and	he'd	bring the bracelet – he knew the
31 and he'd bring the bracelet –	he	knew the delights that awaited him
32 the delights that awaited him but	he	also knew deep down inside that
33 of shape, trying to raise money that	he	knew would lead him eventually
34 eventually only to trouble. Where would	he	raise enough money to pay it all ba
35 made at school. But what the hell –	he'd	worry about it later. Right now he
36 he'd worry about it later. Right now	he	needed to raise the money and Rita
37 probably let him get under her sweater.	He	rang the doorbell of a rich-looking

Note: These concordance lines were obtained manually by noting each instance of *Tubs* and *he* as they occurred in the passage in narrative sequence. When working with larger databases such a method would be both tedious and unreliable and there are software programs available to aid the researcher with his/her endeavours. MicroConcord (Scott and Johns: 1993) is one that the author has used in the past. MicroConcord provides the researcher with a concordance known as KWIC concordance or KeyWord In Context. Once the KeyWord or SearchWord is decided upon, the programme then finds that item and presents all its occurrences in lines of context showing the words both to the left and to the right of the SearchWord. Concordance lines can also be classified or sorted in various ways as part of an editing process by, for example, a consideration of grammatical or sense categories. Scott and Johns provide the example of *bank*, where the researcher might wish to separate *bank* as a verb from *bank* as a noun or *bank*(river) from *bank*(money). MicroConcord is published by Oxford University Press.

Relational processes can also be possessive as in *Sarah has a gun*. Here *Sarah* is the Carrier (Possessor), *a gun* is the Attribute (Possessed) and *has* represents the Relational process (Possession).

The usefulness of transitivity as an analytic tool lies in how it allows us to classify processes, participants and circumstances in fictional worlds. In sustaining a narrative an author may well change the selection of processes for a participant to engage in. Participants can be assigned different roles, they may 'think' more than they 'do'; they may be the Affected more than the Actor; they may be ascribed attributes which will lead the reader to form opinions concerning the participants.

Mental processes seem to be important in the Cormier extract. I noted above the frequency of what I then called 'thinking' verbs collocating with *Tubs* and *he*. Tubs is in the world of his thoughts. He is often the Senser. The concordance lines do not provide sufficient text for us to obtain a clear picture of all Tubs's thoughts. Nevertheless, as readers we are aware that money (or the lack of it) and desire for Rita are inextricably entwined as Phenomena in the boy's Mental processes which are predominantly those of Cognition. Collocation complements transitivity as an additional tool for constructing a framework for analysis.

Transitivity shows Tubs as being in a highly charged emotional state. I noted also how Tubs is not always in control of his own physical actions. In concordance line 1 we have the clause:

The short fat legs of Tubs Caspar carried him

We can consider the clause from the point of view of the roles specified by the transitivity system:

The short fat legs of Tubs Caspar	carried	him
{Actor}	{Material process}	{Affected}

This is the introductory clause of the extract. As such, it is important in influencing the reader's perception of Tubs and of the particular role he has been assigned in his fictional world. This is not the role of an agent in command of his own actions.

It is also important to note that the nominal group *The short fat legs of Tubs Caspar* is not only the Actor of the process but the first element in the clause. As such, it occurs in Theme position, or as 'the point of departure of the message' (Halliday 1994: 37). Cormier has organised the informational content of the clause for the reader in such a way that we are immediately aware that this boy is not 'tall, dark and handsome'; he is *short* and *fat*, and the inference is 'physically undesirable'. This is a much more subtle opening – accomplishing as it does more than one purpose linguistically – than merely to state in a Relational process 'Tubs Caspar was short and fat'.

130

3 THE TEXT AND THE ANALYSIS

Here is the full text I will analyse in detail. The sentences – or clause complexes – are numbered for ease of reference:

(1) The short fat legs of Tubs Caspar carried him through the neighbourhood in what for him was record time. (2) He'd have made better time if one of his bicycle tyres wasn't flat, not only flat but definitely beyond repair and he didn't have money to buy a new tyre. (3) In fact it was a desperate need for money that sent Tubs scurrying around town like a madman, from one house to another, lugging the chocolates, knocking at doors and ringing doorbells. (4) He also had to do it furtively, afraid that his father or mother might see him. (5) Small chance that his father would come across him – he was at work at the plastic shop. (6) But his mother was another thing altogether. (7) She was a nut about the car, like his father said, and couldn't bear to stay home and was always driving around.

(8) Tubs's left arm began to ache from the weight of the chocolates and he shifted his burden to his other arm, taking a moment to pat the reassuring bulge of his wallet. (9) He had already sold three boxes – six dollars – but that wasn't enough, of course. (10) He was still desperate. (11) He needed a hell of a lot more by tonight and nobody but nobody had bought any chocolates at the last six houses he'd visited. (12) He had saved every cent he could from his allowance and had even sneaked a folded and greasy dollar bill from his father's pocket last night when he arrived home, half drunk and wobbly. (13) He hated doing that – stealing from his own father. (14) He vowed to return the money to him as soon as possible. (15) When would that be? (16) Tubs didn't know. (17) Money, money, money had become the constant need of his life, money and his love for Rita. (18) His allowance barely made it possible for him to take her to the movies and for a Coke afterwards. (19) Two-fifty each for the movies, fifty cents for two Cokes. (20) And his parents hated her for some reason. (21) He had to sneak out to meet her. (22) He had to make phone calls from Ossie Baker's house. (23) She is too old for you, his mother said. (24) What his mother should have said was, she looks beautiful. (25) She was so beautiful that she made Tubs all shaky inside, like an earthquake going on. (26) At night he could have one without even touching himself, just thinking of her. (27) And now her birthday was tomorrow and he had to buy her the present she wanted, the bracelet she'd seen in the window of Black's downtown, that terrible and beautiful bracelet all sparkles and radiance, terrible because of the price tag: $18.95 plus tax. (28) 'Hon –' she never called him Tubs – 'that's what I want most in all the world.' (29) Jesus – $18.95 plus the 3 per cent sales tax which Tubs figured out would make a grand total of $19.52, the sales tax

amounting to fifty-seven cents. (30) He knew that he didn't have to buy her the bracelet.

(31) She was a sweet girl who loved him for himself alone. (32) She walked along the sidewalk with him, her breast brushing his arm, setting him on fire. (33) The first time she rubbed against him he thought it was an accident and he pulled away apologetic, leaving a space between them. (34) Then she brushed against him again – that was the night he'd bought her the earrings – and he knew it wasn't an accident. (35) He'd felt himself hardening and was suddenly ashamed and embarrassed and deliriously happy all at the same time. (36) Him – Tubs Caspar forty pounds overweight which his father never let him forget. (37) Him – with this beautiful girl's breast pushed against him, not beautiful the way his mother thought a girl was beautiful but beautiful in a ripe wild way, faded blue jeans hugging her hips, those beautiful breasts bouncing under her jersey. (38) She was only fourteen and he was barely fifteen but they were in love, dammit, and it was only money that kept them apart, money to take the bus to her house because she lived on the other side of town and they'd made plans to meet tomorrow, her birthday, at Monument Park, a picnic sort of, she'd bring the sandwiches and he'd bring the bracelet – he knew the delights that awaited him but he also knew deep down inside that the bracelet was more important than anything else . . .

(39) All of which rushed him along now, out of breath and out of shape, trying to raise money that he knew dimly would lead him eventually only to trouble. (40) Where would he raise enough money to pay it all back when the returns were made at school? (41) But what the hell – he'd worry about it later. (42) Right now he needed to raise the money and Rita loved him – tomorrow she'd probably let him get under her sweater.

(43) He rang the doorbell of a rich-looking house on Stern's Avenue and prepared his most innocent and sweetest smile for whoever opened the door.

(Cormier 1992: 102–5)

I noted earlier how Tubs is not in control and clause complex (3) gives us more information: 'In fact it was a desperate *need* for money that sent Tubs scurrying around town like a *madman*, from one house to another, lugging the chocolates, knocking at doors and ringing doorbells' (my emphasis). And, further down, in clause complexes (10) and (11), after the reader has been informed that Tubs had earned $6: 'He was still *desperate*. He *needed* a hell of a lot more by tonight and nobody but nobody had bought any chocolates at the last six houses he'd visited'.

Tubs may be physically undesirable, but it is nonetheless *desire* that is driving him forward. The succeeding sentences, including our extract above, focus on this desire by involving the reader in the boy's thought processes. More precisely what we have here is Cormier representing the thoughts of this character so that the reader is invited to see life from Tubs Caspar's point of view. In this way, Cormier makes Tubs the Reflector (see Leech and Short 1981: 341–51). There is no speech here but an omniscient narrator presenting the thoughts of this character (for a detailed discussion of the categories of thought presentation see Leech and Short 1981: 337–51). Tubs's thoughts, as we shall see, are inflamed by desire; if this were a dramatic production he would, no doubt, share them with the audience in a soliloquy.

Tubs is out in the neighbourhood selling chocolates which are supposed to raise money for school funds. As we enter the soliloquy sequence we learn that Tubs has other plans for the money because, to quote partly from clause complexes (3), (10) and (11), respectively:

it was a *desperate need* for *money* that sent Tubs scurrying around

He was still *desperate*. He *needed* a hell of a lot more [money] by tonight

At this point we do not know what he needs the money for. What we do have is the key lexical item *desperate* collocating with the item *need* twice within a short space of text. In the item *need* in clause complex (3) we have a nomina- lised example of the concept of modality mentioned earlier, boulomaic mod- ality. This is then realised by the verb form *need* in the second.

Tubs is so desperately in need of cash that the reader is informed the boy has stolen from his father. The soliloquy reaches its first climax with the fol- lowing clause complex (17): 'Money, money, money had become the *constant need* of his life, money and his love for Rita.' Note how this time a Relational process is used to considerable effect in this clause complex:

Money, money, money	had become
{Carrier}	{Relational process}
the constant need of his life	
{Attribute}	

When dynamic verbs of transition such as *become* realise a Relational process, the Attribute then exists as the result of the process. *Become* is an 'ascriptive' verb, which means that '. . . an entity has some quality ascribed or attributed to it' (Halliday 1994: 120). In clause complex (17), the 'quality ascribed' is *the constant need of his life*. In addition in the latter part of the clause we have the reiteration of *money*, but this time co-ordinated with *his love for Rita*. Thus, there are two Carriers and we could rewrite the clause as: 'Money and his love for Rita had become the constant needs of his life.' Rewriting the clause underlines the central point that one need, *money*, is the result of the other need or desire, *Rita*.

133

The item *need* occurs in this way in the entire text in clause complexes (3), (11) and (17):

(3) In fact it was a desperate *need* for money that sent Tubs scurrying around town like a madman, from one house to another, lugging the chocolates, knocking at doors and ringing doorbells.

(11) He *needed* a hell of a lot more by tonight and nobody but nobody had bought any chocolates at the last six houses he'd visited.

(17) Money, money, money had become the constant *need* of his life, money and his love for Rita.

Note the reiteration of the lexical item *money* in theme position in clause complex (17). *Money, money, money* is a refrain to be repeated again when it co-ordinates with *Rita*. The key lexical item is *need*, which collocates with the two Carriers. The overwhelming force of this need is further emphasised by its modification by *constant*. This collocational pairing underlines the fact that his desire for the girl is addictive. His *need* is *constant* as well as *desperate* and, like many addicts, he has turned to stealing. The importance of this clause is also that it introduces the reader to Rita as she exists in the consciousness of the Reflector. The limits of the boy's view of the world have been set as we are admitted to his thoughts.

Clause complexes (18) and (19) reinforce Tubs's plight in terms of cash flow as his thoughts become even more desperate. Clause complex (18) provides the reader with a general statement of his problem. Note the collocation of *barely* and *possible* where the modality, this time epistemic, underlines the thinking boy's attitude towards what is contained in the proposition. This proposition, which we as readers can infer from clause complex (17), is that 'to keep Rita, money is essential'. In his thoughts, Tubs is assessing the possibility of being able to do so; whether he is consciously aware that he will lose her if he fails to acquire money has not yet been articulated to the reader. Clause complex (19) provides a specific lexical underpinning of his desperation with the reference to cost. We can assume, therefore, that it is not just the possibility of going to the movies that he is assessing but that there is another reason why he *must have* more money. It is now that Tubs's contemplations are directed towards the object of his desire, Rita. She had not appeared in his thought presentation at all until clause complex (17) where, as we saw, she was linked with his need for money.

Clause complexes (20)–(23) focus directly on Rita and a clearer picture of the girl begins to emerge for the reader as Tubs's thoughts move from money back to Rita. The item *And* plays a significant role in the narrator's presentation of the boy's troubled thoughts as it fulfils a linking function in the cataloguing of them, as in a child's story-telling:

(20) *And* his parents hated her for some reason.

In his mind the boy is bewildered; his parents *hate* Rita. This event is represented in his mind as:

. . . his Parents	hated	her
{Senser}	{Mental process of Affection}	{Phenomenon}

and his bewilderment is expressed in the prepositional group *for some reason*.

The consequences of this hatred are expressed in the two Material processes represented by clause complexes (21) and (22) where we are informed that Tubs:

(21) . . . *had to sneak out* to meet her.

(22) . . . *had to make* phone calls from Ossie Baker's house.

He is hemmed in on every side; his love/desire for Rita, his lack of money, his parents' disapproval which is articulated by his mother:

(23) She is too old for you, his mother said.

Here we have a Verbal process with the Verbiage *she is too old for you*. This, however, is part of his thought presentation; the dialogue is inside his head and we have the effect of the inversion of the reporting and reported elements, and thus of the foregrounding of his mother's objection to Rita. An objection for which Tubs provides this response:

(24) What his mother should have said was, she looks beautiful.

What Tubs feels his mother should have said is, of course, his own point of view:

she	looks	beautiful
{Carrier}	{Relational process}	{Attribute}

The process verb *looks* here carries a sensory evaluation which provides a strong contrast with the mother's more prosaic assessment of Rita as being too old for her son.

In clause complexes (25) and (26), the meaning of the sensory perception of Rita's beauty takes on a more physical dimension in terms of desire. First, we have: 'She was so *beautiful* that she *made* Tubs *all shaky inside, like an earthquake going on.*' This leads the reader into clause (26) where Tubs's thought presentation now focuses on the sexual and on the acuteness of his desire for her.

From clause complexes (27)–(29), the intensity of Tubs's thought processes are explained by the immediacy of the temporal circumstance. This immediacy is rendered particularly acute by the *And now* fronting. The birthday may be tomorrow, but the implications of this should he not have the money to buy Rita the present she desires are already there in his mind: 'he *had to* buy her the present she *wanted*.' It is her desire, signalled by *want*, which is compelling him to spend money which is not his. It is at this point that the whole notion of desire becomes concentrated in the items *need, want, have to*. He is not in control, he *had to* buy the present: 'that *terrible* and *beautiful bracelet* all *sparkles* and *radiance*'. *Beautiful* now collocates with the object of Rita's desire where previously it had collocated with the object of Tubs's desire, Rita herself.

Beautiful and its collocates provide one of the most significant lexical patternings in the soliloquy. The connotations of *need, want, desire* and *have to* are, I suggest, connected with the semantic prosody of *beautiful*. Consider the concordance lines in Table 6.2. There are eight occurrences of *beautiful* in the extract, seven of which collocate with Rita or her breasts (that is, all but concordance line 3). Thus we have the following prosody of associations for Tubs with the item *beautiful*:

Tubs - - - - - - - - - - - *beautiful*   {Rita
                                            {Rita's body

For Tubs *beautiful* is physical and sexual. The semantic prosody of *beautiful* for Rita, on the other hand, can be represented, thus:

Rita - - - - - - - - - - - *beautiful*   {material objects, i.e. not Tubs

Note also *terrible* co-ordinating with *beautiful* in line 3. Terrible things can be beautiful (it is, after all, a not unknown literary collocation) but it does not mean that the *terrible* is desirable. It is the cost that is *terrible*, undesirable, as is highlighted in the feverish financial calculations. It is, however, in Rita's words, what 'I *want* most in all the world'. Again note the significance of this verb and its realisation of a type of desire. Rita's modality is one of greed, of desire for material possessions.

Table 6.2

1 have said was, she looks	beautiful.	She was so beautiful that she
2 looks beautiful. She was so	beautiful	that she made Tubs all shaky
3 downtown, that terrible and	beautiful	bracelet all sparkles and radia
4 him forget. Him – with this	beautiful	girl's breast pushed against hi
5 pushed against him not	beautiful	the way his mother thought a
6 mother thought a girl was	beautiful	but beautiful in a ripe wild wa
7 a girl was beautiful but	beautiful	in a ripe wild way, faded blue
8 hugging her hips, those	beautiful	breasts bouncing under her jer

Finally, in clause complex (30) of the extract we have one of the most important transitivity patterns in the whole passage:

136

He	knew
{Senser}	{Mental process of Cognition}

that he didn't have to buy her the bracelet
{Phenomenon}

This appears to be a strange assertion for him to make given what has gone before. This mental process means that Tubs can comment on and evaluate an interpretation of reality. But it is the 'reality' he wants to believe, that Rita wants him for himself. His thoughts now become entirely focused on his desire for Rita.

At this stage of the thought presentation, (31)–(38), a clearer picture of Rita emerges for the reader who will already have inferred the manipulative nature of her character. Tubs, however, prefers to see Rita as described in clause complex (31) even though he may well be repressing or denying the reality of Rita's nature. It could also be argued that he is denying his own reality, that of wanting to get as far as he can sexually with the girl by buying her favours with expensive presents. Here is a clausal analysis of clause complex (31):

She	was	a sweet girl
{Carrier}	{Relational process}	{Attribute}

[She]	loved	him
{Senser}	{Mental process of Affection}	{Phenomenon}

The reality for the boy, the reality he wants to believe in is that of 'a sweet girl who loves him for himself'. This *reality* of selfless love allows for Tubs's thoughts to turn to sex as he recalls: 'She walked along the sidewalk with him, *her breast brushing his arm, setting him on fire.*' Note how the girl's breast is ascribed agency here and there is indeed a concentration on *brushing against, rubbing against, pushing against* (see clause complexes (32), (33), (34), (37) either by Rita or her breast. One result of this is the physical manifestation of desire in Tubs (after he'd bought the girl some earrings):

He	'd felt	himself hardening
{Senser}	{Mental process}	{Phenomenon}

As a result of his sexual arousal:

[He]	was
{Carrier}	{Relational process}

ashamed and embarrassed and deliriously happy
{Attributes}

The items which constitute the Attributes present us with a set of collocates where *Tubs* is node in clause complex (35):

137

hardening   ashamed   embarrassed   deliriously happy

The physical sensation represented by *hardening* causes the emotional sensations of shame, embarrassment and, paradoxically, delirious happiness.

This section of the extract is dense with items and combinations of items that might be regarded as typical of the erotic fantasies of the heterosexual male adolescent. As well as the processes above where Rita or her breast were Actors we have other stereotypical representations, such as these from clause complex (37):

faded blue jeans	hugging	her hips
{Actor}	{Material process}	{Affected}

and:

those beautiful breasts	bouncing	under her jersey
{Actor}	{Material process}	{Circumstance}

These are images which would seem to me classifiable as register features of so-called 'soft-pornographic' writing (or *pornoglossia*; see Cameron 1985: 77) as are the collocates generated by *Rita* as node in clause complex (37), *ripe* and *wild*. Thus, we have *ripe* with its connotation of sexual maturity, and readiness for consumption, and *wild* which connotes the possibility of behaviour where emotions are out of control. This reinforces the sexual imagery I referred to above where the use of metonymy ascribes agency, first, to part of the girl's clothing and, second, to part of her body. In addition, the alliteration of *beautiful breasts bouncing* is hardly accidental.

I referred earlier to the importance of the lexical item *beautiful* and we see it used five times in clause complex (37). Thus, we have *beautiful* as perceived by Tubs's mother, which is not stated but, we can assume, would be articulated in a very different manner linguistically from Tubs's perception. We can be sure that *beautiful* for Mrs Caspar would not involve the use of items like *ripe* and *wild*; were she to describe Rita, her description would be devoid of positive modifiers. *Ripe* and *wild* are in any case not items of everyday discourse patterning.

So, Cormier presents to us Tubs Caspar obsessed with desires that he cannot control either physically or emotionally. In clause complex (38), their complexity reaches a pitch: 'he knew the *delights* that awaited him but he also knew deep down inside that the bracelet was more important than anything else'.

he	knew
{Senser}	{Mental process of Cognition}

that the bracelet was more important than anything else
{Phenomenon}

His thoughts as expressed in the Mental process in clause complex (38) and cited above are therefore a case of self-delusion. If his desire for Rita is to reach any degree of fulfilment – encoded as *the delights* (that is, the probability of getting his hand under her sweater) – then he has to provide for Rita's desire for the bracelet. This desire controls him. Tubs is not his own master and this is reiterated for the reader in the closing stages of the soliloquy. All the strands of anxiety which make up this desire – sexual frustration, worry about his parents, anxiety about money – 'rushed him along now, out of breath and out of shape, trying to raise money that he knew dimly would lead him eventually only to trouble'. And yet despite this albeit dim awareness of impending doom 'Rita loved him – tomorrow she'd probably let him get under her sweater'.

Thus ends the soliloquy. We are returned to the real world outside Tubs's head and we see that the corruption is complete because, having rung a doorbell, he 'prepared his *most innocent and sweetest smile*'.

4 CONCLUSION

In taking the Tubs Caspar 'soliloquy' from one of the best-known novels for adolescents I have attempted to show how desire is represented to young readers in a particular context. That context is one of corruption. The transitivity and lexical patternings that structure the soliloquy demonstrate clearly the powerlessness of the main protagonist. In fact, the whole of *The Chocolate War* is a book where there is 'no longer any trace of the happiness and simplicity that traditionally are associated with childhood' (Egoff 1981: 44). It is the realistic adolescent novel in the extreme. Desires in the form of hopes, wishes and illusions are stripped away. Power is what matters and what governs the lives of the characters. For Tubs and Rita it is in the modality of desire expressed in the words and structures of lust and greed. Tubs thinks he is in love with Rita but he is the object of very confused emotions and ripe for exploitation.

We saw how the system of transitivity represented Tubs as powerless, as being propelled along by some force which he could not withstand. We noted the key item *need* and the fact that Tubs was *desperate* for money and how this *need* was linked to his *need* for Rita. Key vocabulary items and patterns of collocation represented Rita to the reader and highlighted her power over Tubs. Rita's *ripe, wild* beauty is a corrupt beauty which she uses to manipulate Tubs and which, we can infer, will ultimately destroy him. The language is the language of adolescent fantasy but there is no hope in the language patterns, no redeeming feature. All adolescents have fantasies but the language employed by Cormier when representing them to the reader would make it appear that all such experiences are futile and degrading.

REFERENCES

Blume, J. (1975 (1986)) *Forever*, London: Pan.

Cameron, D. (1985) *Feminism and Linguistic Theory*, London: Macmillan.

Carter, R. (1992) *Vocabulary: Applied Linguistic Perspectives*, London: Routledge.

Chatman, S. (1978) *Story and Discourse*, Ithaca, NY: Cornell University Press.

Cormier, R. (1975 (1992)) *The Chocolate War*, London and Glasgow: Lions Tracks, HarperCollins.

Egoff, S. (1981) *Thursday's Child: Trends and Patterns in Contemporary Children's Literature*, Chicago: American Library Association.

Firth, J.R. (1957a) *Papers in Linguistics 1934–1951*, London: Oxford University Press.

— (1957b) *A Synopsis of Linguistic Theory 1930–55* (special volume of the Philological Society), Oxford: Basil Blackwell.

Halliday, M.A.K. (1966) 'Lexis as a linguistic level', in C. Bazell, J. Catford, M.A.K. Halliday and H. Robins (eds) *In Memory of J.R. Firth*, London: Longman, pp.148–62.

—— (1994) *An Introduction to Functional Grammar*, 2nd edn, London: Edward Arnold.

Hasan, R. (1985) *Linguistics, Language and Verbal Art*, Victoria: Deakin University Press.

Holland, Isabelle (1972) *The Man Without a Face*, Philadelphia: Lippincott.

Kennedy, C.J. (1982) 'Systemic grammar and its use in literary analysis', in R. Carter (ed.) *Language and Literature*, London: George Allen & Unwin.

Knowles, G.M. and Malmkjær, K.M. (1996) *Language and Control in Children's Literature*, London: Routledge.

Leech, G.N. and Short, M. (1981) *Style in Fiction: A Linguistic Introduction to English Fictional Prose*, London: Longman.

Louw, B. (1993) 'Irony in the text or insincerity in the writer? The diagnostic potential of semantic prosodies', in M. Baker, G. Francis and E. Tognini-Bonelli (eds) *Text and Technology: in Honour of John Sinclair*, Amsterdam and Philadelphia, Penn.: John Benjamins, pp. 157–76.

Montgomery, M. (1986) *An Introduction to Language and Society*, London: Methuen.

—— (1993) 'Language, character and action: a linguistic approach to the analysis of character in a Hemingway short story', in J. Sinclair, M. Hoey and G. Fox (eds) *Techniques of Description: a festschrift for Malcolm Coulthard*, London: Routledge.

Musgrave, P.W. (1985) *From Brown to Bunter: The Life and Death of the School Story*, London: Routledge.

Perkins, M.R. (1983) *Modal Expressions in English*, London: Frances Pinter.

Peyton, K.M. (1970 (1994)) *Seventeenth Summer*, London: Point, Scholastic Children's Books.

Prince, A. (1986 (1987)) *Nick's October*, London: Teens, Methuen Children's Books.

Scott, M. and Johns, T. (1993) *MicroConcord: Program and Manual*, Oxford: Oxford University Press.

Simpson, P. (1993) *Language, Ideology and Point of View*, London: Routledge.

Sinclair, J. (1966) 'Beginning the study of lexis', in C. Bazell, J. Catford, M.A.K. Halliday and H. Robins (eds) *In Memory of J.R. Firth*, London: Longman, pp. 410–30.

—— (1987) 'Collocation: A progress report', in R. Steele and T. Threadgold (eds) *Language Topics: Essays in Honour of Michael Halliday*, vol. 3, Amsterdam: John Benjamins, pp. 319–31.

—— (1991) *Corpus, Concordance, Collocation*, Oxford: Oxford University Press.

Toolan, M. (1990) *The Stylistics of Fiction*, London: Routledge.

Part III
VOICES

7

'I JUST CALLED TO SAY I LOVE YOU'

Love and desire on the telephone

Joanna Channell

1 INTRODUCTION

In the week beginning Monday 11 January 1993, British newspapers published first extracts and then the full transcript of a private conversation – a telephone call between a man and a woman. Journalists believed from the content of the conversation that the couple were lovers and the man was said to be the Prince of Wales. Hence transcripts of the conversation circulated widely in the public domain and were much analysed and commented upon in the press.

The publication of the transcript provides an opportunity to investigate several issues relevant to the purpose of this volume:

1 How does this couple express love and desire?
2 What is the effect of the telephone on their talk?
3 Apart from the obvious references to sex and love, what other features does the conversation have which mark it out as being the talk of two people who are in a close, loving and sexual relationship?

The transcript of the call (as published) is the primary data analysed here. At the time of publication, there was a large amount of press commentary, which is also of interest. Generally the journalists commented on the content rather than the linguistic features of the transcript (apart from choice of lexis). However, their comments do provide some insights into folk-linguistic beliefs about the language of desire and intimacy. Some of the journalistic comment was prurient, some moralistic, much of it attempted pop-psychological analyses of the couple on the tape.

This chapter differs substantially and deliberately from all of the previous comment about the telephone call. It is not a discussion of the possible identities of the co-participants, nor is there discussion or judgement of their morals, sexual preferences or psychological states. The aim is to analyse what this particular conversation shows about the language of love and desire.

143

2 THE DATA AND THE PARTICIPANTS

Six minutes of conversation were recorded by a radio enthusiast listening in to a cellphone network. Press reports make it clear that such recording is illegal – however, the tape came into the possession of newspapers. Hence transcripts came to be published. The published transcript, reproduced at the end of this chapter in an Appendix, consists of the end of a conversation (it clearly does not begin with the start of the transcript). We may assume that the transcript as it appeared in the press will have been 'cleaned up' in the sense that many features will have been eliminated by a transcriber who I imagine would be without linguistic training – such features as false starts, overlaps, interjected material and *ums* and *ers*. Conventional punctuation has been imposed. The quality of the transcribed data is therefore not as high as a linguist would usually wish to have.

The conversation takes place on a Sunday evening with frequent references to the days in the coming week. From the talk, we learn that the female participant is with her family ('those rampaging children'). We do not learn where the male participant is. They refer to the fact that at least one of them is using a mobile telephone.

Normally for linguistic analysis, the permission of the co-participants would have been agreed, and the investigator would take appropriate steps to protect their identities (see British Association for Applied Linguistics 1994). In the present case, international media coverage has ensured that there are few people in the literate world who do not know their presumed identity. Since it is not the purpose of this chapter to contribute to the identity debate, the participants are referred to as M (male) and F (female) and any other names which appear to be 'clues' to their identity have been changed.

It must be said that while it is true that the privacy of these two people can hardly be infringed any more than it already has been, there remain doubts about the ethics of using this data. My solution has been to concentrate my work on how the linguistic systems and resources of English which are available to all are deployed by these two participants, and to avoid any judgements about them or their conversation.

3 LANGUAGE AND DESIRE ON THE TELEPHONE

Telephone conversations generally present co-participants with a number of linguistic special circumstances which they need to design their talk around. Most obvious is the fact that they cannot see each other, that they are not in the same place together. In the case of parted lovers, these factors are not just present, they constitute their main problem – which is that they want to be together and cannot be. One feature of telephone calls between lovers which contrasts with many other telephone calls is the overt expression of a wish to be together. So the lovers' call 'enjoys' the problematic status of being both a way of overcoming separation and an acutely painful sign of that separation. There is also a specific question as to how the couple express sexual desire and love through a medium which is far from ideal. When lovers are together, much of the work of establishing and maintaining intimacy and desire is accomplished through touch and gaze, neither of which is available to these co-participants.

I have therefore made reference to some of the large amount of literature on telephone conversation, mostly carried out in a Conversation Analysis (CA) framework, in order to compare and contrast this lovers' conversation with other findings about telephone conversation.

Having now completed these preliminaries, my analysis of the transcript covers topics and topic management, the expression of love and caring, the expression of sexual desire, the sequence about making arrangements to be together, and lastly the goodbye sequence.

4 TOPICS AND TOPIC MANAGEMENT

I begin with a common-sense assessment of 'what the talk appears to be about', presented in Table 7.1, whose main purpose is to orient the reader. I am not claiming that these topic names would be valid for the participants. However, I will show that the participants orient their talk to these topics and that the transitions from one topic to the next are handled by well-recognised ploys used by either or both participants, so that on the surface, these are the topics which they are agreeing to talk about. At another level, however, I will argue that these topics provide opportunities to accomplish other, non-propositional, affective communication which is at some stages more important to the co-participants than the propositional content they appear to be speaking about.

Table 7.1 Topics to which the participants orient their talk

No.	Topic 'name'	Turn numbers
1	'anxious' person	1–5
2	desire	5–36
3	people who might help the couple to be together	36–53
	check	54–55
4	planning how to be together	56–129
(5	when they will speak to each other	84–106)
((6	M's lectures	91–101))
7	tiredness	130–132
8	phoning the next morning	132–145
9	goodbye sequence	146–200

One question is whether these topics and their management constitute specific features of intimate discourse. Topics 2 and 3 are those which would not be expected to occur in non-intimate conversation. The others occur in many other domains (though in different forms). Planning how and when to get together is something we regularly do both with work colleagues and with friends. Topics 7 and 8 are standard pre-sequences to a goodbye sequence (see Schegloff and Sacks 1974). Indeed, topics 4, 5, 6, 7, 8 and 9 could occur in a telephone conversation between persons who have not met. The number of turns taken for topic 9 would appear to be a key marker of intimate discourse, goodbyes between other co-participants tending to be brief and consisting of two adjacency pairs (see below, p. 160).

While this list shows what the participants 'talked about', it does not tell us what they saw the conversation as being for (often referred to in the CA literature as the reason-for-calling (RFC)). The transcript is characterised by its lack of many of the features of telephone conversations, much analysed in previous work, which show how the participants manage the orientation of their interaction towards the reason for calling. Admittedly, the absence of the opening lessens the strength of this claim.

The beginning of the transcript lacks any features which usually occur during the opening of a telephone call (greetings, how-are-yous, introduction of the RFC) and for these reasons I am claiming that this is not the beginning.

The literature on telephone calls suggests that a caller may signal their RFC in various ways. Most obviously by a metadiscourse comment ('the reason I'm ringing is . . .'). The RFC is also signalled (by either participant) by moves to return to it following a digression (e.g. 'anyway . . .'; see Owen 1985). Further references to the RFC may be contained in the closing sequence (Schegloff and Sacks 1974). The only candidate here which might be a direct orientation to the RFC is turn 56 which introduces the sequence about how the couple will next meet. Logically, this could be the RFC, but there is no real discourse evidence for this – the RFC could equally be topic 1 or 2. Furthermore, the couple do not accomplish any arrangements for when they will next meet, which supports the contention that 'making arrangements' is not the RFC.

On this basis I speculate that the RFC of a call between lovers who are apart does not have to be a propositional one, but can be that of relationship maintenance (without there being anything specific to 'talk about'). The evidence for this in this particular call is the absence of orientations to the RFC. Further evidence will be found in the ways in which the particular topics are handled, which, I will argue, are different from the ways such topics are handled in other conversations. The idea that the RFC is affective has support in the folk-linguistic comment of some of the journalists. For example:

146

We all do this sort of thing, don't we? The inarticulate rambles and 38 line goodbyes (in desperation not to hang up), the risqué word-plays and silly pet names, these are the stuff of all lovers' private conversations.

(A. Sampson, *Sunday Times*, 17 January 1993)

. . . it is intensely private, full of the silly remarks, repetitions and non-sequiturs that characterise the unguarded exchange of two people who arc fond of cach othcr.

(S. Faulks, *Guardian*, 14 January 1993)

Such conversations are liable to be of that nature. The twitterings of love-birds tend to be rather banal to the rest of the world.

(N. Stone, *Daily Mail*, 15 January 1993)

It is also the idea behind the popular song of some years ago which I chose as the title of the chapter. The point of the song lyric is that people do not say *I just called to say I love you*. If someone said this, it would be an on-record RFC. The appeal of the song was precisely to make overt something which is normally covert. Notice also that the choice of *just* marks those introductions to an RFC whose importance the speaker wishes to downgrade. Usually, the RFC (to maintain their relationship and be lovers) is part of the shared knowledge of the two participants, and therefore they do not need to orient to it on the surface of what is said (in fact we might speculate that it is part of the sharedness of a close relationship precisely not to do this on the record).

Turning now to the management of the topics which are on record, I observe that the majority of topic changes are initiated by the female participant F, who deploys clear on-record topic-change markers, for example in:

53 M Really?
54 F I don't. (Pause) Gone to sleep?
55 M No, I'm here.
56 F <u>Darling, listen</u>, I talked to Duncan tonight again. It might not be any good.
57 M Oh, no!
58 F I'll tell you why. [continues]

At turn 53 M is responding to F's last point on topic 3. At 56 she opens a new topic which is accepted by M's 57; and at 58 signals that she will continue with it.

The one place where both co-operate to shift topic is the following:

36 F Desperately, desperately. Oh, I thought of you so much at Yalford.
37 M Did you?
38 F Simply mean we couldn't be there together.

39   M   Desperate. If you could be here – I long to ask Nuala sometimes.
40   F   Why don't you?

In 36 F initiates a topic shift away from expression of present desire ('desperately'). She refers to another occasion when she felt desire. At 39 M introduces the new topic (3) with 'I long to ask . . .', and this is accepted by F with her question at 40.

At turn 103, the topic 'M's lectures', which is doubly nested inside two other topics, is ended by M who initiates a return to 'when are we going to speak to each other'. At turn 129, M offers a possible new topic. However, this is directly refused by F:

129   M   Wouldn't it? To wish you a happy Christmas.
130   F   (indistinct): Happy Oh, don't let's think about Christmas. I can't bear it. (Pause) Going to go to sleep? I think you'd better, don't you darling?

This may be because she is already planning to initiate closing, which she does in the same turn, but after a pause noted by the transcriber.

To summarise, here are two skilled conversation managers who both feel comfortable to initiate, to close or to refuse topics. At one level, there is nothing about their management of topics which appears to be specially a feature of the language of love and desire. Clearly there is a sense of equality – this is not a conversation where one person rather than the other has control of topics, but it is not possible to claim from this that conversation about love and desire always shows equal rights in its management. I would suspect that it does not. On the other hand, at another level, I think there is a highly marked feature of this conversation which I suspect is characteristic of telephone conversations between lovers and this is that it is not clear what the RFC is, that there is no particular orientation to it and this makes me think that the RFC is something that is not on the record. The RFC then is that of being lovers and doing affective work, and part of the way that affective work is accomplished is by not placing the RFC on record as a topic which is oriented to.

5 LOVE AND CARING

A feature which obviously distinguishes this conversation from others is the occurrence and frequency of occurrence of expressions of feelings about the other co-participant. I want to make a distinction between this, and the expression of one's feelings about other things. Trawling my intuitions for an example: when I telephone a friend, I may feel safe to disclose that I was really distressed to have a proposal turned down by a publisher, but I probably will not say much about how I feel about this friend. There are other settings where on-record disclosure of feelings for the other occurs, for example parent–child talk, sibling–sibling talk. It also might occur in the expression of negative feelings in a row or complaint. But I am arguing, intuitively of course, that what makes this conversation different is the *number* of occurrences.

Disclosures of feelings include sexual feelings:

32   F   Repeating yourself . . . (laughing). <u>Oh, darling, oh I Just want you now.</u>

Supportive feelings:

96   F   Well at least I'll be behind you.

Pride in the other:

152   F   I do love you and <u>I'm so proud of you.</u>
153   M   Oh, <u>I'm so proud of you.</u>

This one is a matched pair, by which I mean an adjacency pair where the two parts show lexical repetition of key content words. In some examples the members of the matched pair are identical (as here). I think matched pairs are a way of showing orientation to the other, agreement and/or feelings of closeness, and there are several in this conversation (see below). Turns 152–3 are also a compliment and its adjacent receipt token. There are several ways of receiving a compliment including thanking or downgrading, and, as here, returning the compliment (see Psathas 1995 for a summary of Pomerantz's work on compliments).

The co-participants mark their love in several ways. One is by their use of *darling* as a form of address. These uses often occur as a matching pair where if one says *darling* the other one does too, as in:

130   F   [. . .] (Pause) Going to go to sleep? I think you'd better, don't you <u>darling</u>?
131   M   (sleepy): Yes, <u>darling</u>.
132   F   I think you've exhausted yourself by all that hard work. You must go to sleep now. <u>Darling</u>?
133   M   (sleepy): Yes <u>darling</u>.

Unless they have been edited out by the newspapers, neither participant uses the other's name during the conversation.

Expressions of love which use the verb *to love* to describe the feeling occur towards the end of the conversation, after turn 140, which is the first time that F says *night night*. Intuitions suggest that expressions of feelings for the other are a canonical part of closings. Between acquaintances these will be limited to, e.g. 'thanks for your help' whereas between lovers there are stronger feelings to express.

142	F	I do love you.
143	M	(sleepily): Before . . .
144	F	Before about half past eight.
145	M	Try and ring?
146	F	Yeah, if you can. Love you darling.
147	M	Night darling.
148	F	I love you.
149	M	Love you too. I want to say goodbye.

Notice that overt expressions of love appear as matched pairs, both here and elsewhere in the transcript.

Love and caring are also shown by expressions of support and praise for the other.

150	F	Well done for doing that. You're a clever old thing. An awfully good brain lurking there, isn't there? Oh, darling I think you ought to give the brain a rest now. Night night.
151	M	Night darling. God bless.
152	F	I do love you and I'm so proud of you.
153	M	Oh, I'm so proud of you.
154	F	Don't be so silly. I've never achieved anything.
155	M	Yes you have.
156	F	No I haven't.
157	M	You're [sic] great achievement is to love me.
158	F	Oh, darling. Easier than falling off a chair.
159	M	You suffer all the indignities and tortures and calumnies.
160	F	Oh, darling, don't be so silly. I'd suffer anything for you. That's love. It's the strength of love. Night, night.

Turn 150 from F is a compliment, though it is not clear to me as an eavesdropper exactly what she is praising M for. This might be a reference back to the missing portion of the conversation. The follow-on to the return compliment at 153 is for F to disagree with the compliment. Psathas (1995: 41) notes that this is often followed (as here) by a reassertion of the praise and in fact M does this three times (155, 157 and 159).

Other examples are:

| 48 | F | And you're . . . I think, as usual, you're underestimating yourself. |

and:

95	M	A rather important one for Wednesday.
96	F	Well at least I'll be behind you.
97	M	I know.
98	F	Can I have a copy of the one you've just done?
99	M	Yes.
100	F	Can I? Um. I would like it.

All the journalistic comment takes the conversation as evidence of a deep relationship between the co-participants:

> . . . the couple on the tape are clearly in love – anyone who can tell someone else that their life's greatest achievement is 'to love me' and not risk a thick ear must be.
>
> (A. Sampson, *Sunday Times*, 17 January 1993)

> The transcript portrays two people who profess their love in an almost teenage way.
>
> (*Guardian*, 13 January 1993)

> . . . the language of frustrated lovers who mean the world to each other and long to be together.
>
> (*Sun*, 18 January 1993)

> The frank language reveals the depth of a long-standing relationship and the agony they feel at being apart.
>
> (*Sun*, 18 January 1993)

While such talk is easily interpreted as showing how much this particular couple love each other (and this is how the journalists see it), the point needs to be made that such language is not reserved for conversations between lovers. Some talk between parents and children features declarations of love, as does some talk between platonic friends. Supportive talk of the 'you're underestimating yourself' type is a regular feature of between-friends talk. The difference appears to be in the quantity of feeling-disclosure talk.

In considering why there is a large amount of on-record disclosure of feelings, it is relevant to recall that the co-participants are on the telephone. They are deprived of the many ways in which lovers together may show their feelings and do affective work, such as taking the other's hand, squeezing hands, putting arms round each other, gazing into each other's eyes, hugging, touching. Hence, affective non-verbal communication, when on the telephone, must be diverted to the verbal channel, if it is to be communicated at all. This is what we see happening in the conversation under study.

6 THE LANGUAGE OF DESIRE

Two sections of the transcript feature on-record expressions of sexual desire. In looking at these, it is necessary to separate out several strands of interest. There is an interest in how this couple talk about their sexual relationship. Related to this there is an interest in how they talk about it on the telephone. Why do they talk about it on the telephone? It might be more appropriate to describe this not as 'talk *about* sex' but as talk which *does* sex or replaces sex in the circumstance of being separated.

Generally, the talk is celebratory – it is pleasurable and it makes both participants laugh. Unlike much other talk (particularly telephone talk) it has no particular outcome – it is not transmitting information (as in direction-giving, or gossip), it is not negotiating (as in making arrangements). It is there for the encoding and transmission of feelings and for each to engender a physical effect in the other (in the absence of the possibility to accomplish this through sexual contact). Both of them laugh and each tells the other that their words are having an effect ('oh stop').

There are several features of the talk which I want to comment on. First how it starts. Here is the relevant extract:

5	M	Anyway you know that's the sort of thing one has to beware of. And sort of feel one's way along with – if you know what I mean.
6	F	Mmm. <u>You're awfully good at feeling your way along.</u>
7	M	Oh stop! I want to feel my way along you, all over you and up and down you and in and out
8	F	Oh!

At 5, M is talking about the 'anxious' person. In turn 6, F draws on his words and their potential for ambiguity (as between *feel one's way along* literally versus metaphorically) to switch topic and talk about sex and desire. She takes the metaphorical use of *feel one's way along* and brings it back to a concrete meaning in a domain where it does not normally apply (the expected collocations of *feel one's way along* used literally might include *a dark path* or *a cave*, but not a human body). While without the tape we cannot know exactly how she shows through intonation that she intends that move, the evidence is there that M hears it that way. Otherwise one cannot account for his *oh stop!*

In the rest of turn 7 he accepts her move to talk about sex and develops the topic himself. Lexical repetition, which I highlighted as the main feature of matching pairs in the previous section, occurs again here. In M's 7 he uses the identical expression which F has just given him in turn 6 and continues with her creative extension of it to apply to her body.

The main question is how do the participants express their desire? M's turn 7 shows several features, which may be the result of general strategies for talking sex and/or showing desire. These strategies are:

1 Talk about what you would like to do to/with the other person.
2 Show that you are orienting closely to the other person by paying attention to the details of their talk and then go on record with this by repeating their words.
3 Use vague, unspecified expressions which have a conventional pragmatic interpretation as being about sex (e.g. *in and out*).

Other examples of such unspecified expressions occur later:

152

187 M   Going to press the button.
188 F   All right darling. I wish you were pressing mine.
189 M   God, I wish I was. Harder and harder.

Another way to show desire is to talk about the need for sex with the desired person:

10   F   Oh, that's just what I need at the moment.
11   M   Is it?
12   F   I know it would revive me. I can't bear a Sunday night without you.
[...]
19   M   What about me? The trouble is I need you several times a week.
20   F   Mmm, so do I. I need you all the week. All the time.

Turns 19 and 20 again show lexical and syntactic parallelism.

   The theme of needs thus introduced leads on to the opportunity to draw on a number of metaphors for sexual experience, and the couple use these as another way to talk playfully about their mutual desire. In addition, using metaphors fosters intimacy. Gibbs and Gerrig (1989) argue that 'metaphorical talk presupposes and reinforces an intimacy between S [Speaker] and L [Listener], and the cultivation of intimacy is, perhaps, a primary function of such language' (Gibbs and Gerrig 1989: 153). In their use of metaphors, the couple draw on metaphors for love and sex which already exist, for example: SEX IS FUEL. (My analysis of metaphor depends largely on that used by Deignan 1995 and Chapter 1 above.)

15   M   I fill up your tank!
16   F   Yes you do.
17   M   Then you can cope.
18   F   Then I'm all right.

This one is an extension of a widely used metaphor discussed by Deignan: DESIRE IS FIRE. The grounds for the 'sex is fuel' metaphor are double. First, it picks up on the idea that love and sex are activities which create heat and energy through the combustion of fuel ('burning desire', etc.); second, it brings in the idea that sex is a requirement to sustain life, already alluded to by F in her turn 12. A car cannot operate without fuel, a woman cannot operate without sex is the paraphrase.

   This metaphor is followed by four others which become progressively more and more creative in the sense of not being already used and available. I speculate that the creation of metaphors for and around their sexual relationship is part of the linguistic repertoire of lovers.

   The linguistically playful sequence of metaphors is framed by two turns from F which are direct on-the-record expressions of desire (though still

153

euphemistic), turn 10 and turn 32. I hypothesise that what triggered journalistic comment on the strength of the relationship between the couple is the juxtaposition of playful metaphor with direct expressions of sexual desire.

Another analytical angle on the sequence of metaphors is that they transgress taboos which operate in public and non-intimate discourse. References to underwear in public discourse are never neutral and simply propositional. They can be neutralised as jokes or they can be part of an impolite/threatening/derogatory intervention, such as 'don't get your knickers in a twist' 'be caught with your pants down'. The tampon/box of tampons metaphor transgresses a stronger taboo. Menstruation is a topic to be avoided in almost all settings and direct references to it are suppressed (television advertisements for sanitary wear do not say what a sanitary towel does or when someone should wear it). If menstruation is talked about, this is accomplished through a set of euphemisms (for example, 'have my period', 'have a friend'). Linked to the tampon metaphor in the talk is another topic protected in public by taboo rules – lavatories and their function. Again, I would speculate that a feature of the discourse of lovers is that they feel permitted to break taboos and that doing this marks their relationship as different and special.

It is important that this talk about a very intimate topic, well surrounded in British society by taboos, is managed without the appearance of any signals that either party wants to refuse the topic or the way it develops. This is in marked contrast to conventional deflections of sex talk ('you are awful'). It contrasts interestingly with the management of a same sex conversation studied by Jefferson et al. (1987) where one participant discloses a pleasurable sensual experience she had during a nude swim, and the other participant disengages from talk about it. Jefferson et al. describe this as 'disaffiliation'. (They also describe the incident as 'obscene', which is itself of interest.) Neither member of our couple disaffiliates from anything which is said about sex.

The journalists interpret the talk as clear evidence that the couple on the tape have an on-going sexual relationship:

> In the . . . tapes there is no room for doubt . . . it's hard not to notice the two indulging in the familiar codes of aural sex.
>
> (R. Coward, *Observer*, 17 January 1993)

> The conversation reveals two people who have a deeply satisfying sexual relationship that they need to maintain on a regular basis.
>
> (L. Lee Potter, *Daily Mail*, 14 January 1993)

At the start of the chapter I posed a question about how this couple orient to the problem of being parted when they want to be together. We have seen that one feature of their conversation is frequent disclosure of feelings for the other. Another feature is their talk about sex. I would suggest that this talk

154

about sex would again be different from that which would occur face to face since, as with the expression of affection, the participants are deprived of non-verbal communication. More markedly, they are deprived of the opportunity to actually do sexual things with each other. This talk, then, replaces the sexual activity which would occur if they were together.

7 MAKING ARRANGEMENTS TO BE TOGETHER (TURNS 56–129)

I have already commented that the topic of this section is not one which would be restricted to conversations between lovers. However, there are some obvious differences between how it is managed, and its outcome, here and in other possible settings (for example where the co-participants are business associates). The first point is that no firm arrangements are made. This could happen in other settings, but it is also interesting that there is no reference to the fact that no arrangement has been made; and there is no specific commitment to come back to this topic in a later conversation and actually make an arrangement, although this is implied by F's turn 120. Conversely, the choice of tense (*it would be so wonderful* . . .) in F's turn 128 allows the possibility that eventually no meeting will take place.

We might speculate therefore that while at a propositional level this section is about 'making arrangements to be together', at another level it is a kind of play between the lovers which allows them to imply longing and desire simply from the effort they are prepared to put into talk which has no definite outcome. It also has a playful analogy with the on/off, yes-you-can/no-you-can't, 'playing hard to get' events which traditionally happen in the early stages of forming a close sexual relationship. The twist is that here it is 'yes-*we*-can/no-*we*-can't'.

The second point of interest is that the participants show that they assume shared knowledge which we as eavesdroppers do not have. Thus, in turn 56:

56 F Darling, listen, I talked to Duncan tonight again. It might not be any good.
57 M Oh, no!

It has no prior referent in the conversation. All there is to guide interpretation is the shared knowledge of why F would have been talking to Duncan. *Again* shows that prior conversations on the topic have occurred, which F knows M knows about. M displays understanding with his response. Similarly in turn 60, what is meant by *do it* is clear to the participants but not to us.

60 F And see if we could do it there.

It is not until the end of this section, at turn 128, that there is on-record evidence of what this section is about:

155

128   F   It would be so wonderful to have just one night to set us on our way, wouldn't it?

Going on now to look at the details of this topic sequence in the order in which they occur, turns 61 to 78 show a misunderstanding and its repair. The misunderstanding is caused by an assumption of shared knowledge by F which turns out to be unwarranted. This is that her reference to *Mike* in her turn 58 will identify a place for M. In turns 62–70 they talk at cross purposes, until in 71, M seeks a direct clarification of what was actually meant back at turn 58, and then goes on record that he had misunderstood ('I thought you meant somebody else').

71   M   Which Mike then?
72   F   What Mike do you think I was talking about?
73   M   I didn't know, because I thought you meant . . .
74   F   I've got lots. . . .
75   M   Somebody else.

Potentially part of what may be happening here is some shared joking because the person's name causing the confusion is the same as M's first name. Without intonational information, though, it is impossible to substantiate this. F's turn 76 –

76   F   I've got lots of friends called Mike.

– could be teasing rather than factual. Turns 71–2 might suggest another reading which is that F reacts badly to the fact that M does not get the right referent for *Mike*. Her turn 72, a question, is a dispreferred response to follow a question. There is plenty of evidence that this couple enjoy and are proud of the high level of their shared knowledge so M's failure to understand could be a disappointment to F, prompting her dispreferred response.

There is no point where F actually answers the question posed by M at turn 71. At turn 77 he makes clear who he was erroneously thinking of. However, by turn 81, M shows that he now knows what F is thinking of because he checks how to get to the implied location. This kind of understanding, which draws so much on shared knowledge that it hardly makes sense to an outside observer, is clearly a feature of conversations between people who know each other very well.

The feature of turns 81 to 84, which is much remarked on by media commentators, is that they are about road directions and traffic, which are judged not to be an appropriate topic for parted lovers: 'mundane' is an adjective which occurs more than once in the press commentary. I think that what is interesting here is not what is said, but again what is not said. No route is actually agreed before they leave this topic, and in any case, the whole idea is hypothetical since it will only apply if 'the other place' 'falls through'. The sequence can be interestingly compared with direction-giving examples in Psathas (1991) which canonically contain 'a marked ending of the set with such possible moves to end as [. . .] an acknowledgement/ acceptance, understanding display by the recipient' (Psathas 1991:198). What is striking is not that they talk about directions, but that they do so without reaching any conclusions or agreement on the topic.

Turns 84 to 106 are a digression from 'arranging to meet' onto the related topic 'when are we going to talk on the phone'. F initiates this:

84   F   So it would be, um, you'd miss the worst of the traffic. Because I'll, er . . . You see the problem is I've got to be in London to-morrow night.

It does not become clear until later what the nature of the 'problem' is, which is that while this conversation is taking place on Sunday, there is no evening before Thursday (when they hope to meet) when they will be able to talk. This is on record at turn 103 and this pair of turns also shows what the *Sun* calls 'their anguish at being apart':

103   M   But I, oh God, when am I going to speak to you?
104   F   I can't bear it . Um . . .

Turns 88–91 acknowledge that both parties already believe that they will not be able to speak on either of the next two evenings.

88   F   [. . .] But, darling you wouldn't be able to ring me anyway, would you?
89   M   I might just. I mean, tomorrow night I could have done.
90   F   Oh darling, I can't bear it . How could you have done tomorrow night?
91   M   Because I'll be (yawns) working on the next lecture.

Turn 88 is not a request and we know this because M does not treat it as a request – his choice of *could have* shows that he agrees with the unasserted but assumed proposition 'M will not be ringing F' (because *could have* presupposes that the action in the verb will not take place). The function of *anyway* in 88 is to indicate that F is not nourishing a hope that M will ring her. We know this because the paraphrase required to make sense of it is something like, 'even if I was free, you would not be able to ring' (this explanation of *anyway* uses the analysis in Owen 1985 of four distinct *anyways*).

Since turns 88–91 show that both parties already know that they will not be talking on the two evenings referred to, an interesting question is why these turns occur at all (because they are not there in order to negotiate that there will be a telephone call). One answer to this might be that it gives an opportunity to express anguish and longing and to play more of the game of 'yes-we-can/no-we-can't', in other words to do affective work.

Nested inside the already intruded 'when are we next going to talk' section is another one, also initiated by F: 'M's lectures'. Here it is:

157

94 F   Oh no, when's that for?
95 M   A rather important one for Wednesday.
96 F   Well at least I'll be behind you.
97 M   I know.
98 F   Can I have a copy of the one you've just done?
99 M   Yes.
100 F   Can I? Um. I would like it.
101 M   OK, I'll try and organise it.
102 F   Darling.

What happens during this is that F makes two different affective moves which indirectly show her love for M. At turn 96 she states her support on record and at 98/100 she shows her interest in his work.

During turn 106, F moves the topic on from 'when are we going to talk' to revert to 'arrangements to meet'. Having earlier mentioned a reason why the plan they have may not happen ('he's got these children . . . staying'), she now introduces talk about another reason, although it is not clear to us, or to M, until turn 110 exactly what she means and even then the reason is left unstated:

109 M   Why?
110 F   Well, because if it stops he'll come down here on Thursday night.
111 M   Oh no.

A gloss on turn 110, including what it implies (partly warranted by M's response) is: 'if the ambulance strike stops then the person referred to as A (whose identity we do not know) will come "down here" and (implied) this will prevent them from meeting'.

The topic closes with this pair of turns:

128 F   It would be so wonderful to have just one night to set us on our way, wouldn't it?
129 M   Wouldn't it? To wish you a happy Christmas.

In these the co-participants agree a shared emotional 'label' which seems to summarise the preceding section as it ends. Again there is a matching pair of forms (*wouldn't it/wouldn't it*) which may help to signal the sharing.

This brings me back to a consideration of what the whole section on 'making arrangements' is really about. While at first glance, what appears to be going on is about arrangements to meet, it is in fact the case that at the propositional level nothing concrete has been achieved about any potential arrangements either to meet or even to talk on the telephone. It is also interesting that neither participant draws attention to that or thinks it out of order. I could imagine that in most conversations where the topic 'arrangements' has been covered, the preferred closing of the topic involves reiterating the arrangement, as in this example (also Owen 1985, with this time a different use of *anyway*):

M: anyway |
G: mmm |
M: mm | so I'll see you Saturday morning
(Owen 1985: 83)

Dispreferred closings probably include an acknowledgement that nothing can be arranged. Neither of these two possibilities actually occurs. Arguably, the following pair is the nearest to an acknowledgement that nothing can be arranged:

124   F   Well I talked to him briefly, but you know, I just thought I – I just don't know whether he's got any children at home that's the worry.
125   M   Right.

But there is nothing in the transcript to substantiate this reading.

To summarise, then, I am arguing that while this section appears to be about 'arrangements', what it mainly achieves for the participants is an opportunity to communicate their longing, their desire and their need to be together.

8 SAYING GOODBYE

Conversational closings have been widely studied and my analysis here draws extensively on Schegloff and Sacks (1974). The journalists thought that the conversation was 'odd' because the couple use many turns to say goodbye but beyond that, they did not know how to comment. In fact, the goodbye sequence conforms to all of what was observed by Schegloff and Sacks about the sequential organisation of a goodbye.

First, the 'warrant' (Schegloff and Sacks' term) for initiating the close of the conversation is to allude to the best interest of the other party in the call; in this case, F attends to the needs of M:

130   F   (indistinct): Happy Oh, don't let's think about Christmas. I can't bear it. (Pause) Going to go to sleep? I think you'd better, don't you darling?
131   M   (sleepy): Yes, darling?
132   F   I think you've exhausted yourself by all that hard work. You must go to sleep now. Darling?

Other features of closings noted by Schegloff and Sacks also occur: '. . . closings may include "making arrangements" with varieties such as giving directions, arranging later meetings, invitations, and the like; re-invocation of certain sorts of materials talked of earlier in the conversation'

159

(Schegloff and Sacks 1974: 256). Turns 134–46 are about making arrangements for the next time the couple will speak.

A key observation about closings is that they occur when the two parties each signal by their non-initiation of any new topic that they are willing to close the conversation. Hence many conversations looked at by Schegloff and Sacks feature a move towards closing by one party which is followed by topic initiation by one or the other, in which case the closing does not occur. Thus:

146	F	Yeah, if you can. Love you darling.
147	M	Night darling.
148	F	I love you.
149	M	Love you too.

– where at 148 F develops the topic of turn 146 instead of saying *night*. This occurs again with M going on record that he wants to continue the conversation:

161	M	[. . .] Night night, before the battery goes. (Blows kiss) Night.
162	F	Love you.
163	M	Don't want to say goodbye.
164	F	Neither do I, but we must get some sleep.

Turn 161 shows another warrant for closing which is to refer to something external to the call (examples in Schegloff and Sacks include a television programme and a date). Calls from public phones employ 'there's someone else waiting' and 'my money has run out'.

A minimal closure could consist of two matched pairs of turns, as follows:

A	OK
B	OK
A	Bye Bye
B	Bye

(Schegloff and Sacks 1974: 256)

It is noteworthy that the presence of such matched pairs does not lead to closure of the conversation between the taped couple, for example:

170	F	Bye. I do love you.
171	M	Night.
172	F	Night.
173	M	Night.
174	F	Love you forever.
175	M	Night.
176	F	G'bye. Bye my darling.
177	M	Night.
178	F	Night, night.

179 M   Night.
180 F   Bye bye.
181 M   Going.

The conversation continues for another nineteen turns after this.

The journalists thought that the long goodbye occurs because the parties do not want to hang up (Sampson) and I want to pursue this a little. I will also propose some other explanations which together would account for what occurs.

First the idea that the parties do not want to finish the conversation. There are other conversations where this happens and my observation is that if either party wishes to continue a conversation, they do this by introducing a new topic or by continuing an already introduced topic, *not* by drawing out the goodbye. As Schegloff and Sacks note, what characterises many closings is neither party introducing a topic. Not to take up an offered topic is dis-preferred behaviour (it is a potential affront and gets handled as such) so the best way to continue talk (when you want to) is to continue the process of offering and accepting topics. The couple on the tape continue to do this until the point where they both offer and accept pre-closing and closing moves. So I do not think the long closing is caused by the fact that they are 'reluctant to say goodbye' (*Daily Mail*, 14 January). A better and more subtle analysis is to say that the couple exploit the conventional mechanisms of closing in order to indicate their reluctance to say goodbye.

Another angle is that the goodbye is long because it is important that a number of things are accomplished during it. Schegloff and Sacks observed that closing sections typically contain components that seem to give a 'signa-ture' to the type of conversation that has taken place. We can note, therefore, that the couple on the tape revisit all the main themes of their earlier talk during the goodbye sequence. This is shown in Table 7.2.

Combining a number of possible components in a closing section, say Schegloff and Sacks, results in 'extended closing sections' as we have here. The two parties demonstrate their commitment to each other and their strong affective links simply by the amount of work they put into this closing. This is consistent with my contention that the RFC of this conversation is the simple one of doing affective work.

Another factor which could help to account for the 'long goodbye' is that F, although she has initiated both pre-closing and several closings, is not

Table 7.2 Themes revisited during closing

next time they will talk	143–46
mutual approval	150–60
expressions of love	throughout
expressions of desire	188–90

willing herself to hang up first. She waits for M to do this. Thus, she is the last speaker, and his last turn consists of hanging up. She gives him many opportunities to close the connection and near to the end she actually tells him to do so 'press the button'. Hence the power to finish the conversation seems to be with him.

9 CONCLUSION: 'IT AIN'T WHAT YOU SAY . . .'

I began my work on this text with an interest in the interaction between the private world of the speakers and the public stage on which their private conversation was exposed. In the course of the work, I came to realise that their talk was itself so rich that it would be a distraction to confuse the chapter with the intrusion of press commentary. Alongside this, I also came to believe that a good way to address the ethical problem I perceived was to ignore the issue of the participants' identity and to deal only with the text, seeing it as a celebration of a close and loving relationship between an anonymous man and woman. In this way a text which first appeared in public as negatively framed by some unpleasant attitudes (prurient interest, superior moralising judgements, humour at someone else's expense) has been transformed for readers so that it appears positively framed instead. I hope that is the case.

To summarise what has been learned about the language of love and desire as it appears in this telephone call, I have argued that:

- The language is special because the lovers are parted and want to be together. They use their conversation to show each other how much they want to be together and to accomplish actions which would normally be non-verbal.
- They do this by exploiting topics which allow them to dwell on themes of longing, hoping and bad luck.
- Another feature is the on-record expression of feelings towards the other. These lovers show each other sexual desire, love, support, pride in each other and recognition of what the other has to suffer.
- A more subtle way to demonstrate feelings for the lover is to pay close attention to the exact language forms they use and to then use the same forms in replies (what I have called matching pairs).
- The actual topics covered at propositional level are shown to be downgraded in importance because there is little or no orientation to ensuring an appropriate outcome for them (no arrangements are made, nothing is decided). In particular there is no clear orientation to any topic as an RFC.
- 'Sex on the telephone' is accomplished by talking playfully about sex, by expressing need, by saying what one would like to do to the other, by

accepting and agreeing to whatever topic development the other suggests; by provoking laughter and by provoking feelings of longing.

- The language is playful and plays with linguistic resources (puns, metaphor, repetition, implicature).
- It is also playful at the level of playing with the resources of conversation management. In the goodbye sequence the speakers draw on the shared 'rules' of how to do closings but they wilfully transgress them by repeating over and over the simple formulas which normally occur once or at most twice.

REFERENCES

British Association for Applied Linguistics (1994) *Recommendations on Good Practice in Applied Linguistics*.

Deignan, A. (1995) *The Collins COBUILD Guides to English: 7: Metaphor*, London: HarperCollins.

Gibbs, R.W. and Gerrig, R.J. (1989) 'How context makes metaphor comprehension seem special', *Metaphor and Symbolic Activity* 4(3): 145–58.

Jefferson, G., Sacks, H. and Schegloff, E. (1987) 'Notes on laughter in the pursuit of intimacy' in G. Button and J.R.E. Lee (eds) *Talk and Social Organisation*, Clevedon: Multilingual Matters, pp. 152–205.

Owen, M. (1985) 'The conversational functions of *anyway*', *Nottingham Linguistic Circular* 14: pp. 72–90.

Psathas G. (1991) 'The structure of direction-giving in interaction', in D. Boden and D.H. Zimmerman (eds) *Talk and Social Structure*, Cambridge: Polity Press, pp. 195–216.

—— (1995) *Conversation Analysis*, Qualitative Research Methods Series Number 35, Thousand Oaks, Cal.: Sage.

Schegloff, E. and Sacks, H. (1974) 'Opening up closings', in R. Turner (ed.) *Ethnomethodology*, London: Penguin, pp. 233–64.

APPENDIX: THE TRANSCRIPT

[M = male participant, F = female participant; turns are numbered; turn 1 is not the beginning of the conversation.]

1   M   He was a bit anxious actually.

2   F   Was he?

3   M   He thought he might have gone a bit far.

4   F   Ah well.

5   M   Anyway you know that's the sort of thing one has to beware of. And sort of feel one's way along with – if you know what I mean.

6   F   Mmm. You're awfully good at feeling your way along.

7   M   Oh stop! I want to feel my way along you, all over you and up and down you and in and out.

8   F   Oh!

9	M	Particularly in and out.
10	F	Oh, that's just what I need at the moment.
11	M	Is it?
12	F	I know it would revive me. I can't bear a Sunday night without you.
13	M	Oh God.
14	F	It's like that programme 'Start The Week'. I can't start the week without you.
15	M	I fill up your tank!
16	F	Yes you do.
17	M	Then you can cope.
18	F	Then I'm all right.
19	M	What about me? The trouble is I need you several times a week.
20	F	Mmm, so do I. I need you all the week. All the time.
21	M	Oh, God. I'll just live inside your trousers or something. It would be much easier!
22	F	(laughing): What are you going to turn into, a pair of knickers? (Both laugh.) Oh, you're going to come back as a pair of knickers.
23	M	Or, God forbid, a Tampax. Just my luck! (Laughs)
24	F	You are a complete idiot! (Laughs) Oh, what a wonderful idea.
25	M	My luck to be chucked down a lavatory and go on and on forever swirling round on the top, never going down.
26	F	(laughing): Oh darling!
27	M	Until the next one comes through.
28	F	Oh, perhaps you could just come back as a box.
29	M	What sort of box?
30	F	A box of Tampax, so you could just keep going.
31	M	That's true.
32	F	Repeating yourself . . . (laughing). Oh, darling, oh I just want you now.
33	M	Do you?
34	F	Mmm.
35	M	So do I.
36	F	Desperately, desperately. Oh, I thought of you so much at Yalford.
37	M	Did you?
38	F	Simply mean we couldn't be there together.
39	M	Desperate. If you could be here – I long to ask Nuala sometimes.
40	F	Why don't you?
41	M	I daren't.
42	F	Because I think she's so in love with you.
43	M	Mmm.
44	F	She'd do anything you asked.
45	M	She'd tell all sorts of people.

46	F	No, she wouldn't because she'd be much too frightened of what you might say to her. I think you've got – I'm afraid it's a terrible thing to say – but I think, you know, those sort of people do feel very strongly about you. You've got such a great hold over her.
47	M	Really?
48	F	And you're . . . I think, as usual, you're underestimating yourself.
49	M	But she might be terribly jealous or something.
50	F	Oh! (Laughs) Now that is a point! I wonder. She might be, I suppose.
51	M	You never know, do you?
52	F	No. The little green-eyed monster might be lurking inside her. No. But, I mean, the thing is you're so good when people are so flattered to be taken into your confidence. But I don't know they'd betray you. You know, real friends.
53	M	Really?
54	F	I don't. (Pause) Gone to sleep?
55	M	No, I'm here.
56	F	Darling, listen, I talked to Duncan tonight again. It might not be any good.
57	M	Oh, no!
58	F	I'll tell you why. He's got these children of one of those Cardwell girls and their nanny staying. He's going. I'm going to ring him again tomorrow. He's going to try and put them off till Friday. But I thought as an alternative, perhaps I might ring up Mike.
59	M	Yes.
60	F	And see if we could do it there. I know he is back on Thursday.
61	M	It's quite a lot further away.
62	F	Oh, is it?
63	M	Well, I'm just trying to think. Coming from Newmarket.
64	F	Coming from Newmarket to me at that time of night, you could probably do it in two and three quarter. It takes me three.
65	M	What to go to, um, Beeford?
66	F	Nelby.
67	M	To go to Beeford?
68	F	To go to Beeford would be the same as me really, wouldn't it?
69	M	I mean to say, you would suggest going to Beeford, uh?
70	F	No, not at all.
71	M	Which Mike then?
72	F	What Mike do you think I was talking about?
73	M	I didn't know, because I thought you meant . . .
74	F	I've got lots . . .
75	M	Somebody else.
76	F	I've got lots of friends called Mike.
77	M	The other one, Susie's.

78	F	Oh! Oh, there! Oh that is further away. They're not . . .
79	M	They've gone . . .
80	F	I don't know, it's just, you know, just a thought I had. If it fell through, the other place.
81	M	Oh, right. What do you do? Go on the M25 then down the M4 is it?
82	F	Yes, you to, um, and sort of Royston or M11, at that time of night.
83	M	Yes. Well, that'll be just after, it will be after shooting anyway.
84	F	So it would be, um, you'd miss the worst of the traffic. Because I'll, er . . . You see the problem is I've got to be in London tomorrow night.
85	M	Yes.
86	F	And Tuesday night A's coming home.
87	M	No.
88	F	Would you believe it? Because, I don't know what he's doing. He's shooting down here or something. But, darling you wouldn't be able to ring me anyway, would you?
89	M	I might just. I mean, tomorrow night I could have done.
90	F	Oh darling, I can't bear it. How could you have done tomorrow night?
91	M	Because I'll be (yawns) working on the next lecture.
92	F	Oh no, what's the next one?
93	M	A Vocational Education one.
94	F	Oh no, when's that for?
95	M	A rather important one for Wednesday.
96	F	Well at least I'll be behind you.
97	M	I know.
98	F	Can I have a copy of the one you've just done?
99	M	Yes.
100	F	Can I? Um. I would like it.
101	M	OK, I'll try and organise it.
102	F	Darling.
103	M	But I, oh God, when am I going to speak to you?
104	F	I can't bear it . Um . . .
105	M	Wednesday night?
106	F	Oh, certainly Wednesday night. I'll be alone, um, Wednesday, you know, the evening. Or Tuesday. While you're rushing around doing things I'll be, you know, alone until it reappears. And early Wednesday morning, I mean, he'll be leaving at half past eight, quarter past eight. He won't be here Thursday, pray God. Um, that ambulance strike, It's a terrible thing to say this, I suppose it won't have come to an end by Thursday.
107	M	It will have done?

108 F Well, I mean, I hope for everybody's sake it will have done, but I hope for our sakes it's still going on.
109 M Why?
110 F Well, because if it stops he'll come down here on Thursday night.
111 M Oh no.
112 F Yes, but I don't think it will stop, do you?
113 M No, neither do I. Just our luck.
114 F It just would be our luck, I know.
115 M Then it's bound to.
116 F No it won't. You mustn't think like that. You must think positive.
117 M I'm not very good at that.
118 F Well I am going to. Because if I don't, I'd despair. (Pause) Hm – gone to sleep?
119 M No. How maddening.
120 F I know. Anyway, I mean, he's doing his best to change it, Duncan. But I just thought, you know, I might just ask Mike.
121 M Did he say anything?
122 F No, I haven't talked to him.
123 M You haven't?
124 F Well I talked to him briefly, but you know, I just thought I – I just don't know whether he's got any children at home that's the worry.
125 M Right.
126 F Oh, darling. I think I'll . . .
127 M Pray, just pray.
128 F It would be so wonderful to have just one night to set us on our way, wouldn't it?
129 M Wouldn't it? To wish you a happy Christmas.
130 F (indistinct): Happy Oh, don't let's think about Christmas. I can't bear it. (Pause) Going to go to sleep? I think you'd better, don't you darling?
131 M (sleepy): Yes, darling.
132 F I think you've exhausted yourself by all that hard work. You must go to sleep now. Darling?
133 M (sleepy): Yes darling.
134 F Will you ring me when you wake up?
135 M Yes I will.
136 F Before I have these rampaging children around. It's Tony's birthday tomorrow. (Pause) You all right?
137 M Mmm. I'm all right.
138 F Can I talk to you, I hope, before those rampaging children . . .
139 M What time do they come in?

140 F Well usually Tony never wakes up at all, but as it's his birthday tomorrow he might just stagger out of bed. It won't be before half past eight. (Pause) Night, night, my darling.
141 M Darling . . .
142 F I do love you.
143 M (sleepily): Before . . .
144 F Before about half past eight.
145 M Try and ring?
146 F Yeah, if you can. Love you darling.
147 M Night darling.
148 F I love you.
149 M Love you too. I want to say goodbye.
150 F Well done for doing that. You're a clever old thing. An awfully good brain lurking there, isn't there? Oh, darling I think you ought to give the brain a rest now. Night night.
151 M Night darling. God bless.
152 F I do love you and I'm so proud of you.
153 M Oh, I'm so proud of you.
154 F Don't be so silly. I've never achieved anything.
155 M Yes you have.
156 F No I haven't.
157 M You're [sic] great achievement is to love me.
158 F Oh, darling. Easier than falling off a chair.
159 M You suffer all these indignities and tortures and calumnies.
160 F Oh, darling, don't be so silly. I'd suffer anything for you. That's love. It's the strength of love. Night, night.
161 M Night darling. Sounds as though you're dragging an enormous piece of string behind you, with hundreds of tin pots and cans attached to it. I think it will be your telephone. Night night, before the battery goes. (Blows kiss) Night.
162 F Love you.
163 M Don't want to say goodbye.
164 F Neither do I, but we must get some sleep. Bye.
165 M Bye, darling.
166 F Love you.
167 M Bye.
168 F Hopefully talk to you in the morning.
169 M Please.
170 F Bye. I do love you.
171 M Night.
172 F Night.
173 M Night.
174 F Love you forever.
175 M Night.

176	F	G'bye. Bye my darling.
177	M	Night.
178	F	Night, night.
179	M	Night.
180	F	Bye bye.
181	M	Going.
182	F	Bye.
183	M	Going.
184	F	Gone.
185	M	Night.
186	F	Bye. Press the button.
187	M	Going to press the button.
188	F	All right darling. I wish you were pressing mine.
189	M	God, I wish I was. Harder and harder.
190	F	Oh, darling.
191	M	Night.
192	F	Night.
193	M	Love you.
194	F	(yawning): Love you. Press the tit.
195	M	Adore you. Night.
196	F	Night.
197	M	Night.
198	F	(blows a kiss).
199	M	Night.
200	F	G'night my darling. Love you.
201	M	[disconnects the call]

8

'BUNNIKINS, I LOVE YOU SNUGLY IN YOUR WARREN'

Voices from subterranean cultures of love

Wendy Langford

1 INTRODUCTION

Love relationships, like all relationships, rely for their existence on the maintenance of some kind of common ground, some kind of intersubjective space
where those communications which go to make up what we mean by a relationship can occur. In an earlier essay (Langford 1995), I began to explore
the phenomenon whereby a love relationship is partly, sometimes very substantially, negotiated through the adoption of alter personalities who play
out their interactions within a mutually constructed imagined world, safe
from the dangers and conflicts which beset 'real' relationships in the 'real'
world. Using a variety of methodologies: literary examples taken from two
famous plays (Ibsen 1981; Osborne 1960) and a short story (Woolf 1991), an
analysis of St Valentine's Day messages from the *Guardian* (14 February
1993), and empirical evidence from in-depth interviews with participants in
two alter relationships, I focused specifically on issues of gender and power
within heterosexual couples. I argued that within the bounds of an alter relationship, individuals can find a comfort, pleasure and security which is often
precluded by the gendered emotional dynamics that commonly characterise
love relationships in the post-romantic phase.

There is certainly no evidence that the adoption of alter personalities is
confined to heterosexual love relationships. I have encountered two lesbian
'Pooh and Piglet' couples and similar phenomena occurring in parent–child
relationships, all of which suggests that there is much room for interesting
research in these areas.

In this chapter, however, I am going to move away from the question of
how the use of alter personalities might be linked to particular patterns of
emotional dynamics in particular kinds of relationships. Instead I will draw
on some different aspects of the material outlined above to develop a broader
picture of how alter relationships function as 'micro-cultures' which have
their own languages and customs and exist in a particular kind of relation to
the social world. Focusing especially on the secrecy and 'childishness' which

characterise these private cultures of love, I will investigate their relation to 'adult' love and the 'public' world of 'adulthood'. Then, drawing on psycho-analytic theory, I will offer an explanation of why adult relationships based on falling in love are particularly likely to harbour these 'subterranean' worlds and suggest there are important reasons why their inhabitants might find it hard to 'grow up'.

2 I JUST WANNA BE YOUR TEDDY BEAR

While 'cultures of love' may take many forms, my investigations so far suggest that between adults, alter relationships are frequently conducted through personae of specific kinds. An analysis of Valentine's Day messages in the *Guardian* (from which the names and 'voices' in this chapter are quoted) reveals that names adopted by couples are commonly 'babyish' (*Fluffy and Higgly, Bobo and Pippy, Mootle and Dootle, Poodge and Biffo*), and frequently evocative either of household pets, or the kinds of soft toys given to small children by adults. The most common species are bears, bunnies, pigs and pussycats:

> *Honeymonster*, big kisses and love from *Bearlet*.
>
> *Flopsy Bunny* I love you. *Fierce Bad Rabbit*.
>
> To *Wee Pig* from *Big Pig*. Grunt! Grunt!
>
> *Ginger* loves *Tom* very much. Meow, preow, purr.

Other mammals and marsupials including dogs, mice, squirrels, hamsters, wombats, tigers and monkeys also number highly among the menagerie of love, along with some birds and a few toads. Reptiles, spiders, insects and fish are rare, confirming that our tendency to identify ourselves and our partners with other species generally increases in proportion to the degree to which these are furry, warm and podgy.

Within the genre there can be a celebration of coupledom but with a denial of humanness, as in:

> *Mrs Mouse*, Cotswold mornings are habit forming! . . . *Mr Mouse*.
>
> *Honey-bee* . . . with all my love now and always!!! *Hubby Bee*.

Or separate identities might be lost:

> *Fluffy* wants *Fluffy*.
>
> To *Winkle* with all my love. *Winkle*.

171

There may be an implicit denial that one or both partners are adults:

Toad, I love you. Love from *little Toad*.

Baby 2. It's getting better all the time . . . *Baby 1*.

Or a declaration that being of different species is no barrier to lasting love:

Bears and *Dormice* love each other.

Mr Wombat loves *Mr Pussycat*. Thanks for the best year ever.

The 'voices' in many Valentine's messages are animalistic, consisting of woofs, grunts, miouws, etc.:

Cobbsie. *Woof woof*! Your big hearted shaggy Labrador.

Others suggest that conversations in 'alter worlds' often involve the use of babyish or childish voices:

Love you *Wuggy Buggy*.

Linlin. Snugglebunnies and *Giggles*.

Muges . . . let's *snuggle-buggle* now! *Windy-Bags*.

This was confirmed by 'inside information' from the interviews which further revealed the utilisation of behaviour such as whining, sulking or the adoption of child-like postures or facial expressions in order to elicit a desired response from the partner.

Asexuality also appears as a striking feature of alter relationships, although a few Valentine's messages are suggestive in a furry, animalistic sort of way:

Big Bear. Hold me tight forever. I love your *lick and gentle growls. Loving nips* from *Fat Hamster*.

Fluffy likes *squeezing a pink thing* at bed time! Oink says *Porker*.

In general, however, a child-like innocence reigns supreme, an impression confirmed in the interviews where it was revealed that the overtly sexual aspects of the couples' relationships occurred outside the confines of the alter relationship. To quote Claire, one of my interviewees, part of the appeal of playing *Furball* to Mark's *Monster* was that it allowed 'a kind of safe play area where you could still express affection, but it wasn't sexually charged in any way'.

3 ARE YOU COMING OUT TO PLAY?

It is not only from the difficulties of adult sexuality that alter relationships provide refuge. In sharp contrast to prevalent constructions of adulthood as responsible, sensible, serious, routine and worldly, alter personalities can be carefree, foolish, silly, adventurous and naive. While adult humans strive to remain controlled and undaunted in the face of life, death and mortgage repayments, bunnies and bears can snuffle and growl at the smallest hurt. And while grown-ups involve themselves in more sophisticated activities, pigs and possums can romp and frolic their days away. In Ibsen's *A Doll's House*, for example, Nora acts the part of a 'frisking' squirrel and a 'chirruping' skylark, 'drooping her wings' in response to the reprimands of her authoritarian husband. Similarly, in Osborne's *Look Back in Anger*, Alison is able to turn the cruel and moody Jimmy into a 'jolly super bear' by jumping up and down excitedly making little 'paw gestures' – 'a dance squirrels do when they're happy'. In 'real life', too, it seems that the fun and happiness afforded by an alter relationship is often in sharp contrast to the 'real' relationship between the partners. Claire, for example, recounted in her interview how she and Mark came to have so much trouble relating as 'people' that for the last few years of their unhappy human relationship they rarely tried. *Furball* and *Monster*, however, played happily on as 'friends, like two children'.

The public disclosure of infantile behaviour might predictably attract disdain from those who like to think of themselves as more mature. My research suggests, however, that it may be hasty and simplistic to write off alter relationships as pitiable and deficient in relation to some notion of proper or authentic adult love. For instance, although Claire readily admitted that her relationship with Mark would not have survived as long as it did without *Monster* and *Furball*, she resisted the implication that the personae were thus an entirely negative phenomenon. Indeed Claire stressed that even when compared to the earlier, happier days of her 'adult' relationship with Mark, *Monster* and *Furball* had a better relationship in many ways. They were friendlier and more companionable and had a happy domestic life. Their interactions lacked the accumulating tensions and frustrations which eventually led Mark and Claire to separate.

Such experiences suggest that while on the one hand alter relationships may be branded as escapist, on the other they may tell us something important about the constraints and privations of adulthood and the restrictions it places on emotional expression. Alter relationships may offer important spaces for the expression of friendliness, playfulness, humour and creativity which, it seems, is often lacking in long-term love relationships and in the adult world more generally. This is certainly suggested by interviewees Katherine and Patrick whose experience of relating as *Pooh* and *Piglet* involves 'going out to play' together, having fun and adventures in their own version of Hundred Acre Wood. Interactions with the 'real' world may be prefaced with reluctant comments about having to pretend to be 'humans' or 'grown-ups', in order to re-engage with a world where sober and streetwise conduct is the mark of legitimate adulthood and long faces and bad tempers pass for maturity.

4 DOWN IN THE BURROW

Alter relationships may also have the potential to tell us something of how constructions of adulthood and humanity as superior to childishness and animality are integral to the construction of the 'public' as superior to the 'private'. Alter relationships are constructed precisely to be 'private' and it is this that enables them to flourish as sites of humour and subversion. This is illustrated well by Virginia Woolf's short story of how Rosalind was able to survive her marriage to the upper-class Ernest Thorburn, whose very name reminded her of 'the Albert Memorial' and 'mahogany sideboards'. Noticing on their honeymoon that when Ernest ate, his nose twitched rather like her pet rabbit's had done, Rosalind seduces him into an alter relationship where he is 'King Lappin' – 'a rabbit that makes laws for all the other rabbits' – and she is 'Queen Lapinova' – 'A white hare . . . a smallish animal; with eyes popping out of her head, and two front paws dangling.' Their secret animal identities enable an intimacy otherwise precluded by the formality of the carnivorous Thorburn family:

> Thus when they came back from their honeymoon they possessed a private world, inhabited, save for one white hare, entirely by rabbits. No one guessed that there was such a place, and that of course made it all the more amusing. It made them feel, more even than most young married couples, in league together against the rest of the world. Often they looked slyly at each other when people talked about rabbits and woods and traps and shooting. Or they winked furtively across the table when Aunt Mary said she could never bear to see a hare in a dish – it looked so like a baby: or when John, Ernest's sporting brother told them what price rabbits were fetching that autumn in Wiltshire . . . But it was all a secret – that was the point of it; nobody save themselves knew that such a world existed.
>
> (Woolf 1991: 263)

The alter relationship is thus an underground relationship. While on the surface its participants take up their parts in public discourse, voices from below belie appearances and whisper 'we know it's not like that at all'. These subterranean communications may be covert and childish, but they have the power to reveal the constructedness of the wedding photograph on the sideboard.

The alter world is of course itself constructed. It comes into being through the creation of a private counter-culture with its own language, codes and customs. Familiar words and phrases convey meanings to be found in no dictionary:

All the *bananas* in the world. *BLP.*

Darling *Chocolate Weasel* please marry me and have lots of *rug rats.*

Lots of special kisses and *starbursts* from your loving cuddly *Koala.*

– and foreign languages and cryptic expressions test the would-be interpreter, who is finally thwarted by codes which are simply untranslatable:

Oink oink!

Grunt grunt.

Dow Bowow ow lowv mow bowbow lowv bowbow.

Hooch hooch, Hooch hooch hooch.

Paradoxically, the exclusivity of these private languages of love is in part
maintained by the very public annual custom of publishing Valentine's Day
messages. Love is declared for all to see, yet at the same time it remains
incognito and unlocatable. Lovers can indulge in the contradictory pleasure
of 'revealing all' whilst remaining anonymous:

No one guessed Squidgy . . . Love you my *Hunny*, from your *Honey Bunny*

– while newspaper readers are offered tantalising glimpses of worlds where
'official' names are a rarity and the nearest thing to an address is a warren,
nest or den of unspecified location. Thus the motley menagerie remains just
on the private side of the public/private divide, always threatening to put a
paw over the line but never quite 'coming out'.

5 SAFE IN THE NEST

While alter relationships may be subversive, however, it is no mere desire for
subversion that provides the motivation for their secrecy. Neither is it simply
a person's fear of what their colleagues at work might think if it came to light
that they spent much of their private life as a 'hamster'. Rather, these alternative worlds of love have positive attractions of their own, attractions
which must be protected from encroachment by the pressures and dangers
that lurk beyond the entrance to the burrow. Alter relationships are exciting
and special:

Come wallow with me in a muddy world of *wonder.*

They provide somewhere to belong:

Kingfisher loves his Swanbeat. *Joint nesting facilities* available.

They are cosy and safe:

Mouse: Thanks for the *comfortable month's hibernation.*

175

And they are timeless and lasting:

> Pigs are *forever, always together*; grunts, snorts, porkers – *come whatever . . . never to sever*.

Hunger is always satisfied with limitless supplies of honey, nuts and acorns, and conflict is reduced to an occasional tiff. In a big, bad, impermanent world of short-term contracts and soaring divorce rates, who could fail to see the attraction of 'Petlet's' plea to 'share nests of Burpies and Raggies for evermore'?

The privacy, exclusivity and security of the world of the alter couple is sometimes extended to an 'alter family' of children, animals or others. This was the case with Claire and Mark's *Furball and Monster* relationship. *Furball* was a furry rodent-like creature whose identity crystallised at a time when Claire kept various pet gerbils and hamsters. These became, in Claire's words, a 'pseudo-family' which *Furball* and *Monster* (a large bear-like creature) looked after in their cosy domestic world where bedtime was referred to as 'going up to the nest'. Some Valentine's messages also include references to a wider group:

> A Big Ook from me and *a certain young primate*.

> Lamb Pie: After ten years I love you more and more *and so do the Pigs*. Poopy.

> Bugs. Be *our* Valentine. Lots of love *Chubby, Meep, Baby Bear and Golden Whiskers*.

Just as 'real' couples settle down and have families, so it seems do some alter couples.

6 CULTURES OF LOVE

While alter relationships themselves thrive in seclusion, there are many points at which connections may be made between the 'private' languages and customs through which they are expressed, and more general and more immediately visible cultural phenomena. For example, some of the busiest shops on any high street are those trading in sentimental soft toys and soft toy-like images, through which and in relation to which affection between partners and family members can be expressed. Such practices suggest that even if we do not adopt personae and live in dens or warrens, many of us are nevertheless readily inclined to identify ourselves and our 'significant others' with representations of bears and bunnies. Perhaps, like alter personalities themselves, cute cards and fluffy keepsakes elicit fun, warmth and security, easing the negotiation of difficult and ambivalent love relationships.

For those who prefer to avoid relating to humans at all, the direct expression of love and desire for soft toys by adults is catered to by a widespread and growing 'bear culture'. Traditional teddy bears are now so widely manufactured, traded, collected and treasured by adults that a new class of shops has come into being which sell nothing but bears and their accessories. The desires of bear-lovers are further pandered to by *Hugglets Teddy Bear Magazine* which carries features on readers' bear collections and instruction on such matters as how to make a pinafore dress for your bear, while the British Teddy Bear Association advertises for new members to 'join paws with over 2,000 bear lovers'. Anecdotal accounts concerning adults who collect and 'play with' soft toys suggest there is much scope for interesting research into the hidden worlds of activity and meaning which lie behind such phenomena.

These examples demonstrate that the micro-cultures of alter relationships are by no means distinct from wider cultures in which adult affection and desire are mediated through, and are sometimes focused upon, soft toys and animals and their representations. This readily suggests the discursive formation of the alter relationship, with popular culture providing an extensive cast of possible 'voices' for the nascent alter personality, some of which are readily recognisable both as those of nursery characters and as popular messengers of adult love:

Mole seeks *Toad* for love *in the willows*.

Pooh Bear, love you now and always, your furry friend *Piglet*.

However, it seems doubtful that an appeal to popular culture is a sufficient explanation, especially when considering the extent to which alter personalities are developed and played out within some relationships. My interview with Claire, for example, revealed that throughout several years of her cohabitation with Mark, practically their entire domestic relationship was conducted through the *Monster* and *Furball* personae. Clearly, this is a far more substantive phenomenon than a simple exchange of cute Valentine's Day cards or the occasional use of nicknames, and it raises a number of interesting questions. How can we account for the fact that adults create 'in the privacy of their own homes' such extensive secret cultures, worlds of escape where they play like children, and which are remarkably similar to worlds created by other adults with whom they have no direct communication? How do couples know the formula through which to seek respite from the adult world? What are the emotional investments and motivations which fuel these paradoxical relationships, on the one hand not objectively 'real' at all, yet where at the same time individuals may experience themselves and their partners as 'being' a bear, pig or rabbit?

Without wishing to foreclose the explanation of similar phenomena which may occur in other kinds of private relationships, it seems of further importance to consider more precisely how the development of alter personalities is connected to romantic love. While it is evident that alter relationships frequently occur in relation to romantic love relationships, and that the 'fluffy bunny phenomenon' is not entirely distinct from romantic narratives at the more general cultural level, there is no precise correlation. In particular, there is little evidence that alter personalities 'fall in love' with each other, and no Mills & Boon novel tells of torrid passion between *Puppylion* and *Bunnymouse*; falling in love is for adults. Only at some later point, hidden beyond the 'happily ever after' closure, do Lucinda and the Count of Monte Varena cease gazing into the depths of each other's souls and take to snuggling and nesting.

It is with these questions and considerations in mind that I now want to turn to psychoanalysis, both because of its general explanatory power in relating infancy to adult sexuality, and because the work of one particular writer offers a useful way to make some interesting theoretical connections between the world of the nursery, popular culture and adult love.

7 BE MY 'TRANSITIONAL OBJECT'

Central to the work of the child psychiatrist and psychoanalyst Donald Winnicott is the concept of the 'transitional object' (or transitional phenomenon) and its crucial importance in the psychic life of the developing child. Winnicott observes the regularity with which the human infant develops a strong attachment to a particular thing or phenomenon which it uses as a defence against anxiety. This may be a particular word, a tune, a mannerism or commonly the corner of a blanket or one of the toys provided by adults:

> Among the various dolls and teddies belonging to a child, there may be one particular, probably soft, object . . . which the infant treats in a most brutal as well as in a most loving manner, and without which the infant could not conceive of going to bed; this thing would certainly not have to be left behind if the child had to go away; and if it were lost it would be a disaster for the child and therefore for those caring for him or her.

> (Winnicott 1950a: 143)

Among the special qualities of this intense attachment are a sense of security gained through possession of the object and, above all, a need for the object not to change unless changed by the child: 'The mother lets it get dirty and even smelly, knowing that by washing it she introduces a break in continuity in the child's experience' (Winnicott 1953: 4). The transitional object must survive the child's powerful emotions of hatred and aggression as well as love towards it, and 'it must seem to the infant to give warmth, or to move, or to have texture, or to do something that seems to show it has vitality or reality of its own' (*ibid.*: 5). The infant's relationship to the object thus has a paradoxical quality; it is perceived both as having come from without and as having been created by the child itself.

I want to suggest that, even apart from the obvious similarity of the objects themselves, parallels can readily be drawn between the uses to which transitional objects and 'alter objects' are put. In other words, for the purpose of maintaining a sense of existential security, the infant (adult) attempts to create an attachment to an object which is reliable and unchanging and which survives the emotional traumas of infancy (adulthood). To sustain this 'relationship', the infant (adult) needs to experience the object as sentient at the same time as 'knowing' that it is not objectively 'real' – it must be both 'created by' the infant (adult) themselves, and have an existence apart from them ('Jill, you are the only *teddy* I want to cuddle in bed. Love Tony').

However, there is one feature of the infant's relationship with *its* teddy which poses a question in respect of a straightforward comparison:

> Its fate is to be gradually allowed to be decathected, so that in the course of years it becomes not so much forgotten as relegated to limbo. By this I mean that in health the transitional object does not 'go inside' nor does the feeling about it necessarily undergo repression. It is not forgotten and it is not mourned. It loses meaning.
>
> (*ibid.*)

If the original transitional object loses meaning for the growing child, how can we explain the phenomenon whereby the adult once again invests meaning in a new one? To answer this, we need to look more closely at the developmental significance of the original object.

8 MEET ME IN THE 'INTERMEDIATE AREA'

For Winnicott, as for Freud, the human being at birth experiences itself as merged with the mother and the world, and psychic development can partly be understood in terms of the various stages of separation through which it passes on the way to autonomous adulthood. At the outset, the mother (if she is 'good enough') protects the infant against too sudden a realisation of its separateness and vulnerability through 'the *illusion* that there is an external reality that corresponds to the infant's capacity to create, i.e. the mother offers the infant the breast at the same time the infant is ready to create the object' (*ibid.*: 11–12).

However, inevitably (and ideally, according to Winnicott, gradually) the infant must become aware that it is indeed separate from the mother, and that there is a lack of congruence between its subjective experience and external reality. It is as a defence against the anxiety induced by this growing awareness that the transitional object first appears: 'The use of an object symbolises the union of two now separate things, baby and mother, *at the point in time and space of the initiation of their state of separateness*' (Winnicott 1967: 96–7).

The purpose that it plays in the psychic life of the infant gives the object its paradoxical qualities:

This object is halfway between everything . . . From the infant's point of view . . . it is the perfect compromise. It is neither part of the self nor part of the world. Yet it is both. It was conceived of by the infant and yet he could not have produced it, it just came. Its coming showed him what to conceive of. It is at one and the same time subjective and objective. It is at the border between inside and outside. It is both dream and real.

(Winnicott 1950b: 29)

For the infant to successfully negotiate the transition in its relationship to the world, adult collaboration in respect of its 'precious illusions' is crucially important. The paradoxical character of the transitional object must be accepted and respected: no one must claim either that Teddy has an independent existence in the world, or that the child created Teddy. It is understood that both these things are true. The object thus functions to 'start each human being off with what will always be important for them, i.e. a neutral area of experience which will not be challenged' (Winnicott 1953: 12). This neutral area is an 'intermediate area' of human life to which inner reality and external life both contribute, yet which is identical to neither. The intermediate area retains a vital importance throughout life 'as a resting-place for the individual engaged in the perpetual human task of keeping inner and outer reality separate yet interrelated' (*ibid.*: 2).

Thus for Winnicott the child's cathexis of the transitional object, its first 'not-me' possession, is synonymous with its entry into culture. It represents the first use of symbol and illusion, the first experience of creativity and play, and often one of the earliest uses of language as it starts to organise sounds and invent a word for the beloved object. As cultural participation develops through ever more sophisticated play, transitional objects and phenomena are decathected, and meaning becomes progressively 'spread out over the whole intermediate territory between "inner psychic reality" and "the external world as perceived by two persons in common", that is to say, over the whole cultural field' (*ibid.*: 5). While Winnicott does not develop his cultural theory beyond the world of the small child, he does usefully point to how the 'intermediate area' remains throughout life as the location of 'the intense experiencing that belongs to the arts and to religion and to imaginative living, and to creative scientific work' (*ibid.*: 14) and exists as a theoretical place where human beings 'may collect together and form a group on the basis of the similarity of our illusory experiences' (*ibid.*: 3).

Winnicott's account of the coming into being of the 'intermediate area' lends itself readily to the suggestion that it is at this time and in this place that alter relationships of the kind I am looking at here have their psychic location. Each partner can be seen to adopt the subject position of the child in relation to her or his transitional object and to consent at once to 'be' the other's transitional object. Thus, the couple form a 'group' based upon a shared cultural illusion. We saw earlier the paradoxical and illusory character of alter personae, both and at the same time a creation of the self and part of external reality. We have seen how alter relationships are 'neutral' areas of experience, free from the conflicts and emotional traumas that may beset the 'real' couple, and how they thus proceed on the tacit understanding that neither partner will destroy the 'precious illusions' of the other. And we have seen the playfulness, the creativity and the linguistic innovation involved in the construction of private cultures which are nothing if not 'imaginative living' ('Great Seal of England claps for his Dormouse. Oink-oink!').

However, recognition of the psychic and cultural significance of transitional objects is not a sufficient explanation for why micro-cultures of love should take the 'infantile' forms that they often do. In Winnicott's account, even the five-year-old is poised on the threshold of an exciting world of comics and toys and 'a whole cultural life waiting to enrich the child's experience of living' (Winnicott 1962: 38). Yet in love relationships we find adults who are hardly weaned ('To Booby from Bear, you are my booby and my bear'). How can we explain why grown adults capable of such sophisticated interests as opera, astrophysics and advanced linguistic theory should negotiate their love relationships in 'intermediate areas' characterised by such cultural primitivism? To answer this question, it is necessary to turn our attention to what, in Western culture at least, is the common foundation of the adult couple relationship – the experience we know as 'falling in love'.

9 OH BABY, BABY

For Sigmund Freud there is no 'normal' experience more likely to return us to infantile states of consciousness than falling in love: the finding of a new love object is always, in fact, the refinding of the first one (Freud 1905: 145). While this knowledge remains unconscious, it is evidenced by a sudden and dramatic loss of the sense of the separateness that normally characterises the adult psyche:

> At the height of being in love the boundary between ego and object threatens to melt away. Against all the evidence of his senses, a man [sic] who is in love declares that 'I' and 'you' are one, and is prepared to behave as if it were a fact.
>
> (Freud 1930: 66)

Powerful sensations reported by lovers of having 'merged' with the Beloved, of feeling they can 'see into their soul', etc. echo Freud's observations. Evidence of extreme ego regression can also be seen in the disturbing symptoms that being deeply in love can produce, such as a temporary inability to structure time sequentially, an incapacity to objectify and an inability to distinguish between past and present loves (Verhulst 1984). The common feeling that the experience is 'beyond words' can also be seen to reflect its origins in the pre-verbal stage of the mother–child bond (Altman 1977; Verhulst 1984).

'Psychic bonding' can be a profound and blissful experience; lovers are able to gaze into each other's depths and enjoy a passionate sensuality, untrammelled by the fumblings which beset those with more intact ego boundaries. Furthermore, in a culture where falling in love is esteemed as a fortuitous and foundational life event, it is no surprise that happy couples often pledge to stay together 'forever'. There are many reasons, however, why this generally proves an ambitious undertaking. Not least of these is that since their love exists in an extra-temporal, extra-verbal realm, the lovers face the cultural and linguistic challenge of emerging from a 'homogeneity of babyness' as two separate adults capable of conducting a reasonably amicable 'relationship'. In the 'real' world of course, they are already two grown-ups with sophisticated cultural competencies, and it may be suggested that it is here where they can build a life in common. In practice, however, the harmonious unity of the love bond is placed in severe peril by such a scheme. Typically, romantic lovers have little if any prior knowledge of each other. They may be from different social classes, different 'races', different age groups or different 'ethnic' backgrounds. They may not even speak the same language. And perhaps not least of possible impediments to cultural compatibility, they are commonly of different genders. Indeed, since it appears to be difference and not similarity which fans the flames of desire, may luck be with the couple who set out to live happily ever after in the 'real' world.

Falling in love thus creates a profound existential dilemma for the lover. On the one hand, a lifetime of happiness cannot easily be constructed from inarticulate, unlocatable, selfless oneness. Yet to separate from someone who is felt to be the 'whole world', and begin to experience the extent of their 'otherness' and one's own alienation is a terrifying prospect indeed. What can the lover do who 'cannot live without' a love which cannot exist in the world? It can seem that there are just two choices: to accept the fleeting and transitory nature of romantic love and suffer a 'broken heart' sooner rather than later, or maintain a naive or delusory hopefulness and 'stay together' anyway, in which case the heart is more likely to succumb to a prolonged and tortuous strangulation involving extensive emotional trauma and destructive power struggles (see Langford, forthcoming, for an account of the latter in heterosexual relationships).

I want to conclude by suggesting, however, that there is a third possible response to the lovers' dilemma, which may or may not occur alongside the second – the mutual creation of a new culture, a world in common.

10 A WORLD WHERE LOVE CAN LIVE

One way in which love can be 'saved' is in precisely the same way that the
infant seeks to save its love for the mother: through the development of an
intermediate area, starting with the 'creation' of an object which 'stands for'
the union, an object which is both and at the same time the breast/mother/
lover/world and not-the-breast/mother/lover/world. Should the lover assent
to 'be' the object, separation anxiety is assuaged and a new world is created,
a secret world where lovers are safe, where love *can* have a future ('Snooze.
So now you're my wife, we'll share our lives together. The two daft bears go
on forever! Love Smelly'). In an alter world, a couple can continue to experience and express affection for one another long after love in the 'real' world
has died.

John Osborne illustrates this perfectly in *Look Back in Anger*. The final
scene finds Jimmy and Alison completely alienated; the adult, gendered
otherness that characterises their 'real' relationship has allowed no vestige of
respect or affection to survive, and Alison is nearly destroyed by Jimmy's
cruelty and rage. All hope for the future of love is not abandoned, however,
for the curtain falls on a different world, a world where love lives on, articulated through shared illusions which evoke an earlier, less corrupted time:

Jimmy: We'll be together in our bear's cave, and our squirrel's drey,
  and we'll live on honey, and nuts – lots and lots of nuts. And we'll
  sing songs about ourselves – about warm trees and snug caves, and
  lying in the sun. And you'll keep those big eyes on my fur, and help
  me keep my claws in order, because I'm a bit of a soppy, scruffy sort
  of a bear. And I'll see that you keep that sleek, bushy tail glistening
  as it should, because you're a very beautiful squirrel, but you're none
  too bright either, so we've got to be careful. There are cruel steel
  traps lying about everywhere, just waiting for rather mad, slightly
  satanic, and very timid little animals. Right?

Alison nods!

Alison: *(Pathetically)*. Poor Squirrels!
  (With the same comic emphasis) Poor bears! *(She laughs a little. Then looks
  at him very tenderly, and adds very, very softly)*. Oh, poor, poor bears!

Slides her arm around him.

CURTAIN

Look Back in Anger is a harrowing portrayal of a modern world where love
is born but struggles to survive at all, where love has retreated into a private
world of childish illusions. The 'cruel steel traps' remind us that the boundaries of the alter world are necessary and must be patrolled. The 'real' world
is a dangerous place for animals, and 'adult' love too hard for those who are
still children in their hearts.

The boundaries between the two worlds are, of course, not fixed or distinct. The 'public' and the 'private', the 'real' and the 'illusory', the 'adult' and the 'childish': all are categories which are constantly under construction and negotiation. Moreover, like all our cultural dualisms, they imply hierarchies of value which are open to question. Part of such questioning can involve listening to the voices from subterranean cultures of love, the voices of those who can tell us about the kinds of worlds where love can live. They tell us that alter personalities are playful, kind and constant; that alter relationships are creative, friendly and fun; and that alter worlds are worlds where everyone is cared for and has enough to eat.

Perhaps then we should celebrate 'life in the burrow'. It might be illusory – its illusoriness is obvious – but is not romantic love the greatest illusion of all? It might be 'childish' – its childishness, too, is obvious – although in comparison to the 'newborn' adult lover, bunnies and bears may be positively mature. And it may, for now, be a private affair. But who knows? Maybe the time has come for *Flopsy Bunny* and *Teddy Edward* to break out of the toy cupboard and proclaim their place as cultural pioneers of love. If we hear what they have to say, maybe alter worlds and their inhabitants will not have to stay so small.

REFERENCES

Altman, Leon. L. (1977) 'Some vicissitudes of love', *American Psychoanalytic Journal* 25: 35–52.

Freud, Sigmund (1905) 'Three essays on the theory of sexuality', in Sigmund Freud (1977) *Three Essays on the Theory of Sexuality and Other Works*, Harmondsworth: Penguin.

—— (1930) 'Civilisation and its discontents' in J. Strachey (ed.) (1961) *The Standard Edition of the Complete Psychological Works of Sigmund Freud*, vol. XXI, London: The Hogarth Press, pp. 64–148.

Ibsen, Heinrik (1981) 'A Doll's House', in *Heinrik Ibsen Four Major Plays*, Oxford: Oxford University Press.

Langford, Wendy (1995) 'Snuglet Puglet loves to snuggle with Snuglet Piglet': alter personalities in heterosexual love relationships', in Lynne Pearce and Jackie Stacey (eds) *Romance Revisited*, London: Lawrence & Wishart, pp. 238–51.

—— (forthcoming) *The Subject of Love*, London: Routledge.

Osborne, John (1960) *Look Back in Anger*, London: Faber & Faber.

Verhulst, Johann (1984) 'Limerance: notes on the nature and function of passionate love', *Psychoanalysis and Contemporary Thought* 7: 115–38.

Winnicott, Donald (1950a) 'The deprived child and how he can be compensated for loss of family life' in Donald Winnicott (1965) *The Family and Individual Development*, London, Tavistock, pp. 132–45.

—— (1950b) 'Growth and development in immaturity', in Donald Winnicott (1965) *The Family and Individual Development*, London: Tavistock, pp. 21–9.

—— (1953) 'Transitional objects and transitional phenomena', in Donald Winnicott (1971) *Playing and Reality*, London: Tavistock, pp. 1–25.

—— (1955) 'Group influences and the maladjusted child: the school aspect', in Donald Winnicott (1965) *The Family and Individual Development*, London: Tavistock, pp. 146–54.

—— (1962) 'The five-year-old', in Donald Winnicott (1965) *The Family and Individual Development*, London: Tavistock, pp. 34–9.

—— (1967) 'The location of cultural experience', in Donald Winnicott (1971) *Playing and Reality*, London: Tavistock, pp. 95–103.

Woolf, Virginia (1991) 'Lappin and Lapinova', in *Virginia Woolf: The Complete Shorter Fiction*, London: Triad Grafton.

9

THAT GREAT SUPERMARKET OF DESIRE

Attributes of the desired other in personal advertisements

Celia Shalom

TALL, GAY professional, 26, with bicycle, seeks nice guy *with lots of adjectives*: funny, intelligent, thoughtful, stable, n/s, tall etc. Box 1452.[1]

1 INTRODUCTION

The personal ad may be considered as a distinct generic form which is linked to the small ad. While the small ad offers something, the personal ad both offers and, most essentially, seeks. The personal ad can be dated back to at least the eighteenth century in Britain (found in the matrimonial columns) and today it enjoys the status of a popular-culture genre. Personal columns (variously called 'Lonely Hearts', 'Heartsearch', 'Heart to Heart', 'Eyelove', 'Soulmates', etc.) are found in a wide range of publications in Britain including local and free papers, national papers and general- and special/specific-interest magazines. Measures of the generic institutionalisation of the personal ad are its use in publicity (advertisements for mortgages and men's perfume) and exploitation as a creative enterprise (the *New York Review of Books* holds an 'Erudite Personal Ad Contest', for instance). It is fast adapting to a range of different technological forms: many written ads are now linked to 'voicemail' (a special 0891 number which contains a further spoken message and space for respondents to leave their own messages), which makes the contact process much speedier than using 'snail mail'; there are teletext and videotext ads; and Usenet personals have taken off in the United States, partly as a reaction to the expense of the 0891 calls.

The ad has truly taken the private search for the desired other into the public domain. The mushrooming of the personal ad reflects the large number of single people (there are six million single-person households in Great Britain today, representing 26 per cent of all households, and this figure is predicted to reach nearly eight million by the year 2000). The trend seems to be towards 'serial mono-living', whereby people enter into two or more relationships involving marriage or co-habitation in their lifetime, with intervals when they may live alone (Mintel Special Report 1992).

The personal ad resonates with ambiguity. People feel ambivalent about taking their personal world of relationships into the public sphere. There is still a stigma attached to the personal columns: while many people happily state that they read them, far fewer admit to actually using them. Personal ads also seem strategically to employ vagueness. Descriptions of self, desired other and sought-after relationship provide a conventional format for the encoding – and decoding – of a personal fantasy and constitute thus a generic form of wishing. The brevity of the text forces a kind of summary which is actually remarkable for its density of information. Yet there is a curious paradox between this orientation towards efficiency of information and the imprecision and vagueness that seems to permeate the lexis of many ads.

The lonely hearts ad has, perhaps unsurprisingly, been criticised for restricting and commodifying the advertiser (and, by extension, the reader). The genre has been accused of promoting old conventional stereotypes where men are tall, rich and mature, and women are slim and beautiful. Evidently, the limitation of space disallows complex individualised descriptions of self and other, and forces simple description. It is also true that some advertisers try to imprint a sense of individuality and difference from the other advertisers by 'subverting the genre' (see Coupland 1996) through creativity shown in word-play, humour and metaphor. However, I suggest that even the frequent, so-called stereotypical lexis of the personal ad represents deliberate selections on the writer's part which do not simply describe and reinforce stereotypes. On the contrary, the lexis chosen is *deliberately* vague and impressionistic: lexical selection flows from the intrinsic communicative purpose of the genre which is to seek a desired other. Hence the lexis is selected with a view to engaging the intended reader in a kind of 'do I fit?' dance with the text.

In order to explore the interactivity of the personal ad, I will consider the ad on two levels. First, I will look at the written personal ad as a genre which aims to set up a certain type of communication between writer and reader and to attract the desired other. Second, I consider a database of personal ads from the London magazine *Time Out*. I look at some of the frequent lexis used by four groups of advertisers (gay and straight men and women) to encode that component within the personal ad that describes the desired other, invariably an inventory of attributes. Focus on some of these attributes enables me to argue my case that, in fact, the most 'stereotypical' lexis is imbued with a vagueness and/or sets off resonances in the reader, both of which are intrinsically interactive devices.

2 THE PERSONAL AD

2.1 Wishing and inferring

One sense of the word 'advertising' is 'drawing attention to something', or notifying or informing somebody of something (Dyer 1982: 2). The writers of most personal ads not only inform but also explicitly state the speech act they are performing. Lexis indicating requests (*would like to meet*), wishes (*seeks, hopes to meet, looking for*) and desires (*desires, wants, lacks*) is found. The frequent term *seeks*, itself a familiar signal of the personal ad, is about searching with intention, with desire. The Western personal ad is the advertiser's quest for a romantic partner, for a perfect mate (Nair 1992). Through self and other description, and description of the desired relationship, the advertiser anticipates a form of partner selection (Erfurt 1985).

It has been noted that the reader of the personals becomes good at inference, or going beyond the information given to form a concept in their mind. This is discussed in relation to specific lexis later in the chapter. Here I simply wish to draw attention to the importance of this reading between the lines, of cracking codes, in the reading process of lonely hearts advertisements. Some lexical items are clear enough: 'discreet lunchtime liaisons' or 'uncomplicated afternoon fun' are hard to misinterpret. However, the coding is often more complex. One researcher, for instance, claims that people indicate wealth by 'identifying what job they do, whether they are educated, or what kind of car they drive' (Dunbar, quoted in O'Kelly 1994). While structured research into readers' interpretation of personal ads would help shed light on such language codes, informal research of my own indicates quite a high degree of idiosyncrasy in reader decoding.

2.2 A colony text

The personal columns are actually a kind of 'colony text' (Hoey 1986) made up of individual and separate entries whose order does not change their meaning. Like other classified advertisements, the entries or 'components' may be sequenced alphabetically, numerically or simply temporally. Arrangement will vary from publication to publication.

There may be different sections within the columns. For instance, the gay paper *Boyz*, which has many pages given over to personal columns, uses rubrics like '1 to 1', 'Locker Room', 'D.I.Y', 'Leather Men', 'Yellow', etc., which ease access as any reference text does. Hence the reader uses particular strategies to read colony texts and these relate particularly to the physical layout (typography) and reader motivation. The first few words of each entry usually appear in bold typeface, and sometimes in capitals, and enable the eye to follow this typeface down the page, scanning for specific information.

Explicit advice on writing effective personals for the Usenet lends support to their being a type of colony text. Esmay sent out a detailed e-mail posting, 'Usenet personals: advice for straights' (Esmay 1996). In the section 'How do I write my own Ad?', he advises senders to 'START EVERY AD WITH THE BASICS ABOUT YOURSELF'. For instance, 'Bostonian GWM, 42, ISO GBM, 40–50, for romance', which, translated, means 'Bostonian Gay White Male, aged 42, In Search Of Gay Black Male, age 40–50, for romance'. For Esmay, the 'basics' include senders' gender, sexuality, age, race, where they live, and what type of contact they are looking for. He advocates efficiency for both the reader and writer:

> By making sure your subject line contains your basic information, you will not only be doing everyone who would NOT be interested in you a favor, but you will increase the likelihood of someone who DOES want to meet you of actually spotting your Ad.
>
> (Esmay 1996)

2.3 Genre chains

There may be a genre chain of interaction between participants that is initiated by the ad. A genre chain is 'a system of interrelated genres that interact with each other in specific settings' (Bazerman 1992). Such a chain may be constituted by both public and private texts and will involve spoken and written language which may be face-to-face, electronic or telephonic. The basic chain is

Ad → (response) → (follow up) → (meeting)

and is not unlike the process followed for a job application. The biodata (CV) is sent in the response (or application), selection from a number of applicants may occur by follow-up, and the interview takes place. Indeed, some advertisers talking on the Radio 4 'Photo Appreciated' series made exactly this comparison between the initial meeting and a job interview. Another metaphor is that of the audition, which this *Time Out* advertiser plays with:

> ALL THE WORLD'S A STAGE but this slim, black female, 32, is still missing a key player. Auditions now being held for witty, intelligent men under 40. Photo essential. Box 1134.

Hence the genre chain is a cross-textual and cross-media process and a variety of combinations of interactions are possible. For instance, there may be a written ad, written response, phone follow-up, face-to-face meeting, or a written ad, voicemail response, phone follow-up and face-to-face meeting, or the ad might be on the Internet and involve e-mail initially, and so on. While the medium of the personal ad evidently affects the discourse (e.g. Coupland's 1996 analysis of the voicemail ad shows that it involves more personalisation than the written ad and allows more verbal hedging), it is still the case that the communicative function of the ad is to set up a genre chain with the desired other. The end point of this chain may be a long-term relationship, or a successful affair, which will set up repeated meetings and interactions between the two participants.

2.4 The genre

The written personal ad is a minimalist genre (Nair 1992). In a small number of words, the seeker has to give a kind of shop-window description which casts out a net that hopefully catches the desired other as one of the respondents. The simplified typical schematic structure of the ad may be described as:

X seeks Y for Z; where X is the desiring subject, Y the desired object, and Z the desired relationship.

Coupland's description of the most frequent schematic structure for the ads labels the X, Y and Z slots as advertiser, target and goals, thus characterising the ad as a directive, goal-orientated genre. She includes an optional comment component in the structure.

1. ADVERTISER	2. seeks	3. TARGET
4. GOALS	5. (COMMENT)	6. REFERENCE

(Coupland 1996)

Thus a typical ad would be the following:

FEMALE GRADUATE, 35, fit and fairly attractive, seeks intelligent, professional male, 35+, for friendship, fun and maybe more. Photo appreciated. Box 906.

– which breaks down as:

1 ADVERTISER: Female graduate, 35, fit and fairly attractive
2 seeks
3 TARGET: intelligent, professional male, 35+
4 GOALS: for friendship, fun and maybe more
5 (COMMENT): Photo appreciated.
6 REFERENCE: Box 906.

As in this example, the ads usually talk about both self and other using the third person, and this creates a sense of objectification. (Use of the terms *female* and *male* add to this sense of objectification.) This style of reference probably has its roots in the marriage advertisement which was usually written about the seeker by a relative or close friend. However, the interactive device of using first and second pronominal forms, typical of advertisements, is often employed. Three examples follow. Note particularly the indeterminate 'you' in the texts.

WISH WE'D MET SOONER. You? Bi/gay female friend/lover. Me? Bi-female, 25, attractive, warm, witty and awaiting you. Box 1421.

YOU AND I are professional people. YOU: male, tall, handsome, humorous, n/s, 27–38. ME: female, slim, attractive, lively, individual, 32. TOGETHER: we'll enjoy weekend adventures and each other. Photo appreciated. Box 1278.

IN DREAMS I WALK WITH YOU male, 37, veggie, divorced, average looking. No beard or sandals though! You: female, 30ish, calm, collected, passionate, committed. Into cinema, books, beaches, picnics. Send letter, photo and share the dream. Box 1444.

The informal, spoken style further reinforces the interactivity of the text. Further features of advertising found in the personals are the use of the imperative, exploitation of punctuation, ellipsis and contraction. Lexical vagueness (Crystal and Davy 1975: 111–14; Channell 1994) is often present in the self or other description. Imprecise references to age are found, e.g. *fortysomething*, and attributes are made fuzzy through use of what Crystal and Davy call the 'approximating' suffix *-ish*, e.g. *tallish*, *youngish*. Colloquial lexis abounds too: e.g. *veggie, into* (as in 'into cinema'). Humour in personal ads has been noted – the reference to beard and sandals conjures up an image of the ageing hippie, while this man emphasises he is walking in other footwear!

Passive variation on the active verb form (generally *seeks*, component 2) may occur, hence giving first position to the other, the object of desire. For instance:

INTO OASIS male 22–28 sought by Japanese female. Photo appreciated. Box 1155.

Ads may draw on intertextuality, thus emphasising the connections between writer and reader. This intertextuality may take the form of extra-textual cultural references, like those to the band Oasis, Dudley Moore, or to cross-textual references such as 'A Man for all Seasons', 'Life is Short'.

LIFE IS SHORT and so am I. Witty, attractive, Dudley-Moore type (young 50), seeks smart, funny lady to look up to. Go on, make my day. Box 1048.

A MAN FOR ALL SEASONS. Spring walks, summer sun, Autumn bonfires and winter cuddles for attractive, n/s, young 40's female. Box 1305.

The amount of self description, projected other description and relationship description varies. Occasionally, there is little or no self-descript in an ad. This ad, for instance, only specifies the sexuality of the writer:

> LESBIAN seeks feminine woman for romance and friendship. Must be affectionate honest and genuine 1-2-1. London area. No bisexuals. Box 1473.

– while this ad concentrates on the self-descript:

> SAGGITARIAN WOMAN forty something, intelligent, successful, creative, tall, slim, longs for soulmate. Box 1475.

But above all, it is their reflexive nature, the sense one gets of the writer's awareness of self, other and genre, that comes through in many personal ads. There is a 'meta-' quality, a self-consciousness on the writer's part that may appear as a deliberate distancing of self from the text.

The writer of the next ad shows an awareness of the idealisation of the other, yet asks for that desired other with the humorous 'realistic' qualification, 'if any or all of these apply to you'. Interaction with the imagined reader is explicitly built into the text, as is the knowledge that the reader is matching themselves to the other description:

> GAY WOMAN, 33, seeks the seemingly impossible; intelligent, witty, enthusiastic, thrill-seeking gay female. If any or all of these apply to you please, please write. Box 1012.

And this advertiser both refuses to categorise himself, thus subverting the genre, yet uses the genre to meet his goals:

> UNCATEGORISABLE MALE, 40, abundant qualities, seeks chic, witty female intellectual for discursive badinage, lunch and flights of fancy. Box 1413.

A number of researchers comment on further common linguistic features of personal ads, such as use of acronyms, euphemism and coding (Nair 1992), as well as the omission of non-essential items such as function words, which results essentially from the compression caused by spatial constraints (Bruthiaux 1994). It is interesting to note that some of these features, in particular acronyms and abbreviations, may be found across different publications, while specific publications – and countries – seem to breed their own codes. For instance, wltm (would like to meet), n/s (non-smoking), (g)soh ((good) sense of humour), ala (all letters answered), alawp (all letters answered with photo) seem to be almost universal. The British eye is not yet, however, familiar with two- and three-letter abbreviations such as: WSF (White Single Female), GF (Girlfriend), DBM (Divorced Black Male), which are mainstays of the *New York Review of Books* and other US publications. New domains, too, seem to promote new linguistic expression. Hence we find acronyms like ISO (In Search Of) and FTA (Fun, Travel, and Adventure) and codes such as G*M (Gay Male of any race) in the e-mail personals. Hence there is a well-recognised terminology of personal ads which provides a kind of language for the community of 'singles' or advertisers, to mark and maintain solidarity as well as providing a form of expression, a way of 'doing' the genre.

In sum, the written personal ad is a highly interactive, stylised genre. The writer of the ad uses the genre to establish a link with the potential desired other. If successful, this will result in a link that starts up a genre chain between the two participants, which may develop into an on-going relationship. But that is far beyond the scope of this chapter. In the second part of the chapter, I will examine the Y part of the genre, the desired other (Coupland's 'target'). Using a computerised corpus of personals, I look at some of the most frequent attributes of the desired other. I will argue that, while these descriptors may be seen as stereotypical, many of them are perhaps more fruitfully understood as representing lexical choices that dialogue with the reader through either their imprecision and/or resonance.

3 ATTRIBUTES OF THE DESIRED OTHER

A database of personals enabled me to investigate the most frequent attributes of the desired other of the four groups of advertisers: gay and straight men and women. The database of written personal ads represent the Lonely Hearts sections of four months' issues (end of March–end of July 1995) of the weekly London entertainment guide *Time Out*. The Lonely Hearts section does not have subheadings which divide up gay and straight or men's and women's ads, which meant that allocation was done by the researcher. A small number of ads was discarded since clear allocation to a section was not straightforward. This section only contains ads that still use the box-number system. After repeat ads had been sifted out, the total number of 766 ads was divided into four sub-corpora: straight men (367 ads); straight women (186 ads); gay men (155 ads); gay women (58 ads). One copy of each sub-database then had the X and Z parts of each advertisement deleted, leaving only Y, the 'target', or desired other description.

My interest was in the attributes or descriptors of the desired other in the advertisements. (Note that by 'attribute', I understand adjectives that occur both before nouns as well as those that follow the predicate.) Attributes of gender (*male, female*) and of sexuality (*gay, straight*) were high in frequency because separate sections for the four groups (straight male, straight female, gay male, gay female) are not provided in the magazine; I have not included these four descriptors in my study.

The frequency of occurrence of each descriptor per ad was calculated as a percentage of the total number of ads in each particular database, since the size of each varied. These figures yielded the following table of attributes for

193

each of the sub-corpora. Occurrence in 3 per cent of the advertisements is taken as a cut-off point. Eight frequency bands were established, Band (1) representing a frequency of 35 per cent and over, Band (2) of between 30 and 35 per cent, and so on. The last band, Band (8), represents the narrower frequency range of 3–5 per cent. The frequency results for the four corpora are shown in Table 9.1.

It should be noted that the total number of adjectives in each database varies, which is partly a reflection of the uneven number of ads in each sub-corpus, and it is only when we get down to the lower bands that all groups use a number of adjectives. *Similar* stands out as the only other descriptor that appears in Band 1 and that is for just one subgroup of advertisers, gay women. It appears in nearly half (48.3 per cent) of their petitions for the desired other. It is also the highest descriptor in the gay men's database, at 34.8 per cent, and is in Band 2.

Straight men use *attractive* with greatest frequency (Band 3, at 27.0 per cent occurrence).

Table 9.1 Eight frequency bands of the attributes of the desired other

Band & %	Straight men	Straight women	Gay men	Gay women
(1) 35+				similar
(2) 30-3-5			similar	
(3) 25–30	attractive			
(4) 20–25				
(5) 15–20	intelligent	professional similar		feminine
(6) 10–15	similar slim	intelligent tall(ish) n/s[1]		
(7) 5–10	n/s warm pretty	educated handsome witty kind honest	intelligent younger professional handsome(ish) masculine	attractive
(8) 3–5	independent bright young beautiful younger loving sensual	attractive gsoh[2] humorous passionate sincere solvent aware warm	non-scene n/s special tall nice slim warm	good-looking lovely sensitive bi

Notes: 1 non-smoker.   2 good sense of humour.

194

No descriptors are found in the range of Band 4, between 20 and 25 per cent occurrence.

Moving down to Band 5, descriptors found are *feminine* (gay women, 17.2 per cent), *intelligent* (straight men, 15.3 per cent), *professional* and *similar* (straight women, both at 15.1 per cent).

Band 6 holds *similar* and *slim* for straight men's other attributes, and *intelligent*, *tall(ish)* and *n/s* or *non-smoker* for straight women's desired other.

Band 7, representing a frequency of 5–10 per cent, contains *n/s*, *warm* and *pretty* (straight men); *educated*, *handsome*, *witty*, *kind* and *honest* (straight women); *intelligent*, *younger*, *professional*, *handsome(ish)* and *masculine* (gay men); and *attractive* (gay women).

The final band contains more items for all groups than the other bands and represents the lower frequency range of 3–5 per cent, which is only a small number of the currencies in the smaller gay sub-corpora. For more representative results evidently a larger database is needed. However, for the purposes of this chapter, we shall note the emergence of the following lexical items in Band 8: for the desired other of straight men: *independent*, *bright*, *young*, *younger*, *beautiful*, *loving* and *sensual*; of straight women: *attractive*, *gsoh*, *humorous*, *passionate*, *sincere*, *solvent*, *aware* and *warm*; of gay men: *non-scene*, *n/s*, *special*, *tall*, *nice*, *slim* and *warm*; and of gay women: *good-looking*, *lovely*, *sensitive* and *bi*.

One can note a variation of lexis according to the subgroup of advertiser – for instance, the two gay groups of advertisers make frequent use of the items *masculine*, *non-scene* and *special* (men), and *feminine*, *good-looking* and *bi* (women); items which do not appear in the straight advertisers' frequency bands. Both gay groups use the term *similar* with very high frequency, which merits comment later on. A rough semantic classification of these high-frequency attributes later in this paper gives another perspective on the four subgroups' desired others. In any case, further research on a larger corpus, would give a clearer picture of a gay register and enable comparisons between gay men and gay women as well as on the dimension of gender.

From one perspective, the attributes in Table 9.1 look like a list of stereo-types, and in some sense this may be inevitable for reasons already mentioned. However, it is perhaps more useful to consider these adjectives as either descriptors entailing openness or vagueness of some type, or as instigators of associations or resonances in the reader. I will look at some specific examples below.

3.1 The top three attributes: *similar; attractive; professional*

3.1.1 Similar

As already noted, this word appears in nearly half the gay women's ads and about 35 per cent of gay men's ads. It is also found with 15 per cent frequency in the straight women's corpus, and comes lower in the straight men's corpus, at just over 11 per cent.

The extremely high frequency of *similar* in the gay women's and gay men's databases implies a specific gay usage of this word. Its occurrence for straight women and men (higher for straight women, in Band 5, than for straight men, in Band 6) is also significant, but I would argue that its implications are different for these groups. The use of *similar* implies a direct link between self and other. Questions of similar what? and possible indication of an empathy towards the other are raised here, as well as the possible relevance of same-sex relationship to similarity and opposite-sex relationship to difference.

A typical collocation in all the ads is that of 'seeks similar'. This chunk may be followed by a noun ('seeks similar woman'), or by an adjective or string of adjectives ending with a noun ('seeks similar intelligent sincere male'); it may also, interestingly, be followed by *for* ('seeks similar for fun'), or it may stand alone ('seeks similar'). In the last two cases, *similar* seems to be functioning quasi-nominally, as a container word. Seeks similar what? is the question the reader will have. There is an ellipsis, or omission, of one or more words. In addition to this, omission of the article 'a' reinforces the telegrammatic style typical of the genre of the small ad.

What becomes clear when looking at *similar* across all four sub-corpora is that it is not a transparent token saying "transfer all the list" but it requires much interpretive work on the part of the reader. It always works anaphorically in that some reference back needs to be made when decoding. Such anaphoric reference varies, though, in its specificity. In the gay corpora we find the typical chunk 'seeks similar for'. For instance:

GAY FEMALE, 29, 5′6″, slim, attractive, sporty, fun-loving, seeks similar for evenings out, clubbing, friendship or maybe more. Box 1007.

GAY MALE, 29, professional, shy, non-scene, discreet, ordinary looks, specs, tall, seeks similar for friendship. Box 845.

In neither of the straight corpora does *similar* appear alone, without being followed by (or near to) reference to age and/or gender. We may conclude from this that in the chunk 'seeks similar for' *similar* refers explicitly to sexuality, to being gay.

Again, in the gay corpora we find 'seeks similar' as in:

GAY MALE, fit, 39 yr old, romantic, sensitive, with gsoh, enjoys travel, outdoor pursuits, cinema, theatre and reading. Seeks similar. Box 1192.

All the corpora contain many explicit references to gender: 'seeks similar woman' (gay women); 'seeks similar guy' (gay men); 'seeks similar male/man' (straight women); 'seeks similar female/woman' (straight men).

The next question, then, is how much reach the term has. In the first example, does it include all the self-description, from *gay female* to *fun-loving*? Or does it refer to only part of this list? It could include 'gay female, around 29'. Is height included?, etc. Perhaps the advertiser intends *fun-loving* to be carried forward, since such a person would enjoy going out. In the second example, does the term contain *non-scene* and *discreet*? There is great ambiguity here and readers will tend to differ on their interpretation of *similar* in different ads.

Similar may collocate with an expression of age, yet we are still left asking how much of the self-description it refers back to:

BEAUTIFUL GAY WOMAN, feminine, 36, non-scene, up market, loves travel, art, new age, seeks similar 33–38, 5ft 7in. and over. Photo. Box 877.

And it is unclear how cataphoric it is: is the advertiser 5ft 7in?

There may be some further description after the term:

GAY WOMAN, 45. Young, attractive, feminine, caring, wants similar adventurous, funny, stable, lovely woman to explore life's opportunities. Friendship initially. Box 1718.

But the question remains as to how much of the previous self-descriptors are included in *similar* (and indeed how much of the other descriptors also relate to self).

The other sub-corpora seem to use the term in the same ways as in the gay women's corpus. The chunk 'similar age' is found in the straight women's corpus and this confines the term, as the reader simply has to refer back to the age expression for self:

EVE, 40, arty, Jewish, left-wing, teenage child, seeks tall, intelligent, similar age or younger Adam, to regain paradise. Box 839.

One advertiser shows an awareness of the possible hold-all nature of the term and is keen to separate out gender-specific descriptors:

WOMAN SEEKS MAN for usual reasons. Her: warm, attractive, slim, curvy, fun, fit, bright, interesting, easy-going, positive, open-minded. Him: similar, minus curves, age 40-ish. Photo? Box 1581.

In conclusion, *similar* raises the question of how the reader fits in, or projects herself or himself into the personal advertisement. The ambiguity of the use of *similar*, its indeterminacy in scope, acts as a hook to draw in the reader, the potential desired other. The back-and-forth nature of the term seems to embody a positioning of desires between writer and reader.

3.1.2 Attractive

The ubiquity of *attractive* in the Western personal ad has also been noted by a number of linguists (e.g. Nair 1992). In my corpus, *attractive* is the highest frequency attribute for the desired other in the straight men's advertisements, representing almost 27 per cent of the ads. It occurs with the frequencies of 8.6 per cent in the gay women's ads and 4.3 per cent in the straight women's ads but does not enter the eight frequency bands for gay men's ads (having a 2.5 per cent frequency rate). Hence it attaches particularly to the female desired other. Straight women use *attractive* with great frequency in the self-descript (in over 45 per cent of the ads), but interestingly, straight men use the adjective to describe themselves with the same frequency as they do to describe the desired other.

The first words of the following advertisement wittily depict a straight woman's awareness of the frequency of male use of the term *attractive*, as well as her ready acceptance of the label:

ANOTHER ATTRACTIVE, slim, intelligent, blonde, this one a charismatic, young-looking 48, interests in cinema, politics, music (all sorts but particularly classical), theatre, travel, walking in parks, eating in pubs, in search of unpretentious male complement, similar age or younger, any area. Box 1509.

In the straight men's database, the following three-word clusters are typically found in the 'other' slot:

. . . seeks attractive female . . .
. . . seeks attractive intelligent . . .
. . . seeks slim attractive . . .

In the actual texts, we find what is essentially a list of attributes of the desired other, strung together with commas. For example, there follows the concordance lines for the cluster 'seeks attractive slim':

ks intelligent, witty, active,	attractive, slim idiot who can't believe
, seeks intelligent, educated,	attractive, slim lady, 25–38, shared holi
iterranean bachelor, 36, seeks	attractive, slim lady, 18–34, for wining,
t, cinema, theatre. Seeks very	attractive, slim, tallish, curvaceous fem
taining and intelligent, seeks	attractive, slim, childless lady, 28–38,
, intelligent, nice bum, seeks	attractive, slim, intelligent, open-minde
and would love to meet a very	attractive, slim, petite, intelligent, n/
, expatriate from Japan. Seeks	attractive, slim, friendly woman, 18–25,
en eyes, bohemian, warm. Seeks	attractive, slim, female, 30–36, for last
Thai speaking lady, 21–30 yrs,	attractive, slim, well-educated, for last

In the genre of the personal ad, *attractive* seems to have a kind of catch-all sense, whereby it is emptied of its full force as a word referring to physical appearance. We all like to think we are attractive, and the reader is more likely to include herself or himself in the category *attractive* than in the category of one of its more specific near-synonyms (*pretty*, *good-looking*, *handsome*, *beautiful* and the ambiguous *lovely*). The abundant use of *attractive* in the small ads may thus reflect a kind of delexicalisation of it.

Further, *attractive* is also not just a socially desirable physical attribute – we typically talk of an 'attractive personality' or an 'attractive place'. (Kennedy 1996 monitors the use of *attractive* in job advertisements, noting that before the Equal Opportunities legislation, it was used to describe women – secretaries and PAs – and that after the legislation *attractive* was still used in ads, but describing the office environment.) There is a sense in which the connotation *attractive*, through the range of its non-physical collocates, conjures up an all-embracing concept that most readers would feel able (or wish) to adopt.

Hence *attractive* does not have the precision, or the imposing nature, that *pretty* or *handsome* might have. As such, it seems, it has been placed by the writer for the reader to interact positively with; more positively than could be done with a lexically stronger word such as those mentioned.

3.1.3 Professional

Together with *similar*, this is the most frequent 'other' attribute in the straight women's corpus, occurring in just over 15 per cent of the ads. It also occurs in frequency Band 7 in the gay men's corpus.

The high use of this attribute evidently reflects the social milieu of the readership of *Time Out*. However, it is interesting that straight women, more than the other groups, desire this of the desired other to such an extent. They ask for a 'professional man', or a 'professional male', with qualities such as humour, height and kindness. Typical ads are:

> ATTRACTIVE, INTELLIGENT FEMALE, 27, seeks kind, reliable professional man with a spiritual side for love, laughter and adventure. Photo please. Box 1595.

> ALLEGEDLY BEAUTIFUL, blonde, successful lady, 40ish, seeks tall, humorous, professional man, to share special moments with. Box 1637.

Often there is use of descriptors such as *intelligent* or *educated* collocating with *professional*:

> FEMALE GRADUATE, 35, fit and fairly attractive, seeks intelligent, professional male, 35+, for friendship, fun and maybe more. Photo appreciated. Box 906.

And there is often mention of *intelligent*, *graduate*, *educated* or *professional* in the self-descript as well. These terms seem to reinforce each other. They belong to a semantic network that conjures up social class and way of life. The attribute *professional* holds within it a set of associations or resonances – in this case relating to lifestyle, intellect and possibly reliability – for the reader. Such a characterisation would concur with gay men's use of the word. The following is a typical ad:

> ATTRACTIVE GAY MAN, 37, would like to meet a single, caring professional man 37+, who's looking for romance and a long lasting friendship. No time wasters please. Photo please. Box 1392.

The collocation 'gay professional' is a typical one. The gay men's ads also contain the terms *educated, intelligent* and *graduate*. I have noted that these terms seem to form a network which, while *professional* is the most common, may be interchangeable. They set off connotations of lifestyle and cultural interests.

It is noticeable that the occurrence of *professional* in the straight men's database of desired other attributes is low, at 2.4 per cent, while it is used at over 19 per cent occurrence in the self-descript. However, *intelligent* is used more frequently for the desired female other (15.3 per cent).

Also of note is the relatively high occurrence of the term *professional* in self-descripts: 14.5 per cent of straight women assume this attribute, as do nearly a quarter of gay men. Hence, while *professional* remains dominantly a male attribute, it is one that straight women and gay men seem to be most aware of.

I have argued that *professional* is a term that is not so much vague, but rather is a word that holds within it information and associations that the reader is invited to unpack and respond to.

3.2 Discussion

An attempt at categorising the other attributes on a semantic basis predictably gave rise to difficulties. Previous attempts at classification of trait names of personality and content analysis have all found clusters of terms that overlap in meaning or strong associative networks or semantic fields (see, for example, Bromley 1977 and Berger and Bradac 1982).

In dividing the most frequent other attributes into semantic categories, I wished to gain another picture of the four groups of advertisers. My categories were ostensibly fairly simple: material attributes (i.e. what is written on a form – gender, age, marital status, nationality, job, sexuality, religion, education), physical attributes (height, hair colour, etc.), mental attributes (e.g. intelligence), affective attributes (about emotions), social and relational attributes (e.g. humour and honesty), and erotic attributes (e.g. passionate). Problematic was the characterisation of, for instance, the terms *feminine* and *masculine* – while they seem to be more essentially physical attributes they may also be regarded as social and relational. Similarly, a word like *lovely* seems to have both a physical and a personality sense. While I have considered *professional* as a kind of synonym of *intelligent* or *educated*, I have categorised it as a material attribute since it refers first to profession. Further problems in classifying attributes involve the term *aware* which on one level relates to the mental, yet also suggests ideas of self-awareness and an interest in personal growth, and thus connotes lifestyle. Notwithstanding the difficulties described, I present the classification I arrived at in Table 9.2.

Table 9.2 Semantic categorisation of attributes

material	physical	mental	affective	social and relational	erotic
professional	attractive	educated	kind	n/s[1]	passionate
young	tall	intelligent	warm	witty	sensual
younger	tallish	bright	sensitive	honest	
solvent	handsome	aware	nice	gsoh[2]	
bi	slim		loving	humorous	
	pretty			sincere	
	beautiful			independent	
	good-looking			non-scene	
	lovely			special	
	feminine				
	masculine				

Notes: 1 *non-smoker.* 2 *good sense of humour.*

The difficulty of trying to pin down the meaning of a number of the attributes commonly employed to describe the desired other adds weight to the argument that personals deliberately employ vague lexis or items that are principally associative in their effect – terms which the reader toys with for fit.

A combination of the information in Tables 9.1 and 9.2 shows certain differences between the four groups. All the groups use adjectives of physical attributes: straight men use *attractive, slim* and *pretty*; straight women use *tall/tallish, handsome* and *attractive*; gay men use *handsome, masculine, tall* and *slim*; and gay women use *feminine, attractive, good-looking* and *lovely* (the ambiguity of which has been noted). In fact, in the frequency bands of my data, gay men and women use a larger range of physical attributes to describe the other than do straight men and women.

Gay women's use of *good-looking* is interesting. *Good-looking* usually collocates with a male-identified noun and its use to describe a woman implies a strong, assertive kind of beauty that is distinct from the heterosexually marked terms *pretty* and *beautiful*.

It is noticeable that straight women use a far higher number of descriptors of social and relational attributes than any of the other groups. In particular,

201

they wish for partners who are *witty*, *humorous* and with a *gsoh*. Attributes like *honest* and *sincere* are common. Straight women also ask for a greater range of mental attributes than the other groups: *intelligent*, *educated* and *aware*.

The database for gay women's ads is small and consequently the lack of material or mental attributes found at this level of frequency would need to be further explored.

4 CONCLUSION

I have argued in this chapter that many of the attributes of the desired other are, in fact, open-ended, in a number of different ways. The term *similar* is ambiguous in its reach and reference: the reader has to work with its co-text in order to decode it. *Attractive* has a positive semantic span, evoking an all-embracing notion of pleasing appearance, to the extent that it has almost been delexicalised in these advertisements. Similar items might be *intelligent* and *interesting*. As a result of this – perhaps genre-specific – delexicalisation, *attractive* allows readers of the ad space to interact with it, supplying their own projected meaning and criteria. *Professional* is interactive in a different way: it sets up resonances in the reader's mind relating to person and lifestyle. Another example might be *non-scene* for gay men and women.

Further, in attempting to make a semantic classification of the other attributes, I have shown the difficulties inherent in terms of overlap and association networks; difficulties that reinforce the idea that the small ad is working as a lexically interactive – and reactive – text.

More in-depth study of how gender and sexuality variables affect lexical usage in the personals would certainly yield interesting results. However, a larger corpus than this one is necessary for such work.

In conclusion, the written personal ad is a deceptively simple, highly interactive text. It contains much in terms of the personal investment of the individual advertiser, who exposes publicly her or his hopes and wishes for a desired partner. The linguistic expression of this takes place through a compressed, carefully selected text using general, catch-all lexis or lexis that sets off resonances in the reader. The reader, in turn, interacts with this lexis, questioning if she or he is the intended/desired audience of the ad.

ACKNOWLEDGEMENTS

I would like to thank Susan Hunston for commenting on a draft of this chapter, Angelika Eder for translating the Erfurt article, and Nancy Blachman for the e-mail information by Esmay. Also, thanks to Fiona Maguire and Huriye Rees for those enjoyable readings of 'the columns' at the cottage.

NOTE

1 All examples have been taken from *Time Out*'s 'Lonely Hearts' between 29th March and 27th July 1995.

REFERENCES

Bazerman, C. (1992) 'Systems of genres and the enactment of social intentions', paper presented to the Rethinking Genre Colloquium, Carleton University, Ottawa, April 1992.

BBC (1994) 'Photo Appreciated', Radio 4.

Berger, C.R. and Bradac, J.C. (1982) *Language and Social Knowledge*, London: Edward Arnold.

Bromley, D.B. (1977) *Personality Description in Ordinary Language*, New York: John Wiley.

Bruthiaux, P. (1994) 'Functional variation in the language of classified ads', *Perspectives: Working Papers of the Department of English*, City Polytechnic of Hong Kong, 6(2): 21–40.

Channell, J. (1994) *Vague Language*, Oxford: Oxford University Press.

Cockburn, J. (1988) *Lonely Hearts: Love Amongst the Small Ads*, London: Simon & Schuster.

Coupland, J. (1996) 'Dating advertisements: discourses of the commodified self', *Discourse and Society* 7(2): 187–207.

Crystal, D. and Davy, D. (1975) *Advanced Conversational English*, London: Longman.

Dyer, G. (1982) *Advertising as Communication*, London and New York: Methuen.

Erfurt, J. (1985) 'Partnerwunsch und Textproduktion: Zur Struktur der Intentionalitat in Heiratsanzeigen', *Zeit für Phonetik, Sprachwiss und Kommunikforsch* 38(3): 309–20.

Esmay, D. (1996) 'Usenet personals: advice for straights', esmay@syndicomm.com.

Hoey, M. (1986) 'The discourse colony: a preliminary study of a neglected discourse type', in *Talking about Text*, Discourse Analysis Monograph no. 13, English Language Research, University of Birmingham, pp. 1–26.

Kennedy, C. (1996) '"La crème de la crème": coercion and corpus change – an example from recruitment advertisements', in H. Coleman and L. Cameron (eds) *Change in Language*, Clevedon, Avon: Multilingual Matters, pp. 28–38.

Mintel Special Report on Single Person Households (1992) Mintel.

Nair, B.R. (1992) 'Gender, genre and generative grammar: deconstructing the matrimonial column', M. Toolan (ed.) *Language, Text and Context: Essays in Stylistics*, London and New York: Routledge, pp. 227–54.

O'Kelly, L. (1994) 'Kiss a few frogs, land a prince', *Observer*, 10 July 1994, p. 23.

10

SPEAKING ITS NAME

The poetic expression of gay male desire

Charles Lambert

1 INTRODUCTION

In this chapter I identify some of the linguistic strategies adopted by gay men poets to establish their sexuality as a central factor governing the expression of desire in texts. In order to do this, I shall examine in section 2 the ways in which the work of gay men poets has been categorised over the past twenty-five years, principally by anthologists. I shall show that a commonly held distinction exists between the notion of a naturalised, implicitly heterosexual, poetic expression of desire and a non-naturalised, explicitly gay poetry. In section 3 I will argue that this distinction creates a dilemma for gay men poets, whose specific sexual identity needs to be forged within a genre that tends to elide it by rendering it universal. I shall then discuss in sections 4 and 5 some of the formal and linguistic features gay men poets have adopted in order to make their sexuality explicit and look at some of the problems that may arise as a result of these ostensibly liberating strategic choices.

2 WHAT IS GAY POETRY?

2.1 Life, theme, language

The first question that needs to be considered is what we mean by 'gay poetry'. A common defining strategy is to locate the gayness of the text in the sexual orientation of its writer. In his introduction to the anthology *Not Love Alone* (1985), for example, Humphries states that 'any poetry by lesbians or gay men can be seen as gay poetry [because] our experience as lesbians or gay men is cognitively different from non-gay women and men' (Humphries 1985: 7). Humphries makes the attractive, common-sense claim that the lived experience of the writer is situated firmly at the heart of the defining process. Gay men poets write gay men's poetry. Gay men's poetry is anything written by a gay male poet. According to this – somewhat tautological – position, our knowledge of a writer's biography plays a determining role in our reading of the text.

This approach to reading flies in the face of the reliance on minute textual analysis propounded by many modern schools of criticism, a reliance whose roots can be traced back to statements such as the following by Austin Warren and René Wellek: 'Whatever the importance of biography . . . it seems dangerous to ascribe to it any real critical importance. No biographical evidence can change or influence critical evaluation' (cited in Daiches 1956: 326). Nevertheless, even the most stubborn adherent to exclusively text-based approaches could not deny that some extra-textual awareness of the life of Oscar Wilde creeps in to trouble the reading of a text such as *The Ballad of Reading Gaol*. Awareness of the writer, in other words, cannot be excluded from the activity of reading, and readers cannot be required to suppress their knowledge of events in the writer's biography in order to satisfy a critical fundamentalism that blatantly contradicts the schematic nature of typical reading practice.

Nevertheless, biography is not recognised by most literary critics as an analytical tool. It is important to understand, however, that this is not why Humphries and others insist on its centrality. Biographical criteria are adopted not to explain the text, but to position the reader. Let us say that I, as a gay reader, want to read poems by other gay men. I assume that those poems will not only meet my needs as a reader of poetry by satisfying my formal/aesthetic/literary requirements, but also that they will tell me something about the experience of being gay. This assumption has nothing to do with subverting any presumed 'discrete existence' the text may possess, since it is incidental to what the text may actually contain. In other words, although it is true to say that the relationship between the writer and the text is obscure – even irretrievable – this does not mean that the reader is not free to regard the sexual identity of the writer as a criterion for choosing one text rather than another.

Perhaps the biggest danger with the use of biography is that one of the tasks of a biographer is to explain the subject in terms that render her or him available to the modern reader. When this happens, the gayness of the writer is levelled out into a synchronic cultural constant spanning such diverse figures as Petronius and Marc Almond. There is nothing new about this ahistoricising tendency, nor is it limited to the biographical approach. Thematic notions of 'gayness' frequently inform anthologists. At the beginning of the twentieth century, Edward Carpenter published *Iolaus*, the first anthology to identify and collect texts with 'the manly love of comrades' as their theme. Carpenter commented:

> I have been struck by the remarkable manner in which the customs of various races and times illustrate each other, and the way in which they point to a solid and enduring body of human sentiment on the subject [of friendship].
>
> (Carpenter 1917: v)

205

Leyland takes a similar line in *Angels of the Lyre* (1975; henceforth *AL*), sub-titled 'A Gay Poetry Anthology'. According to Leyland, 'gay poetry' began with the *Epic of Gilgamesh* and includes the work of writers like Catullus, 'medieval Persian poets', Whitman and Cocteau. These writers also appear in *The Penguin Book of Homosexual Verse* (1983; henceforth *PBHV*), the intro-duction to which begins: 'This is a collection of poems by and about gay people', adding: 'A gay poem . . . either deals with explicitly gay matters or describes an intense and loving relationship between two persons of the same gender' (Coote 1983: 48–9). Although emphasis is placed on the sexual orientation of the writer, something called 'gay matters' (whatever they might be) is also introduced as a gesture towards a non-biographical, the-matic approach.

This approach seeks out some element in the poem that would allow for what might be termed a sexually-orientated reading. The anthology *PBHV* thus also contains texts written by heterosexual poets in which 'an intense and loving relationship between two persons of the same gender' is described.

We have, then, isolated two different strategies for defining gay poetry: one based upon biographically-centred criteria, and the other on thematic principles. As I stated at the beginning of this chapter, however, a third approach exists, based not on who the writer is/was, nor on what the text says, but on the way in which it says it. Later, in section 4, I will show that gay love poetry also – and even primarily – differs from heterosexual love poetry because of the deployment of its lexis, syntax and/or discourse.

But first I wish to look more closely at the way in which language allows or elides the possibility of identifying a text as gay. I shall take the example of a group of poems by W.H. Auden that feature in two British anthologies of poetry.

2.2 Gay poetry, gay language: the case of Auden

The Penguin poetry list contains not only *The Penguin Book of Homosexual Verse*, but also *The Penguin Book of Love Poetry* (1973; henceforth, *PBLP*) edited by John Stallworthy. The following English-language poets appear in both collections – Auden, Byron, Coleridge (Mary), Cowley, Dickinson, Gunn, Housman, Marlowe, Mew, Rochester, Rossetti (Christina), Shake-speare, Spender, Swinburne, Tennyson, Waller, Whitman and Wordsworth. The criterion of selection is thus clearly not biographical. Heterosexual poets – such as Cowley and Wordsworth – seem to be as competent as gay poets – such as Gunn and Whitman – at writing both 'homosexual verse' and 'love poetry'. The fact that the poet is demonstrably gay (or not) is clearly less important than the text itself. Two conclusions might be drawn from this: first, that thematic criteria have been adopted; alternatively, we might speculate that the texts chosen possess linguistic features that determine their reception by the reader.

In order to determine what makes a poem a candidate for one anthology rather than the other, let us look at the choices made from the work of one of the twentieth century's most famous gay poets, W.H. Auden. *PBLP* includes four poems by Auden. Two of them begin in the following way:

> Lay your sleeping head, my love
> human on my faithless arm . . .
>
> > (Auden, 'Lullaby', in *PBLP*: 155)

> Dear, though the night is gone,
> Its dream still haunts today,
> That brought us to a room
> Cavernous, lofty as
> A railway terminus . . .
>
> > (Auden, 'A Dream', in *PBLP*: 233)

It would not be difficult to recreate the 'scene' of these poems, the second text being particularly rich in empirical description. It would, however, be impossible to establish the gender of the loved one, who is explicitly addressed in both poems. In the first text, the initial imperative is replaced by a more general disquisition on the nature of love in which the physical presence (asserted and denied by epithets such as 'dreaming' and 'sleeping') of the desired individual is apostrophised as 'the living creature'. The speaker, far from identifying the beloved, uses a number of lexical strategies to produce a universalised figure. It is interesting, for example, that almost every adjective in the poem ('human', 'thoughtful', 'mortal', 'guilty', 'universal', 'abstract', etc.) belongs to a register of ethics, rather than aesthetics, let alone eroticism. Indeed, the only flicker of physical desire within the text is the 'sensual ecstasy' of the hermit, a figure notorious for sexual sublimation or denial.

The speaker in the second poem also addresses another person without indicating gender. There is nothing unusual about this: three other poems on the same two-page spread in the anthology also address a sexually unspecified 'you'. But it is precisely the fact this is the case that makes the two Auden poems being considered here so consonant with the model of love poetry proposed by the anthology, in which 'love' is universalised into 'normality' at the level of theme.

The other two Auden poems in the collection, in their different ways, point in the same direction. The addressee of 'Fish in the unruffled lakes' (*PBLB*: 161) is concealed until halfway through the third and final stanza. The text adopts a series of distancing strategies by which love is rendered abstract in a similar way to 'Lay your sleeping head, my love'. The final poem by Auden in the collection, 'Song of the Master and Boatswain', shares the thematic concerns of the other three: crudely, the triumph of time over love. It is a ballad, and adopts the persona of a sailor. To a male gay reader, a sailor figure may (or may not) be erotically charged. Auden's speaker both sidesteps and obliquely acknowledges this possibility by referring to long-term (heterosexual) relationships as a cage:

> There Wealthy Meg, the Sailor's Friend,
> And Marion, cow-eyed,
> Opened their arms to me but I
> Refused to step inside;
> I was not looking for a cage
> In which to mope in my old age.

(Auden, 'Song of the Master and Boatswain', in *PBLP*: 342)

The world created by the poem, however, makes it difficult to disengage it from the genre of the ballad, a genre that can only respond to explicitly gay demands when its empirical image-complex is drastically overhauled; by presenting the sailor, for example, as sexually available.

The choice of Auden poems in the anthology confirms the hypothesis advanced above, according to which certain elements in a text – for example, the unmediated use of 'you', the avoidance of signalling gender – make it available to a reading which seeks large generalisations about theme, generalisations which can accommodate, and be accommodated by, heterosexual demands on the text. It does not matter, in other words, that Auden was gay as long as his texts fail to make that explicit.

The single Auden poem in *PBHV*, 'Uncle Henry', is very different, however. It too adopts a persona:

> When the Flyin' Scot
> fills for shootin', I go southward,
> wisin' after coffee, leavin'
> Lady Starkie.
>
> Weady for some fun,
> visit yearly Wome, Damascus,
> in Mowocco look for fwesh a-
> musin' places
>
> Where I'll find a fwend,
> don't you know, a charmin' cweature,
> like a Gweek God and devoted:
> how delicious!
>
> All they have they bwing,
> Abdul, Nino, Manfwed, Kosta:

here's to women for they have such
lovely kiddies!

(Auden, 'Uncle Henry', in *PBHV*: 320)

There is no doubt about the sexual orientation of this persona. Even if the reader were blind to the significance of the diction, lisp and choice of holiday venue, the specific details – and patronising misogyny – of the last two verses make Uncle Henry's preferences perfectly clear.

This is minor Auden and its inclusion in *PBHV* is either a lapse of poetic and political taste on the part of the anthologist, or a recognition that much gay humour is directed at itself. Unlike the texts selected for *PBLP*, this text makes clear the form of sexual desire specific to the speaker. What it fails to do is describe a 'loving relationship' in a way the universalising texts in *PBLP* clearly set out to do.

I now intend to explore two discourse strategies available to lyric poets and describe the dilemma they give rise to for gay writers who wish to resist the universalising tendencies noted in Auden's verse in *PBLP*.

3 WHO AM I TALKING TO?

3.1 Addressing the loved one

In his Introduction to *The Faber Book of Love Poems* (1973), Grigson describes an essential characteristic of the love poem as: 'Always an I and You' (Grigson 1973). Nevertheless, this is not always – or straightforwardly – the case. A poem is a curious kind of discourse: a simple discourse model is usually based on the minimal presence of an addresser and an addressee (Hymes 1964). Poems, however, like epistolary novels, deviate from this model, typically addressing someone other than the reader. As we have seen, the Auden poems from *PBLP* address an unmediated second person. The addresser might even be the historical figure, W.H. Auden, but the explicitly interpolated addressee is certainly not the person now reading the text.

In order to avoid confusing addresser with poet and, to an even greater extent, addressee with reader, we need to work with a more accurate descriptive framework. This would place the poem within a larger discourse model, in which the speaker may or may not represent the poet (probably an irrelevant question, anyway), and in which it is extremely unlikely that the addressee within the poem would be the reader (except, in each case, in a possible single instance). A closer examination of the relations that exist within this model might help us to understand not only how the expression of desire is rendered literary by creating its own 'situation of address', but also how desires themselves might be focused and differentiated.

209

Stallworthy commented that 'the poet in love and celebrating the fact is often writing for an audience of one' (Stallworthy 1973: 26). This assumes that intimacy is created by the use of the second person, since 'an audience of one' would appear to exclude – or diminish the status of – the reader who, at this point, becomes an eavesdropper rather than a participant in the discourse. Stallworthy's position is an acute example of the tendency to naturalise the expression of desire as an expression of intimacy, as though it were really happening.

For an explicitly gay male writer, however, the intimacy of the second person is obtained at the cost of the addressee's invisibility, since in English verb forms do not indicate the gender of the loved one. This explains why anthologists such as Stallworthy can dip unscathed into the work of gay writers, excluding any poem in which the addressee is explicitly of the same sex as the addresser. Over half the poems anthologised in *PBLP* – whether by gay writers or not – are addressed to an unmediated 'you'.

In the past, the genderless second person has been exploited by many gay writers, who have been able to write love poetry directly addressed to persons of unidentifiable sex, thus avoiding exposure as 'inverts', etc. (Housman's poem in *PBLP* is a case in point). This fact confirms the remark made by Foucault: 'Renounce yourself or suffer the penalty of being suppressed; do not appear if you do not want to disappear. Your existence will be maintained only at the cost of your nullification' (Foucault 1979: 84). There are ways to confute positions like that of Stallworthy, however. For example, we can posit as digressive a love poem which, while ostensibly addressing the loved one, acknowledges the presence of the reader in some way. Another way to subvert the naturalising norm in which a lover addresses her or his loved one directly, would be to address the reader explicitly, to produce a text in which the object of desire is being described. However, this strategy also leads to difficulties. Let us look more closely at the problems that arise when the speaker directly addresses the (hypothetical) reader.

3.2 Addressing the reader

Whenever a text dealing with desire is addressed to someone other than the object of that desire, a common practice in gay and straight love poetry, a sort of three-way relationship is installed.

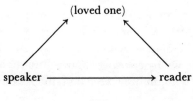

Here, the speaker directly acknowledges the presence of the second person as distinct from the loved one, thus including the reader, in a sense, within the discourse model of the poem. Although passive, and unable to respond, the reader is no longer a mere eavesdropper, but is invited to take part in a relationship with the speaker which, at least pragmatically, is as intimate as the relationship being described. The desired one now becomes the topic of the lover's discourse, rather than a potential addressee, being effectively deprived of the right to respond, to speak. What is established in this kind of strategy is a relationship of equality between speaker and reader in which the third person, the object of desire, is silenced, and rendered 'other'. It might be argued that the reader of the poem is also – necessarily – silenced, and that the use of the second person is no more than formal. Nevertheless, its formal effectiveness depends on the reader's recognition of empirical discourse norms. (For a useful discussion of the way in which the addresser–addressee relationship was maintained, and blurred, in ancient Greek lyric poetry, see Williamson 1995.)

The dilemma faced by gay poetry can be summed up in the following way. If the poet uses the second person to address the loved one directly, other strategies have to be brought into play within the text to ensure that for the reader the addressee has a gender. The argument that 'you' is universal, and should be cherished as such, absorbs individual texts about love into an undifferentiated notion of human desire. If, on the other hand, the text uses a third-person pronoun to make the gender of the desired explicit, the reader inevitably intrudes in the relationship linking the loved one with the lover. The poem becomes a sort of narrative performance in which the desired one is presented as an object. Pragmatically, this is not that different from discussing your partner with your best friend. The intimacy being established by the text is achieved at the expense of the lover.

Indeed, the greater the degree of erotic information or expressed desire within the text, the greater the betrayal of the loved one becomes. A text that succeeds in achieving the explicitness of intimacy actually excludes the loved one, who is reduced to the status of passive victim in a displaced eroticism. The narrative use of the past tense, a common feature of poems in which the loved one is described to a third person, only increases this sense of displacement, since the loved one is not only excluded from the addresser–addressee relationship but is also shifted in time, and is thus no longer there. The following text demonstrates both these features – the use of the third person and the past tense – with their concomitant sense of loss:

> A mean, dark man
> was my lover
> in a mean dark room
> for an evening

till dawn came
we hugged and kissed
ever since, first and last
I have missed

him, his mean dark ways.
(John Wieners, 'How to Cope with This?', in *AL*: 223)

4 RECUPERATING THE SECOND PERSON

While it is true that the unmarked 'you' has allowed gay readers to appropriate 'universal' texts – a phenomenon that reaches well beyond poetry to
inform gay tastes in popular music, opera and so on – many modern gay
poets regard its use as frustrating to a specifically gay agenda. They have
turned to linguistic devices that enable them to employ the second person
without the object of desire within the text disappearing in a non-inflected
genderless blur. These devices, used to rescue the directly addressed loved
one from gender-free oblivion, tend to be lexical. Whereas the British anthology *PBHV*, produced by a mainstream publisher and drawing on English-
language poetry from a period of over five hundred years, continued to show
a bias towards the use of 'he', the texts anthologised in the gay-published *AL*
– all of which were written by modern American male poets belonging to the
generation of, or influenced by, the Beats, the New York School and Black
Mountain College – use 'you' almost as frequently as 'he' in their reference
to the loved one. However, these poets introduce lexical and discourse strategies in order to make the gender of the loved one clear to the reader while
seeking to maintain the immediacy and intimacy of the second-person pronoun. It is to these strategies I now turn.

4.1 Naming and addressing

Perhaps the simplest strategy is to use the lover's name in the title, dedication
or text itself:

> *Rick Asleep*
>
> your naked chest
> breathing
>
> nipples
>
> corks bobbing
>
> on a hot sweet sea
> (Ian Young, 'Rick Asleep', in *AL*: 236)

God love you
Dana my lover
                    (John Wieners, in *AL*: 214)

Alternatively, the speaker might refer to him, as Whitman so often did, by
adopting such gender-specific vocatives as 'Boy', as we can see in the following examples:

Then to the second I step – And who are you my child and darling?
Who are you sweet boy with cheeks yet blooming?
(Whitman 1986: 332, 'A Sight in Camp in the Daybreak Gray and
                                                           Dim')

O tan-faced prairie-boy!
Before you came to camp came many a welcome gift;
Praises and presents came and nourishing food, till at last among the
    recruits,
You came, taciturn, with nothing to give – we but look'd on each
    other,
When lo! more than all the gifts of the world you gave me.
                    (*ibid.*: 344, 'O Tan-Faced Prairie-Boy')

4.2 Itemising the body

Other texts adopt different strategies. In many cases the body of the loved
one, dissected and itemised, becomes a physical presence in the text. In the
following extract, for example:

Delicious form of youth I love your view,
Your feel, your sound, your scent, your taste, your all
                    [...]
Shoulders and armpits savoury with sweat,
Broad breast with nipples, arms and wrists and hands,
Belly and navel, back and shoulder-blades,
Caressing shapely buttocks, groins and hips,
Genitals dangling in a cluster down,
Thick thighs and knees, shins, ankles, calves and feet.
                    (Ralph Chubb, 'The Book of God's Madness,
                                          Part III', in *PBHV*: 300)

This extract, like many of the ones below, contains explicit gender markers.
It refers to 'broad breast' (where *broad* traditionally collocates with *shoulders*)
and to 'genitals dangling in a cluster down', as well as to non-gender-specific
parts of the body which tend to be less erotically charged, such as 'shins,
ankles, calves'. The obsessive taxonomy of the text, in which each segment of
the body is awarded identical status, creates a generalised homoeroticism in

213

which not only the genitals are seen as male. Traditionally feminine lexical items, such as 'breast', 'belly' and 'shapely', are absorbed into a rhythmic, almost monotonous, accumulation of homoerotic desire. What is interesting about this kind of description, of course, is that, despite being ostensibly directed at an addressee within the poem, it flouts all norms of conversational implicature. It is as though the addressee does not know that he has a breast, ankles, and shoulder-blades. Once again, the speaker's 'real' addressee is not the lover, despite his being present in the second person, but the reader. The information provided can only be relevant to the reader, in that it establishes the gender of the loved one and presents the eroticised nature of the relationship between addresser and addressee.

Our second extract also contains an explicit gender marker:

> Like a hot stone your cock weighs on mine, young man,
> and your face has become brutish and congested.
>
> (Paul Goodman, 'Long Lines, Youth and Age',
> in *PBHV*: 326)

This extract exemplifies a more mundane way of establishing the specificity of the desire expressed by the text: its opening reference to 'cock', which is picked up in the second line by the use of 'congested' to describe the lover's face, as though the young man's body were itself a penis. Because of this shift, the word 'cock' acquires a metonymic function, expanding until it represents the loved one as a whole. This is a common feature of pornographic texts. Interestingly, the poem also makes explicit the gender of the addresser, in 'your cock weighs on mine'. If this were not the case, of course, it would be possible in theory to posit a heterosexual woman as the speaker. In practice both these two extracts and the ones that follow are unlikely to have been written by women. One of the reasons for this may be the use of slang.

4.3 Slang, taboo and mixed registers

Gay poetry makes constant use of sexual slang to refer to the bodies and acts that it describes. This language is not only available to gay men. Both gay and straight desire, at least in theory, can be expressed at different levels by employing different registers. The choice to use slang is more likely to reflect the fact that the gay (male) lover and his (male) loved one have the same lexical resources to hand, something that may not be the case when the lover is a man and the loved one a woman. It would be difficult to imagine a male heterosexual poet unproblematically using *cunt* to express desire, yet almost all the texts in *AL* and a substantial number of twentieth-century texts in *PBHV* happily refer to *cocks, asses* and *pricks*, as well as to the activities encoded by the items *blowing, fist-fucking* and *cock-sucking*. These words have an almost performative role to play within the working of the poem since they not only describe the erotics of the text, but serve to enact it. They do this in three ways.

First, and most obviously, they excite their gay readers. Second, taboo words draw on a language that is readily used by gay men to describe gay sexual practices. As they do so, they identify, realise and lend dignity to gay experience, and thus to gay readers. Third, the disruptive incorporation of taboo words into literary language distinguishes the gay text from more traditional desire-motivated literary texts, in which such language is rarely, if ever, used as taboo restrictions still hold. This use of taboo terms may reflect the easier relationship gay men have with gay pornography – less compromised by power imbalances than its heterosexual equivalent. In this case, such words lose their iconoclastic force and become a 'natural' element within the lexis available to the poet as he addresses his peers. On the other hand, slang words may be deliberately adopted – with all their power to disturb – in order to insist on the difference between gay and straight love poetry. Here, their function is that of a consciously liberating discourse.

Poems that take this line often overtly mix register, as we can see in the following example:

> I love your eyes;
> in my dreams
> my breath is on your pants
> fluctuating seashell
> my hand is on the zipper
> starfish opening a shell
> my hand petting your jock
> blue sun warming a salty ocean
>
> (R. Daniel Evans, 'I Praise', in *AL*: 70)

This extract describes a rapid and – in a naturalised reading – bathetic shift from eyes to groin as the addresser prepares to suck the addressee. Although it adopts a register familiar to love poetry, with its use of expressions like 'I love your eyes' and 'dreams' and the construction of an almost mawkishly romantic scenario with such trappings as 'seashell', 'starfish' and 'sun', the juxtaposition in lines 2–3 of two grammatically parallel phrases 'in my dreams'/'on your pants' neatly undercuts the potentially hackneyed romanticism of the opening couplet. The same technique is used in the next two lines, where 'my hand' is implicitly compared and contrasted to 'starfish' and 'the zipper' to 'a shell'. The final couplet resorts once more to the use of structural equivalence: the semantically connected verbs 'petting' and 'warming' oblige a reading in which 'my hand' and 'blue sun', and 'your jock' and a 'salty ocean' are related both grammatically and metaphorically, exploiting the sexual implications of the second phrase to the full.

It might be said that this text is trying to have it both ways (and, in my view, succeeding). On the one hand, the act described is elevated by its insertion into a standard 'love poem' setting. On the other hand, the banality of the setting is being transformed by the presence of unexpected lexical items. The reader is thus positioned as a reader of a lyric belonging to a recognisable tradition of love poetry, but also as a participant in the act of fellatio that is about to take place, alongside – in the place of? – the addresser.

The poem draws on a homoerotically charged lexis, with its use of words such as 'zipper' and 'jock', the latter being a common item in male gay pornography catalogues (e.g. *Young Jocks, Locker Jocks, Coppin' the Jock*). These words serve both to identify the gender of the addresser and to circumscribe the erotics of the poem, since the otherwise undescribed addressee is identified as an athlete (or as having the sexual appeal normally attributed to athletes in the culture of gay pornography). 'Jock', incidentally is an example of the way in which an item of clothing ('jock strap') is transformed into a metonymic reference, or synecdoche, for the person who wears it, in much the same way that 'skirt' has sometimes been used to refer to an individual woman. As with the use of 'cock' in the Goodman extract above, this process diminishes the person to whom it is applied by concentrating on only one aspect, usually sexual, of that person.

Another feature of the poem is that it describes something which is not happening, except 'in my dreams'. We have seen above that when gay poets address the reader directly, adopting the third person to describe the loved one, they run the risk of reducing the latter's role within the discourse, and even of excluding him. In this poem, despite the addressee status of the lover, what is being described is a fantasy. In one sense, the lover is always unlikely to be there at the moment of composition. Nonetheless, a common feature of gay love poetry is that this 'absence' is specifically referred to by the speaker, and incorporated into the text, as in the following example:

> Your body here beside me, warm and still
> this morning, as so many mornings now;
> still webbed in sleep the dusty face; the smooth
> boy's arms are crossed upon the hairless chest;
> only the heart beats the stomach's tender drum;
> the genitals at peace; the strong legs curl
> hunched against mine.
>
> (E.A. Lacey, 'Two Poems for Leobardo', in *AL*: 115)

In this extract the addressee – whose body is carefully itemised as though it were about to be whipped away from beneath the poet's eyes – is sleeping. Lacey continues, exploring the 'absence' still further:

> Surrendered to the other violence of sleep
> you make no protest as my roaming fingers
> explore you, alien continent. I know

> your body in the act, not in repose; I do not
> know you at all.
>
> > (*ibid.*)

4.5 Description, insistence, existence

The four extracts we have just examined come from poems with textual
addressees. However, the same insistence on the physical appearance of the
desired man also features in a high proportion of texts without an identified
addressee, texts in which the loved one is described to a third person:

> Sometimes, when I'm at the beach I see your muse.
> He's tall, goodlooking, has dark blond hair
> and a bulge in the crotch of his blue bikini.
>
> > (R. Daniel Evans, 'Letter to Walt Whitman', in *AL*: 69)

This extract is interesting because of the juxtaposed nature of the detail
offered. The second line contains conventional description, whereas the third
swings the reader down towards the genitals with startling rapidity. In a
sense, the poem uses contrast in a similar way to the other Evans extract,
quoted above, where features of traditional love poetry were folded into an
unadorned description of oral sex. In this case, the framing register is that of
a small ad ('tall, goodlooking, has dark blond hair'), which is less a description of an individual than of a type. It is juxtaposed with a more direct reference – 'bulge in the crotch' – which makes the subtext of that register
explicit. It is as though the need for linguistic identity encouraged this kind
of dogged repetition of explicit, constitutive, reference in order to avoid
nullification within the poem and, by implication, in the world.

AL contains one of the clearest examples of this need: the poem by Allen
Ginsberg, 'Please Master' (*AL*: 88–9). (This appears, significantly, in a
number of other gay anthologies, including *PBHV*.) The poem consists of a
series of requests addressed by the speaker to the Master of the poem's title.
The poem begins:

> Please master can I touch your cheek
> please master can I kneel at your feet
> please master can I loosen your blue pants
> please master can I gaze at your golden-haired belly
> please master can I gently take down your shorts
> please master can I have your thighs bare to my eyes
> please master can I take off my clothes below your chair
> please master can I kiss your ankles and soul

At the level of 'scene', the text appears to be situated in a gay sado-masochistic relationship. This can be established not only by the semantics of the poem (where the gender of the speaker is established by references to his 'bald hairy skull' and 'balls'), but also by the insistence and nature of the requests being made. The speaker is asking permission to perform acts which do not require permission outside the ritualised eroticism of SM.

In terms of voice, the text thickens. Although the empirical scene requires a masochistic speaker, the poem negotiates a series of different registers. The first few lines reveal the use of a religious register, neatly playing on the biblical use of the term 'master' to refer to Christ. 'Can I kneel at your feet' appears early enough in the poem for its full ambiguity to be felt. It is still not clear whether we are dealing with a master of the spirit or of sexual desire. 'Bare to my eyes' also suggests the unveiling of some religious icon. Finally, 'your ankles and soul' explicitly identifies the Master's role as both spiritual and physical. Although a long-standing literary, spiritual and often mystical, tradition has consciously blurred distinctions between the soul and body, providing Ginsberg with a context in which to operate, other lexical elements within the poem – notably taboo words – move beyond the traditional deployment of eroticism in a religious context.

The second register deployed by the poem is explicitly sexual. One of the most striking aspects of male gay pornographic texts is their inventive multiplication of terms used to describe the sexual organs. They not only adopt existing taboo words, but are endlessly resourceful in the minting of new expressions. In the first few chapters of the gay porn novel *Slaves of the Empire* (Travis 1992), for example, the following terms are used to describe the penis: 'shaft', 'long, pale sword of flesh', 'massive pole of flesh', 'mallet', 'rod', 'staff' and 'tower of flesh'. As Ginsberg's poem develops, the master's penis is overlexicalised in a similar way: 'thick shaft', 'prick-heart', 'dumb hardness', 'hot prick barrel', 'shaft', 'cock head', 'droor thing', 'prick trunk', 'sword', 'self' and 'heat-rood'.However, although many of the items used by Ginsberg belong to the register of commercial pornography ('hot', 'prick', 'shaft', 'sword', 'cock head'), the poem also returns explicitly to the lexis of the church in its use of 'self' and 'rood'. According to the *Shorter Oxford English Dictionary* (1973), the secondary meaning of 'rood' is '(local) a linear measure . . . varying from six to eight yards' – giving a whole new dimension to size-queen. However, the text clearly expects the item 'rood' to evoke primarily spiritual associations.

The kind of overlexicalisation we have here is not mere poetic proliferation, but a deliberate attempt to rub the reader's face into the burgeoning physicality of what is being described.

Master grease my balls and hairmouth with sweet vaselines
please master stroke your shaft with white creams
please master touch your cock head to my wrinkled self-hole

please master push it in gently, your elbows enwrapped round my breast
your arms passing down to my belly, my penis you touch w/ your fingers
please master shove it in me a little, a little, a little
please master sink your droor thing down my behind

In this passage too, the repetition of 'please master' becomes a kind of incantation in which noun phrases like 'sweet vaselines' produce startling juxtapositions: one might expect 'sweet' to collocate with 'unguents' or 'perfumes', rather than 'vaselines' (and even the plural lends strangeness to the term). The adverb 'gently' also introduces a perhaps surprising element into an increasingly violent text. In fact, the poem contains many related words and phrases such as 'blond soft fur', 'rosy asshole', 'delicate flesh', 'the softness the softness' and 'body of tenderness'.

Master drive down till it hurts me the softness the
Softness please master make love to my ass, give body to center, & fuck
   me for good like a girl,
tenderly clasp me please master I take me to thee
& drive in my belly your selfsame sweet heat-rood
you fingered in solitude

These expressions inevitably, in this context, recall the traditional notion of 'gentle' Jesus, a link that is emphasised by 'I take me to thee'. They contrast dramatically with the kind of language that sustains the original naturalising reading of the text as the description of an SM encounter: terms like 'rough', 'fuck me more violent', 'plunge', 'brutal hard lash' and 'bamming it in', which feature in the final part of the poem. Although softness and tenderness may actually play a significant part in SM relations, they are rare in pornographic accounts of SM encounters. The contrast in this poem, which recalls the contrast between 'tender' and 'strong' in the Lacey poem considered above, thus problematises the reader's attempts to integrate, or identify, the poem with readily available frames.

The poem is neither an SM encounter, nor a piece of pornography, nor a mystic text, although it adopts the lexis and/or discourse structure of all three to varying degrees. Even though its use of taboo items might seem to relate the poem to the register of pornography in general, what makes these terms particularly available to gay poetry is the need to make space within traditional lyric discourse for the expression of an otherwise invisible, because undifferentiated, desire. Overlexicalising taboo items in literary discourse is one way of doing this.

Ginsberg's poem draws on, and adapts, the 'unpoetic' language of sexually explicit slang. The laurel wreath for lexical invention, however, must go to a text by James Mitchell, entitled 'Gay Epiphany', in *PBHV*. In this poem, a fine example of high camp, the genital apparatus of an otherwise unidentified 'Boy' receives a hymn of praise in which specialised medical vocabulary is folded into the kind of traditional list-based paean that dates back to the *Song of Songs*. The poem begins:

> o sperm, testes, paradidymus! o scrotum, septum, and rectum!
> o penis! o prepuce, urethra!

> o prostate gland! o Dartos muscle! o spermatid and spermatocyte!
> (James Mitchell, in PBHV: 330–1)

Mitchell's poem is an effective comment on the final unavailability of an unmarked sexual lexis. By resorting to the language of medicine to celebrate sexuality, he reveals the inadequacy not only of these terms, but of any other terms on offer. Language, whether obscene or technical, remains tainted.

5 CONCLUSION: RUNNING RISKS

This chapter is concerned with insistence, with the struggle against invisibility, and with the identifiable linguistic and social space that certain strategies of insistence are able to create. Nothing prevents a gay poet from writing about desire in a less explicit way. However, the texts we looked at in section 4 have made a different choice. They draw attention to their sexuality through a series of lexical and discourse strategies.

They may specify the loved one's gender by using a third person 'he' in order to narrate their desire directly to the reader. Alternatively, they may decide to retain the intimacy of the second person 'you' and to specify the gender of the loved one in some non-pronominal way: by naming him in the title, text or dedication, or by addressing him with a gender-specific term such as 'Boy'; by describing his body, often in considerable detail; or by adopting recognisably gay registers either entirely or in juxtaposition with other, more traditionally appropriate, registers. As a result, they oblige the reader to acknowledge the presence of gay desire. They resist the kind of universalising, ahistorical reading in which love is simply absorbed into a cultural absolutism – a reading which reflects neither our own experience as gay readers nor our understanding, as gay men, of the world. (For an examination of the strategies adopted by some contemporary lesbian poets to achieve similar ends, see York 1995.)

In the course of rendering gay desire visible, however, gay poetry runs two risks. First, where the speaker describes or narrates the object of his desire by directly addressing the reader, the displacement of the loved one inevitably entails a displacement of the intimacy the speaker wishes to convey. As a new intimacy is created between speaker and reader, the loved one is objectified and rendered 'other'. He is finally embodied as an absence, as something wanted in both senses of the word.

The second risk involves the compensatory strategies considered above, which are employed to define the second person, or addressee of the poem, as belonging to the same gender as the addresser. We have seen that these also tend to reduce the addressee to the status of object, either by insisting on his physicality through bodily description and lexical proliferation, or by providing the reader with the clues he or she needs to identify the work as gay. Once again, the reader's gain is the loved one's loss as, implicitly, the poem moves the object of desire to one side in order to acknowledge the constant overbearing presence of the eavesdropper.

These risks are probably as inevitable as the need to run them. After all, to say that strategies of displacement are a central feature of explicit gay writing is merely to recognise that language itself displaces gay experience by marginalising it, by forcing it not merely to speak, but to shout, its name. The 'other' of the gay poem, finally, is not only the individual loved one. It is also the very existence of gay desire, referred to, described, embodied and sometimes even excluded, from the discourse whose subject it is.

REFERENCES

Carpenter, E. (1917) *Iolaus*, New York: Pagan Press.
Coote, S. (ed.) (1983) *The Penguin Book of Homosexual Verse*, Harmondsworth: Penguin.
Daiches, D. (1956) *Critical Approaches to Literature*, London: Longmans, Green.
Foucault, M. (1979) *The History of Sexuality*, vol.1, Harmondsworth: Penguin.
Grigson, G. (ed.) (1973) *The Faber Book of Love Poems*, London: Faber & Faber.
Humphries, M. (ed.) (1985) *Not Love Alone*, London: GMP.
Hymes, D. (1964) 'Towards ethnographies of communication: the analysis of communicative events', in P.P. Giglioli (ed.) *Language and Social Context*, Harmondsworth: Penguin.
Leyland, W. (ed.) (1975) *Angels of the Lyre. A Gay Poetry Anthology*, San Francisco: Panjandrum Press/Gay Sunshine Press.
Stallworthy, J. (ed.) (1973) *The Penguin Book of Love Poetry*, Harmondsworth: Penguin.
Travis, A. (1992) *Slaves of the Empire*, New York: Masquerade Books.
Whitman, Walt (1986) *The Complete Poems*, ed. Francis Murphy, Harmondsworth: Penguin.
Williamson, Margaret (1995) 'Sappho and the other woman', in Sara Mills (ed.) *Language and Gender: Interdisciplinary Perspectives*, London: Longman.
York, Liz (1995) 'Constructing a lesbian poetic for survival', in Sara Mills (ed.) *Language and Gender: Interdisciplinary Perspectives*, London: Longman.

11

DISCURSIVE CATEGORIES AND DESIRE

Feminists negotiating relationships

Sara Mills and Christine A. White

1 INTRODUCTION

This chapter analyses the way that feminists negotiate the discursive categories of sexuality and desire to which they are assigned or which they consciously adopt. We have chosen to focus primarily on lesbian and heterosexual feminists, since we consider that feminists are, in general, very aware of the constraints of living under heteropatriarchy, and have analysed the problems entailed in identifying oneself within a sexual category, given the debates within feminist theory of the last five years (see *Feminist Review* 31 for an overview).[1] We aim to challenge the current polarised view that heterosexual feminists feel guilt and discomfort with their categorisation as heterosexual, whereas lesbian feminists embrace the way that they have been categorised and feel comfortable within that categorisation.

Rather than posing lesbianism as a magical zone, where subjects can be truly themselves and express their sexual natures outside the confines of institutionalised heterosexuality – as some lesbians and heterosexuals have tended to do –, we argue instead that the process of categorisation is a difficult negotiation which all subjects engage in, and that subjects learn to experience and express their desires within and against the constraints of these categories. The negotiating process is different for heterosexuals and lesbians, given that many feminist lesbians choose to describe themselves as such as a political choice, whilst for feminist heterosexuals naming oneself is less of an issue, because of the normalisation of heterosexuality, and because of the absence of institutional and social discrimination against heterosexuals.

We wish to question the notion that lesbians necessarily feel more comfortable than heterosexuals with the labels that they have been given or which they have chosen for themselves. We tested out some of these ideas through discussions with two groups of feminists, heterosexual and lesbian, in order to examine the way that feminists inhabit the categories used to describe them, and try to come to some conclusions about the process of the construction of desire within the constraints of discursive categories.

We organised two sets of discussions: one set, largely heterosexual, took place in Loughborough University's Feminist Research Group; and the other consisted of discussions with lesbians and bisexuals in three groups: the Lesbian and Gay societies at Goldsmith's College, London University; the GLINT (Gays and Lesbians in Theatre) group; and teachers in an inner-city school. All members of the groups were largely white, European, working- and middle-class. The sessions were recorded and followed up with a questionnaire (see Appendix). Since we aimed to analyse the way that feminists inhabit categories, it was important for us to explore this in the discussion groups; we therefore intersperse reference to these discussions throughout the theoretical sections of the chapter.

2 THE WHITE HETEROSEXUAL FEMINIST SUBJECT

There has been a noticeable shift in recent feminist politics: those in the so-called mainstream grouping have been considering the politics of their seemingly neutral position (Mills *et al.*, forthcoming). For some time, black feminists have confronted white women with the implicit racism of their universalising theorising which implicitly excludes black women from the category 'women'. White feminists have begun to analyse 'race' as a variable which constructs their own sense of identity, rather than assuming that 'race' concerns only black feminists (see Ware 1992; Frankenberg 1993a and 1993b; Wetherell and Potter 1992; McClintock 1995). This critical work has led to many white feminists beginning to consider both the material benefits which accrue to them on account of their whiteness, and their own unthinking participation in the perpetuation of racism at an institutional and a personal level.

This critique of white feminism's universalising tendencies has led to constructive work by black and white feminists alike on the nature of the problem of identity categories. For example, June Jordan states:

> We have been organising on the basis of identity, around immutable attributes of gender, race and class for a long time and it doesn't seem to have worked . . . I think there is something deficient in the thinking on the part of anybody who proposes either gender identity politics or race identity politics as sufficient, because every single one of us is more than whatever race we represent or embody and more than whatever gender category we fall into.
>
> (Jordan, cited in Ware 1992: 249)

What Jordan is arguing here is that a focus on race or gender as defining categories for our sense of self is insufficient. Race is always a gendered and classed category, and gender is always racial and classed. Anne McClintock has argued that it is precisely this superimposition and interlinking of categories that we should be analysing rather than assuming that gender, class or race are:

> distinct realms of experience, existing in splendid isolation from each other; they (cannot) be simply yoked together retrospectively like armature of Lego. Rather, they come into existence in and through relation to each other – if in contradictory and conflictual ways.
>
> (McClintock 1995: 5)

This discussion of 'race' and white feminism bears interesting analogies to some of the theoretical work currently being undertaken by lesbian feminists, who have consistently critiqued white heterosexual feminism for its failure to consider questions of sexual orientation in formulating its theoretical frameworks concerning women in general. They have also criticised the tendency to assume that heterosexuality is the norm from which lesbianism is the deviation (Bell *et al.* 1994).

Thus, to some extent, mainstream feminists have moved away from the tendency to make universal statements about women in general based on their own experience and the experience of those like them, arguing that these have tended to focus on stereotypical white, heterosexual and middle-class experience (Butler 1990; Fuss 1989; Wittig 1992). Lesbian theorists have demonstrated that the positing of a feminist subject in order to gain visibility and representation for women as a whole often results in only a particular type of woman being represented. Monique Wittig in particular argues that lesbians cannot be classified as women at all, because the term 'women' implies sexual and social servitude to men; since lesbians reject this relation to males, they cannot therefore be women. However, whilst this destabilises the category 'women' and foregrounds its assumed heterosexual nature, Stevi Jackson contends that it is necessary to analyse 'woman/ women' in more materialist terms, seeing it as a social rather than a natural category:

> Lesbianism (as well as heterosexuality) by virtue of its location in relation to patriarchal heterosexuality . . . has a real social existence. This does not mean, as Wittig would have it, that lesbians are not women – we are all defined by our gender and there is no escaping the patriarchal hierarchy within which we are positioned as women.
>
> (Jackson 1995:20)

This critical work has also entailed some destabilising of the category 'lesbian', particularly in the light of Queer theory; as Lynne Pearce argues, writing about the term 'lesbian' in the context of literary criticism:

> Although there have been some persuasive attempts to argue for the strategic preservation of the category 'lesbian', I have little doubt that

the radical de-centring of the term will make it increasingly difficult to identify a body of literature and/or criticism under that heading.

(Pearce 1996)

Perhaps Queer *will* be everywhere in the future, making this analysis of categorisation unnecessary, but at present, it seems rather ironic that, just at the moment when the term 'lesbian' is one which can be inhabited with pride and one which can be viewed with envy by some heterosexual feminists, the term itself is called into question.

Perhaps rather than simply assuming that categories such as 'heterosexual' and 'lesbian' have disappeared, we might consider Judith Butler's notion of the performativity of gender, which has been at the root of much of this work on the instability of sexed identity. She states quite clearly that

> if I were to argue that genders are performative, that could mean that I thought that one woke up in the morning, perused the closet . . . donned that gender for the day, and then restored the garment to its place at night. Such a wilful and instrumental subject, one who decides on its gender is clearly not its gender from the start and fails to realise that its existence is already decided *by* gender.

(Butler 1993: x)

Thus the destabilising of identity which the notion of performativity entails does not mean that the categories 'lesbian', 'heterosexual' and 'bisexual' are meaningless, nor does it imply that we can simply choose to belong to whatever sexual category we desire; rather, it means that the process of being gendered is one which is achieved only through the 'ritualised repetition of norms' (*ibid.*). Butler goes on to say: 'that this reiteration is necessary is a sign that materialisation is never quite complete, that bodies never quite comply with the norms by which their materialisation is impelled' (Butler 1993: 2). Thus, critical analysis of the process whereby gender identities are formed does not mean that lesbians and heterosexuals do not exist, but simply that we are forced to be more aware of the process through which those identities are precariously achieved. Discomfort within the categorisation within which one is positioned is therefore the norm.

3 DISIDENTIFICATION AND FEMINIST HETEROSEXUALITY

Basing our work on this critical material, we would like to consider the possibility of feminists negotiating in productive ways with the identity categories, 'heterosexual' and 'lesbian'. We are aware here that the 'desire for' identity is more important than proving or disproving its existence. But this 'desire for' an identity might be more complex than at first envisioned, for subjects want not simply any position which seems close to their own desires, pleasures and experiences, but rather an identity category which is positively viewed by others. For feminists, this can mean that they want to inhabit a category which has some general approval, or that they want to inhabit a category oppositionally, that is, to use Foucault's term, to *disidentify* with the category.

This will have two results: first, it will clear a theoretical space for hetero-sexuality to be analysed and inhabited in a process of disidentification. Second, it will be possible to examine some of the difficulties which lesbians experience when trying to negotiate with identity categories. Thus, rather than guilt being induced in heterosexual feminists because they are not lesbian, a form of political heterosexuality could be developed, which might be termed feminist-heterosexual. This cannot be the same type of political identity category as that developed by lesbians, since heterosexuality has a different institutional status, and a different set of histories, but it may be possible to map out a space within heterosexuality from which feminists can make choices about the type of heterosexual practices they will 'buy into', at the same time as resisting oppressive practices operating beyond hetero-sexuality (Spraggs 1994). Dorothy Smith has shown that discursive cate-gories should be more usefully thought of as a set of practices which are negotiated, rather than fixed identity positions (Smith 1990).

Celia Kitzinger and Sue Wilkinson's (1993) work on heterosexuality is an important step in beginning to analyse the often unacknowledged benefits that heterosexuality brings, which ultimately are at the expense of lesbians. For example, Mary Crawford, one of the heterosexuals interviewed by Kitzinger and Wilkinson, notes that she is not treated in the same way as a lesbian is:

> No one hassles me at my child's school, at the doctor's office or at work. No one tells me I'm an unfit mother. Because I am legally married, my job provides health care benefits for my partner and family . . . Wills and mortgages, taxes and auto insurance, retirement pensions and school enrolment for the children – all the ways that indi-viduals ordinarily interface with social structures – are designed to fit people like me and my partner.
>
> (Crawford, in Kitzinger and Wilkinson 1993: 10)

A feminist heterosexual might be one who would not simply wear a red ribbon to show token support on issues of AIDS awareness, but who would actively campaign on issues of gay and lesbian rights, and who would inter-rogate and challenge the privileges which heterosexuality confers (for example, in pension rights, immigration laws, child-custody disputes, job security and so on).

However, it is not enough to carve out a disidentified political position for heterosexual feminism, since this would seem to bring the focus back onto heterosexuality again. We would rather focus at the same time on the constraints also operating on lesbians when they identify themselves, and suggest that a similar process of disidentification is at work even though this is often not acknowledged for political reasons. For as one of our lesbian respondents argued:

I resolved some time ago that I would never write on sexuality per se. This is doubtless to do with my own ambiguities (my present inclination is to retreat back into whatever closets are available). What I couldn't stand about the lesbians I have met recently was how it had become not only an 'identity' but a life-project – like one's house was full of lesbian kitsch and art and culture – and this was the centre of everything all day long!

This sense of lesbian disidentification is something which Butler sees as essential:

Although the political discourses that mobilise identity categories tend to cultivate identifications in the service of a political goal, it may be that the persistence of disidentification is equally crucial to the re-articulation of democratic contestation. Indeed it may be precisely through those practices which underscore disidentification with those regulatory norms by which sexual difference is materialised that both feminist and queer politics are mobilised. Such conceptual disidentifications can facilitate a reconceptualisation of which bodies matter, and which bodies are yet to emerge as critical matters of concern.

(Butler 1993: 4)

Some theorists have discussed the possibility of avoiding the binary split of heterosexual/homosexual by the use of the term 'lesbian continuum' whereby women who identify as feminist and are heterosexual can still assert some solidarity with lesbians (Rich 1980). This is a position which many feminist heterosexuals initially welcomed, because it enabled them to continue with their heterosexual relations and yet to foreground the importance of their relationships with other women. As Kitzinger and Wilkinson (1993) point out, whilst this does have some benefit since it marks out a political position from which heterosexuals can critique institutional heterosexuality and politically align themselves with lesbians, it nevertheless may result in the erasure of the specificity of lesbianism, and mask much of the discrimination suffered by lesbians.

Perhaps what is more useful than emptying out the significance of certain categories is the critical analysis of heterosexuality in order to differentiate between a range of different practices. We need to distinguish between: first, having sexual relationships with males; second, the formalising of that sexual practice to constitute an identity, thus entering into narrative schemata for the 'progression' of such relationships, what we will call the narrative of conventional heterosexuality; and third, institutional heterosexuality which is the set of varied discourses which implicitly cast heterosexuality as the norm and make 'ordinary' the privileges which heterosexual women enjoy. By distinguishing between these three elements it will be possible for us to emphasise that these choices about sexuality are more than merely sexual choices (Jackson 1995).

We feel the need to make these distinctions because it is clear that heterosexuality as a practice has changed greatly. Whilst it is still the case that many heterosexual women do remain in relationships which are sexually and physically abusive and do suffer great oppression at the hands of their 'lovers' and husbands, it is also true that far fewer women tolerate such treatment. As Lynne Pearce and Jackie Stacey argue, because of feminist work and other factors, heterosexual relationships have come under pressure and have been transformed as a result (Pearce and Stacey 1995: 35). Thus, many of the women interviewed by Shere Hite had much higher expectations of their relationships with men, especially concerning equal share of housework and concern for the workings of the relationship; these women also stressed that they would be more willing to leave their husbands/partners if their relationship did not meet their expectations (Hite 1987; Ehrenreich et al. 1986).

Whilst there has been a significant shift in what women expect from heterosexual relations, there has also been a change in the way that heterosexuality as a whole is viewed by feminists. Many heterosexual feminists feel that their choice of sexuality is under critical scrutiny. Three reasons can be identified for this. First, choosing a male lover – when they could have (should have) chosen a female one – means that the progress of heterosexuality as an institution that oppresses women continues unchecked. Second, having a male lover is not seen as very hip. For example, many of our female students see the choice of a female lover as something that you simply have to do, as a certain way of presenting oneself. This is not about being gay or even being bisexual, but just part of one's image – streetwise, competent and in control. Having relationships with males does not have this same sense of adding to one's street credibility. (However, whilst heterosexuals may see an occasional lesbian relationship as an attractive option, one lesbian respondent noted that there was no tangible gain in the wider world for lesbians, for example, no tax benefits, no security, no funeral rights.) Third, the choice of a male lover is under critical scrutiny because it entails the progression along the romance narrative pathway resulting in choices being made in relation to having children. Because of a great deal of early feminist work, children are often not seen in a positive light, and are viewed as problems in relation to feminist self-fulfilment (Freely 1995).

228

The sense of unease which many heterosexual feminists experience when discussing their own sexual identity has resulted from lesbian and gay theorising; in a sense, 'heterosexuality' was simultaneously created and destabilised when homosexuality and lesbianism were asserted as positive sexual choices and ways of life. As Ward has shown we can think of heterosexuality as having been invented in the late nineteenth century, by Victorian sexual science, as 'a touchstone . . . to mark the thoroughfare from which . . . bizarre enormities diverged' (Ward 1987: 146). But Ward goes on to show that the currency of the term *heterosexual* is in fact much more recent, and developed only after the 1960s when 'homosexuality, already unique among the perversions in manifesting a viable subculture, proclaimed for itself the legitimacy reserved for married love' (*ibid.*). 'Heterosexuality' presents itself as having no nature, in stark contrast to homosexuality and lesbianism which are simply socially constructed; however, under pressure from gay and lesbian theorising – and from the sheer numbers and visibility of lesbians and homosexuals – heterosexuality has become the category which now feels most socially constructed and most unstable, at least for feminist theorists.[2] As one heterosexual respondent said:

> For many women (both feminist and non) much of life appears to be a balancing act between resistance and compromise. For many feminists, however, room for resistance appears to be always available in some form. How, or if this can be measured and in what form I'm not sure. I'm not sure that all women don't constantly resist/revise definitions of themselves.

The responses from the heterosexual discussion group we set up are in stark contrast to work done by Celia Kitzinger and Sue Wilkinson (1993). They sent a questionnaire to a large number of heterosexual women and asked them to describe the impact their sexuality had made on their feminism. The women they interview are overpoweringly defensive, and Kitzinger and Wilkinson describe the responses as 'a long grey stream of heterosexual misery'. In one of our lesbian discussion groups, however, one respondent remarked that there was a strong possibility that:

> had the individuals surveyed included the general public, as opposed to a highly educated bracket of workers, to identify oneself as heterosexual would have been seen as an extremely positive category, rather than be defined as the 'perverse' and 'deviant' lesbian or bisexual.

In order to examine the process whereby feminists negotiate with identity categories, we will now examine prototypes, narrative schemata and naming (section 4). We will then, in section 5, consider the issues entailed by the question of dominance and passivity within relationships and, finally, examine the function of the parodic acting out of identity categories.

4 NEGOTIATING WITH IDENTITY CATEGORIES

4.1 Prototypical categories

George Lakoff's work on categorisation and thought has revealed that categories do not simply represent 'reality' but that they are themselves constructed in a way which Lakoff terms 'imaginative', that is, they contain an element of negotiation and play between bodily experience, cognitive devices such as metaphor and metonymy and the categories themselves. Further, he has shown, drawing on Eleanor Rosch's work on prototypes, that within categories there are so-called 'best examples' which stand for elements within that category, unless their use is questioned (Lakoff 1987: 7). Lakoff states: 'prototypes act as cognitive reference points of various sorts and form the basis for inferences' (*ibid.*: 45) – that is, unless we distance ourselves from those presumptions.

Lakoff's work is important in much the same way that Foucault's is helpful here, because he stresses the way that the existence of categories encourages us to assume that there are pre-given differences between members of two category groups, as he states: 'Since we understand the world not only in terms of individual things but also in terms of categories of things, we tend to attribute a real existence to those categories' (*ibid.*: 9).

4.1.1 Heterosexual prototypes

Heterosexuality is a category which contains a diverse range of behaviours and emotions but which has as its 'best example' or prototype – standing for heterosexuality as a whole – a very conservative set of practices to which most heterosexual feminists do not subscribe (Langford 1995). Many of the respondents from the heterosexual group stated that, whilst they felt quite comfortable within certain circles of friends to be assumed to be heterosexual, often in the 'outside world' they were treated as prototypical heterosexuals with assumed power-differentiated relationships with men. Most of them wanted to make a clear distinction between institutionalised heterosexuality, which they felt that they were constantly at odds with, and their own negotiation of heterosexuality within their relationships with males. Several mentioned the difficulties that they had trying to combat the assumption that they were married and found it difficult to refuse constantly to be categorised as 'Mrs' or 'Miss'. Others described their decisions not to marry or not to be married within the conventional frameworks as a way of working against assumptions of stereotypical heterosexuality. Certain respondents remarked how they felt it necessary not to act as a couple; for example, one stated that by not going to parties and so on with her husband, she felt that she was resisting stereotypical versions of heterosexuality.

Many of the group recounted anecdotes about not being taken seriously because they were with males. When, for example, a woman was hiring a car and was accompanied by a male, it was assumed that the male was in fact hiring the car, even though the female was paying for it. One lesbian in this group told how once she was in a garage buying petrol accompanied by a male friend and realised that to the outside world she was categorised as being in a heterosexual relationship with her friend; she described the fury that she felt at the assumptions which were being made about her.

Within the group, many remarked that they were aware of the benefits they accrued by being heterosexual, but they also mentioned the potential problems that they encountered from the assumption that they were or should be a particular type of heterosexual; they talked of the difficulty of 'others expecting you to have children, be domestic, to not manage your own finances, etc.' Whilst it is possible to resist heterosexual categories and ways of living, one person noted that this did not seem a very visible resistance, particularly when parents and relatives made assumptions about her and her partner simply on the basis of their being heterosexual. She also mentioned that she felt the pressure of the conventional narrative of heterosexual relationships, because she and her partner do not live together, and there is an assumption that if the relationship is serious it will 'progress'. Indeed, one of the group mentioned that she found her feminism to be always at odds with her heterosexuality in personal and political terms. Another mentioned that she felt 'very unhappy with the assumptions by non-feminists that my heterosexuality somehow cancels out my feminism', or that her 'nice' feminism is being set against 'nasty' lesbian feminism in some way.

4.1.2 Lesbian prototypes

Lesbians also measure themselves against stereotypes of what they assume certain types of lesbian really are. That is not to suggest that these prototypes are equally as conservative as the ones in play for heterosexuals, but that they are no less effective in forcing subjects to evaluate their own position within a category in relation to a proposed norm.

It is clear that there are a range of prototypical notions of what lesbians are. In *Sexual Inversion* (Ellis 1897) lesbians are defined as transvestites who cross-dress as 'butches' in order to define themselves more visibly as 'genuine' lesbians. This form of blatant display is a reaction to the dominant culture which forces women into heterosexual patterns, but all lesbians do not see themselves in this way or define themselves against a heterosexual norm. Feminist lesbians are as diverse a group as any other and balk at being grouped together because of some perceived shared life experience. The reason for this grouping is the dominant culture's hatred of perceived sexual deviance. The groups themselves have little choice as to how they are viewed when the media present them in this way. As Phyllis Nagy (1991) states about lesbian characters in the theatre:

> It is much easier for audiences – both straight and gay – to accept lesbian and gay characters who obsess and fret about gayness as an issue (and who, as a result, enable an audience to feel they are on solid ground) than it is to accept lesbians and gays who sometimes misbehave, and do not present themselves as sexless, vaguely martyred but politically hip individuals who manipulate empathy and equate it with victimhood.
>
> (Nagy, cited in Payne 1994: 1)

A further lesbian prototype is that all lesbians are radical. Lesbianism, by its very existence, is a challenge to heterosexuality, as Dolan comments:

> The lesbian subject is in a position to denaturalise dominant codes by signifying an existence that belies the entire structure of heterosexual culture and its representation . . . The lesbian is a refusor of culturally imposed gender ideology, who confounds representation based on sexual difference and on compulsory heterosexuality.
>
> (Dolan 1988: 116)

However, at the same time, most lesbians in the groups we interviewed expressed concern with such generalisations of a collective identity. They preferred to highlight an awareness of the differences within a category.

4.2 Narrative schemata

A study of narrative schemata can help us to consider the way that narratives seem to structure the forms that sexual and emotional desires take. Schema theory developed in studies of artificial intelligence; there are presumed to be models or narrative formats which individuals use to structure their thought and action sequences, and these sequences are entailed to some extent with the use of categories (see Brown and Yule 1983; Mills 1994a; Semino 1995). The way schema theory is conventionally viewed is that 'we make sense of new experiences . . . by relating the current input to existing mental representations of entities and situations that we have experienced in the past' (Semino 1995: 82).

Where schema theory can be used by feminists in productive ways is when we attempt to trace the way that it is not simply our own experiences in the past which condition the contents of the schemata enlisted, but that there are preconstructed schemata with which we engage in the construction of our own narratives (Mills 1995). Let us take the classic example of a narrative schema: the restaurant schema or scenario. This typically includes opening moves such as 'entering the restaurant', 'being greeted by the waiter/

manager', 'asking for a table', and further moves such as 'being given a menu', 'ordering', 'consuming' and 'paying for food', all within the constraints of behaviour considered appropriate in restaurants. But, whilst this is a useful general framework for considering the way that people negotiate stereotypical action sequences, there is a sense in which it is too simplistic to deal with the complexity of the range of schemata entailed by the use of the categories 'heterosexual', 'lesbian' and 'bisexual'.

However, Semino has stressed that narrative schemata are not rigid structures; rather, 'schemata are dynamic and flexible structures that are not just imposed on incoming information, but are constantly being changed and adapted in the light of new experiences' (Semino 1995: 83). Indeed, one of the integral elements of schemata is the notion of 'schema refreshment', the disruption of conventional narrative schemata by new information resulting in 'the destabilising of old schemata, the creation of new ones and new links being made between existing schemata' (Cook 1990, cited in Semino 1995). It is this sense of acting *on* discursive categories as well as *within* them which we would like to retain here; indeed, this disruption of schemata is a necessary part of our negotiation with identities, in order for us to recognise these categories as useful and real rather than as simple roles that we play. It is precisely this process of schema refreshment which is currently under way with the narrative schemata of heterosexual and lesbian relations and identities, and which is setting out new disidentified positions.

Schema theory can be useful in considering heterosexual and lesbian relations since, for example, as we mentioned above, in a heterosexual relation, there is a constant pressure to progress along a particular narrative pathway or schemata ('we have been seeing each other for several months, therefore we should be thinking of living together', etc.; 'we have been living together for two years and therefore we should be thinking of having a child together, or getting married, or both', etc.). One of the narrative schemata of the progress of conventional heterosexuality is romance. As the collection of essays entitled *Romance Revisited* demonstrates, 'individuals are educated in the "narratives of romance" from such an early age that there is little hope of immunity' (Pearce and Stacey 1995: 12). However, what the essays in this collection stress is that feminists can gain some critical purchase on these narratives and engage with them in order to negotiate a position for themselves. Precisely because romance is a narrative and hence textual in nature, it is subject to revision and rewriting.

The unthought-out nature of this narrative pressure of romance, which Rich (1980) termed 'compulsory heterosexuality', often means that heterosexuals are unable to think beyond the narrative frameworks which to them seem self-evident, and which are ratified by others. There are also narrative schemata which lesbians are subject to which are often modified versions of these heterosexual narratives; these narrative pressures entail that lesbians work within similar constraints to heterosexuals, but that the narrative closure seemingly achieved through marriage is not available.

One of the discussions which took place in the heterosexual group was around whether heterosexual feminists should refuse marriage and refuse to name their partner in terms of gender because this possibility of marriage was not available to lesbians. Lesbians within the group found it rather ironic that heterosexuals were using silence about their relationships as a sign of solidarity with lesbians, when lesbians often had no choice about whether to be open about their sexuality. One respondent from the lesbian group stated:

> I would find it the height of hypocrisy to resist identifying myself as lesbian, since I have spent most of my adult life in relationships with women. For me, to identify as a lesbian is a decision which I have no choice but to make – but, further, to identify publicly as a lesbian is a political choice, made in the teeth of pressures on lesbians to stay invisible and silent. But on the other hand 'lesbian' carries with it stereotypes I cannot identify with at all, and scripts I am less and less interested in acting out.

4.3 Naming

4.3.1 Serious relationships

A significant part in the mapping of narrative schemata for relationships is played by the naming of those with whom we have relationships: lover, friend, partner, husband, wife, fiancé and so on. Heterosexuals have a wide range of terms to describe the 'progress' of their relationships along a narrative schema which begins in friendship and ends in marriage or a settled relationship, and it is necessary to signal the type of relationship (progressive or conservative) through the choice of terms like *partner* and *lover* as opposed to *boyfriend* or *fiancé* or *husband*. Many heterosexual feminists are only too aware that the majority of the population defines their relationships along a pathway leading to marriage, and feminist relationships are defined in opposition to this. Many of the heterosexual group explicitly stated that this was a perpetual problem, for example:

> On the phone, when I am asked if that is Mrs [name] (my partner's surname) I have to make difficult decisions about whether I can be bothered to say no, this is his partner (and give my name) when I know that the caller really doesn't care about our marital status, but just wants to get through to my partner.

Despite the lack of specificity involved in the use of the word *partner*, there is a sense in which *partner* has come to mean a long-term relationship, usually where the couple live together. Both lesbians and heterosexuals use the term to refer to relationships of this type.

Nevertheless, it is still difficult to find terms for those relationships which are more fluid and less clearly defined than those which follow the narrative of compulsory heterosexuality: for heterosexual feminists who are over 16, the term *boyfriend* seems juvenile, whilst *friend* seems overly asexual. For many lesbians, the choice of the word *lover* is crucial in foregrounding the fact that a heterosexual narrative schema is not being engaged with, and that the nature of the relationship is sexual.

There are limited means to refer to those we have relations with: within heteropatriarchal definitions of sexuality, it is only sexual relations which define a relationship as serious. All other relationships are categorised as simply 'friendship', i.e., if same-sex, as peripheral to 'real' relationships, or, if opposite-sex, as the precursor of a 'real' relationship. Thus, there are few terms for love relations which are not overtly sexual or physical. This poses problems for non-sexual heterosexual and lesbian relations, and also for those who have intense relations with others which involve desire but not sexual relations.

Lillian Faderman's (1981) work on female friendship in the nineteenth century is important here for she argues that desire and sexual relations need to be disentangled when discussing same-sex relationships in the past. It is not appropriate to assume that all those women who expressed passionate desire for one another were lesbians in the sexual sense that we have imposed on current models of sexuality. We should be aware that when we currently debate whether a couple is lesbian or not we are drawing on a narrative schema of conventional heterosexuality which assumes that a relationship is only valid if it is sexual.

4.3.2 Self-categorisation

The decision to identify as lesbian was an element of discussion in the Lough-borough Feminist Research Group: a feminist lesbian stated that she did not believe in lesbianism as such, but that political expediency forced such categorisation. She went on to state:

> I think for an awful lot of people sexuality is a pretty fluid thing and if choice of sexual partner were more socially neutral I'm pretty sure it would be more fluid. Maybe if heterosexual feminists were to abandon heterosexual privilege and argue publicly for a less static reified concept of individual sexuality the line would disappear.

Another feminist in the group stated that she totally refused all categorisation: 'I won't label myself, because I don't know what I am. I don't have sexual relationships these days.' This respondent, whilst having been attracted to both males and females, found it a relief not to be in a relationship and valued the 'space, time and choices' which living alone gave her. This decision to live alone and to be celibate were political choices. However, within one of the lesbian groups, an ex-lesbian bisexual pointed out that:

> Being single is not a statement it's a bloody pain in the arse, and it's also a blissful relief on occasion. Others might see it as a statement and find it threatening e.g. wives of male friends, family members at a wedding!

Another respondent stated: 'I sometimes think that I don't want to identify as celibate, or as lesbian, but the desire to identify as something is also so very strong. Maybe not sexuality though.'

One bisexual defined herself as 'bisexual' based on her sexual history but found the meaning of the term in relation to her identity a mystery. She also stated that she rarely spoke of herself as 'a bisexual' and was more likely to express her sexuality as being important only to the person she was partnering at that time. The bisexuals canvassed felt under threat and criticised for their definition of themselves as bisexual in that 'bisexual' still has connotations of 'not having made up one's mind', or of not really being aware of their true sexuality. Bisexuals change their sexual orientation as they meet someone they wish to be sexually active with and may well change again in the future. Perhaps this sense of unease with categorisation can be summed up by one of the feminists in the lesbian group:

> I feel very uncomfortable with identifying myself as heterosexual, bisexual, lesbian etc., because at different times I am all of the above. I think these labels only work for me in terms of relationships at any given point, i.e. I was a lesbian, I am now heterosexual because that describes the nature of those relationships – I guess this would mean that in lifetime terms I am bisexual. But I hate the word for some reason. I don't know why. I also hate saying I am heterosexual because that description excludes a big and important part of my life. I suppose to summarise I use these terms to describe my relationships, not the essence of me.

5 DOMINANCE AND PASSIVITY IN RELATIONSHIPS

Within heterosexuality, there does not seem to be a great variety of sexual experience in categorisation terms – you are either in a sexual relationship or not. Further, heterosexuals do not generally define the type of relationship they are in – i.e. female dominant, male dominant, or whatever. Within the lesbian context, these are issues which are clearly marked in relationships and which are signalled to others, by dress and other elements. Members of so-called 'deviant' groups such as lesbians may focus on sexual categorisation and sub-categorisation as collective celebration, whereas heterosexuals do not have the sub-categories to easily refer to their sexual preferences, nor is this process of detailing sexual preferences one which brings street credibility. It is rare to find feminist heterosexual sado-masochists identifying openly. But it is also rare to find any celebration of heterosexuality as a form of sexuality per se. It is significant that not one of the heterosexuals in our survey brought up the question of the type of sexual relationship they had and those who responded to the questionnaire left these questions unanswered. For heterosexuals, questions of activity and passivity within sexual relationships are categorised as private matters and difficult to discuss even in anonymous questionnaires.

Within the lesbian groups, there was a great deal of discussion of the nature of dominant and passive practices. Some lesbians see these practices as distinct from seemingly similar practices within heterosexuality, which are tabooed (or which, in the case of masochism, are almost seen as a pathological prerequisite for certain types of female/male relationship) (Haug 1987). One of the lesbian feminist respondents stated that she thought she would probably be categorised by sado-masochists as a 'vanilla' lesbian, but she said that she was very resistant to defining herself in this way, since she saw it as an insult. This position of open discussion of sexual practice is also a response to the general homophobic trend of assuming that lesbians are either, on the one hand, sexual and only sexual, or, on the other hand, completely asexual (for after all, what *do* lesbians do?).

Within the lesbian groups, there was a certain amount of debate about the lack of 'fit' between these categories of dominance/passivity and women's relationships with each other. As Susan Ardill and Sue O'Sullivan have shown, the labels *butch/femme* are ones which many lesbians do not feel comfortable with:

> What appears to be happening is a definition of who's butch and who's femme through trial by clothing, or haircuts or makeup. All of us tarted-up femmes running around in cocktail dresses, and all of them butches dressed à la Radclyffe Hall. Or black leather or whatever. A great big mess of dress style, top–bottom terminology – and what else?
>
> (Ardill and O'Sullivan 1990: 79)

What Ardill and O'Sullivan point out is that in this display of fixed identity positions, the flexibility and freedom of lesbian sexuality, in contrast to the seeming constraints of heterosexuality, are lost. Many lesbians in the groups commented that labels such as *butch* and *femme* do not in fact reflect a predisposition to a certain type of personality or sexual practice, but rather they signify a range of exchangeable sexual roles. These roles are open to change and experimentation within relationships, either on a daily basis or in the longer term. Thus the roles which are seemingly signified through dress

codes are not necessarily ones which subjects adhere to in their sexual practices and in the acting out of their desires. This on-going nature of sexual
identity is highlighted by Jan Parker when she states:

> Despite the stereotype of lesbians, changing your sexual/political iden-
> tity is not like changing your clothes or getting your hair cut. Most of
> us who are/have come out as lesbians have been through a difficult,
> complex and often painful process of change that doesn't suddenly
> stop.
>
> (Parker 1987: 140)

Many lesbians in the groups drew attention to the fact that how you identify
depends on the company and context you are in. One's level of butchness,
aggressiveness or femininity is measured in relation to other individuals. The
word *mannish* is used to describe some lesbians and by its very nature is a
derogatory description of a woman 'wanting to be like a man'. *Butch* falls
into a similar category but it has been reclaimed as a positive display of
lesbianism. In practice, however, the context will define what roles and
labels are attributed to an individual.

Thus in a lesbian couple, one partner may be considered 'butch', because
the way they split the household tasks means that one does the more 'manly'
tasks, such as carpentry. However, that same person, in groups of predominantly 'butch' lesbians, will be categorised as 'femme' because of the way she
behaves and looks in relation to them. One respondent in one of the lesbian
groups spoke of being categorised differently when in different company. For
example, amongst a group of lesbians, the more 'butch' the group, the more
the individual felt 'femme', but when in a group of heterosexuals the same
individual appeared 'butch'. Within gay relationships it is also often assumed
that the partner who performs the more 'feminine' tasks is passive sexually.
What all of the members of the lesbian discussion groups argued for forcefully was the necessity of rethinking sexual relationships – and lesbian and
gay relationships in particular – so that un-thought-through prototypes of
male and female roles within conventional heterosexual relationships were
not simply imposed onto lesbian and gay relationships.

What is also required here is a consideration of the way that we categorise
sexual activity, since the terms *top/bottom*, *active/passive* used to define polari-
ties of sexual behaviour – and hence subject roles – assume a purely receptive
and agentless position for the 'bottom'/'passive' subject. This again stems
largely from conventional heterosexual narrative schemata where the role
marked out for women within heterosexual relationships is one of non-
agency and in effect non-participation, as Shan Wareing (1994) has shown.
(Although the receptor position is one which this narrative marks out for
women, it does not map onto women's experience of sexuality (see Mills
1994b).)

It is interesting that, for the general public, the prototypical and stigma-tised category for lesbians is that of the 'butch'/'active' sexual participant, whereas perhaps for gay men both the 'passive' role and the 'active' role are equally stigmatised. This maps onto prototypical categories for males and females where passivity is considered the norm for females and activity for males. As a member of one of the lesbian groups put it:

If you look butch, you are considered a Lesbian and dealt with accord-ingly by society, whether or not you would wish to be so defined. In this respect choosing to be a Lesbian is sometimes not a 'choice' – one is simply that and seen as that; women who look 'Butch' have no choice as to how they are categorised.

Although these categories 'butch' and 'femme' developed within lesbian politics in order to define such relationships as 'active' in the same sense as heterosexuals, there has been a more recent move to avoid comparison with heterosexual partnering, to avoid defining lesbian and gay relationships in terms of their similarity or difference to heterosexual marriages. This has led to a tendency for some lesbians to feel that they should therefore avoid long-term relationships and commitment because this does not challenge stereo-types of relationships; it feels as if politically you have 'sold out', in much the same way that feminist heterosexuals feel that they have 'sold out' through continuing relationships with men. For lesbians, being involved in a long-term relationship may mean aping the heterosexual norm but feeling like only a pale imitation of the original, whilst avoiding long-term relationships means slipping into the stereotype of the promiscuous deviant, condemned to an eternity of pick-ups.

6 THE FUNCTION OF PARODIC IDENTITIES

David Bell *et al.* (1994) have written about the way that lipstick lesbians and gay skinheads should be seen as very particular types of identity category because they represent less a fixed identity position than a parody of hetero-sexuality. Although these are categories which have been invented to describe groups of which one is not a part, they have nevertheless become terms which subjects choose to adopt oppositionally. Bell *et al.* claim that within these categories:

The excessive performance of masculinity and femininity within homo-sexual frames exposes not only the fabricated nature of heterosexuality but also its claim to authenticity. The 'macho' man and the 'femme' woman are not tautologies, but work to disrupt conventional assump-tions surrounding the straight mapping of man/masculine and woman/ feminine within heterosexual and homosexual constructs.

(Bell *et al.* 1994: 33)

239

Thus, if certain lesbian and gay identity categories are performative and parodic, then they cannot be taken as having the same status as heterosexual categories. That is not to say that heterosexuality is not performative, but simply that this political form of identity category is clearly of a different order.

Bell *et al.* go on to describe the different histories of the 'gay skinhead' and 'lipstick lesbian' categories, seeing these histories as determined by a conflictual relation with heterosexuality and stereotypes of gay and lesbian sexual behaviour. They show how the butch category developed as a response to conventional inability to understand women's desire for each other except in masculine terms: 'By differentiating in this way between "men in women's bodies" and "real" women, sexologists were able to explain the impossible – women's sexual desire for each other' (*ibid.*: 39). But lesbians questioned this masculinisation of lesbianism, as Nestle (1984) states:

> None of the butch women I was with . . . ever presented themselves to me as men; they did announce themselves as tabooed women who were willing to identify their passion for other women by wearing clothes that symbolised the taking of responsibility. Part of this responsibility was sexual expertise.
>
> (Nestle, cited in Bell *et al.* 1994: 40)

Nestle goes on to describe the way that she played with butch–femme dress codes and lifestyles and comments that most heterosexuals miss the parodic and playful nature of butch–femme precisely because they are looking for fixed identity categories, such as the prototypical categories within heterosexuality and homosexuality. For Bell *et al.*, lipstick lesbianism has the effect of demonstrating that the performance of femininity is not restricted to heterosexual women, and hence it forces both heterosexuals and lesbians to redefine their own notions of femininity and passivity: 'Lipstick style thus has the potential to make heterosexual women question how their own appearance is read, to challenge how they see other women' (*ibid.*: 42). They assert that lipstick lesbianism can be a productive space within which embracing femininity with enthusiasm can mean that a woman can become a sex object for herself, and can reclaim lesbian sex as an issue of desire rather than of politics.

7 CONCLUSIONS

Thus what emerges from these group discussions and the responses to the questionnaire is that these feminists inhabit heterosexuality and lesbianism in very critical and politically active ways. Many of the heterosexuals were very critical of the power dynamics within their relationship but did not feel that these were simply male/powerful, female/powerless. The limitation of the sexual label 'heterosexuality' is due in part to its being such an amorphous title; it denotes only sexuality – sex with men – and does not suggest a struggle or politics. The difficulty for feminist heterosexuals is linked to the need for an inherent politics overshadowed by the individual 'giving in' to sex with men.

Many of the lesbian respondents disidentified with a unified prototype of lesbian existence. The differences between various sexualities is taken by the members of Gays and Lesbians in Theatre to its ultimate conclusion once the naming and categorisation is over:

> We at GLINT, while recognising our difference as lesbians/gay men/
> queers, dykes and bisexuals, not to mention personal idiosyncrasies,
> continue to work together believing that creating alliances rather than
> getting deadlocked in separatism is the way forward.
>
> (Rapi 1994: 1)

Perhaps a similar sense of alliance amongst feminist heterosexuals is not achievable because of the different contexts within which feminist heterosexuality is positioned, but it is evident from our discussions with these groups that the position of disidentification which we have located in the lesbian, heterosexual and bisexual communities is the starting point for radical critiques of categorisation. This sense of discomfort in relation to categories is a productive stage in the process of rethinking the boundaries of what we see as our identities.

APPENDIX – QUESTIONNAIRE: FEMINISTS AND IDENTITY CATEGORIES

1 How would you identify yourself? (Homosexual, heterosexual, bisexual, other?)
2 Are there other categories which are equally important in identifying yourself? (political categories; mother/guardian; race/ethnicity categories; class)?
3 How do others categorise you (i.e. people who do not know you and people who know you)?
4 How comfortable are you with being categorised? Does it matter to you that you are seen in this way?
5 Are there sub-categories within this category which describe you?
6 What room for resistance is there within this category?
7 Are you currently in a stable relationship? On your own? How important is this to you ?
8 If you are in a relationship, how important do you think power differences are?
9 Are power differences a part of the sexual dynamic of the relationship?

10 Is your choice of sexual category also a political choice?

11 Do you feel that you accrue benefits from being categorised in this way?

12 Have you ever wanted to change your sexual orientation? Why? Have you ever done so ? Do you think you will in the future?

13 Do you feel that your desires are met within this sexual category?

ACKNOWLEDGEMENTS

We would like to thank Gill Spraggs, Lynne Pearce, Tony Brown and Keith Harvey for their detailed and constructive comments on drafts of this chapter. Thanks are also due to Elaine Hobby for discussions on this topic.

NOTES

1 We decided against identifying ourselves as lesbian, straight, bisexual, celibate – being up-front about 'where we are coming from', etc. We both felt that this sense of having to come clean about the category which we have been allocated/have chosen to describe our sexual choices constituted an undermining of our argument.

2 However, many of the respondents also mentioned the fact that institutional heterosexuality continues relatively untroubled amongst the wider population.

REFERENCES

Ardill, S. and O'Sullivan, S. (1990) 'Butch/femme obsessions', *Feminist Review* 34: 79–85.

Bell, D., Binnie, J., Cream, J. and Valentine, G. (1994) 'All hyped up and no place to go', *Gender, Place and Culture: A Journal of Feminist Geography* 1(1): 31–49.

Brown, G. and Yule, G. (1983) *Discourse Analysis*, Cambridge: Cambridge University Press.

Butler, J. (1990) *Gender Trouble: Feminism and the Subversion of Identity*, London: Routledge.

—— (1993) *Bodies that Matter: On the Discursive Limits of Sex*, London: Routledge.

Christie, C. (1995) 'Theories of textual determination and audience agency: an empirical contribution to the debate', in S. Mills (ed.) *Gendering the Reader*, Hemel Hempstead: Harvester/Wheatsheaf, pp. 47–66.

Dolan, J. (1988) *The Feminist Spectator as Critic*, Ann Arbor: University of Michigan Press.

Ehrenreich, B., Hess, E. and Jacobs, G. (1986) *Remaking Love: The Feminisation of Sex*, Glasgow: Fontana/Collins.

Ellis, H. (1897) *Sexual Inversion*, with J.A. Symonds, London: Macmillan, withdrawn before publication at the request of Symonds's executors. Later published as *Sexual Inversion (Studies in the Psychology of Sex)*, vol. I, Watford: The University Press, 1897, reprinted from an earlier edition excluding Symonds's contributions.

Faderman, L. (1981) *Surpassing the Love of Men: Romantic Friendship and Love between Women from the Renaissance to the Present*, New York: Morrow.

DISCURSIVE CATEGORIES AND DESIRE

Feminist Review 31 (Spring 1989) 'The Past Before Us: Twenty Years of Feminism'.

Feminist Review 34 (Spring 1990) 'Perverse Politics: Lesbian Issues'.

Frankenberg, R. (1993a) *White Women, Race Matters: The Social Construction of Whiteness*, London: Routledge.

—— (1993b) 'Growing up white: feminism, racism and the social geography of childhood', *Feminist Review* 45 (Autumn): 51–84.

Freely, M. (1995a) *What about Us? An Open Letter to the Mothers Feminism Forgot*, London: Bloomsbury.

—— (1995b) 'Keeping Mum', *Everywoman*, November, pp. 10–12.

Fuss, D. (1989) *Essentially Speaking: Feminism, Nature and Difference*, London: Routledge.

Haug, Frigga (ed.) (1987) *Female Sexualization*, London: Verso.

Hite, Shere (1987) *The Hite Report*, London: Pandora Press.

Jackson, S. (1995) 'Gender and heterosexuality: a materialist feminist analysis', in M. Maynard and J. Purvis (eds) *(Hetero)sexual Politics*, London: Taylor & Francis, pp. 11–27.

Kitzinger, C. and Wilkinson, S. (eds) (1993) *Heterosexuality*, London: Sage.

Lakoff, G. (1987) *Women, Fire and Dangerous Things: What Categories Reveal about the Mind*, Chicago and London: University of Chicago Press.

Langford, W. (1995) 'Snuglet puglet loves to snuggle with Snuglet piglet: Alter personalities in heterosexual love relationships,' in L. Pearce and J. Stacey (eds) *Romance Revisited*, London: Lawrence & Wishart, pp. 238–51.

McClintock, A. (1995) *Imperial Leather: Race, Gender and Sexuality in the Imperial Contest*, London: Routledge.

Mills, S. (1994a) *Feminist Stylistics*, London: Routledge.

—— (1994b) 'Close encounters of a feminist kind: transitivity analysis and pop lyrics', in K. Wales (ed.) *Feminist Linguistics in Literary Criticism*, Woodbridge: English Association/D.S. Brewer, 137–57.

—— (1995) (ed.) *Gendering the Reader*, Hemel Hempstead: Harvester/Wheatsheaf.

Mills, S., *et al.* (forthcoming) 'Feminist theory', *Year's Work in Critical and Cultural Theory* 3 (review for 1993), Oxford: English Association/Basil Blackwell.

Parker, J. (1987) 'The tables need turning', in G. Hanscombe and M. Humphries (eds) *Heterosexuality*, London: GMP, pp. 137–43.

Payne, B. (1994) 'Between the glitter and the gutter', in *Gays and Lesbians in Theatre Journal* 2(1) (Winter): 1–4.

Pearce, L. (1996) 'Lesbian criticism', chapter 7 in S. Mills and L. Pearce *Feminist Readings/Feminists Reading*, 2nd edn, Hemel Hempstead: Harvester/Wheatsheaf.

Pearce, L. and Stacey, J. (eds) (1995) *Romance Revisited*, London: Lawrence & Wishart.

Rapi, N. (1994) Editorial, *Gays and Lesbians in Theatre Journal* 2(4) (Winter): 1.

Rich, A. (1980) 'Compulsory heterosexuality and lesbian existence', *Signs* 5(4): 631–60.

Semino, E. (1995) 'Schema theory and the analysis of text worlds in poetry', *Language and Literature* 4(2): 79–109.

Smith, D. (1990) *Texts, Facts and Femininity: Exploring the Relations of Ruling*, London: Routledge.

Spraggs, G. (1994) 'Coming out in the National Union of Teachers', in D. Epstein (ed.) *Challenging Lesbian and Gay Inequalities in Education*, Buckingham: Open University.

Ward, J. (1987) 'The nature of heterosexuality', in G. Hanscombe and M. Humphries (eds) *Heterosexuality*, London: GMP, pp. 145–69.

Ware, V. (1992) *Beyond the Pale: White Women, Racism and History*, London: Verso.

Wareing, S. (1994) 'And then he kissed her: the reclamation of female characters to submissive roles in contemporary fiction', in K. Wales (ed.) *Feminist Linguistics in Literary Criticism*, Woodbridge: English Association/D.S. Brewer, pp. 117–36.

Wetherell, M. and Potter, J. (1992) *Mapping the Language of Racism: Discourse and the Legitimation of Exploitation*, Hemel Hempstead: Harvester/Wheatsheaf.

Wittig, M. (1992) *The Straight Mind and Other Essays*, Hemel Hempstead: Harvester/ Wheatsheaf.

INDEX